"*Autism and Crime* is a thought-provoking and essential read that illuminates the systemic barriers faced by autistic individuals in education, society, and the criminal justice system. With its blend of research, lived experiences, and actionable recommendations, it is a vital resource for anyone committed to equity, understanding, and reform."

Professor Amanda Kirby, *Emeritus Professor at the University of South Wales, Honorary Professor at Cardiff University, and Visiting Professor at Trinity College, Dublin*

"This book focuses on increasing our understanding of young autistic people. It is also driven by the critical recognition of the ways in which a subgroup of young autistic people may go from school to prison and outlines in an accessible way how this can be prevented through appropriate support, understanding, and timely intervention."

Professor Clare Allely, *Professor of Forensic Psychology at the University of Salford in England*

"Dr Neil Alexander-Passe continues his important thematic exploration of neurodivergence and the Criminal Justice System through the lens of the 'school to prison pipeline'. Never has the topic been more important."

Matthew Graham, *Partner at Stone King LLP, UK and criminal justice specialist*

"This valuable book highlights how autistic people are at increased risk of becoming involved in the criminal justice system. In most cases, this is for reasons related to their disability, and where they had no intention of breaking the law. Neil makes the powerful case that with greater support at school, autistic people can avoid this pipeline to prison altogether."

Professor Sir Simon Baron-Cohen, *Director, Autism Research Centre, Cambridge University, UK*

Autism Awareness and Crime

Autism Awareness and Crime explores Autism Spectrum Disorder (ASD) and the 'school-to-prison pipeline'.

This book takes the reader through a journey from understanding autism, how it manifests and how it is diagnosed. The author looks at how circumstances in schools including isolation, misunderstanding meltdowns, lack of autism awareness, and training have criminalised autism, leading to suspensions, exclusions, and the use of restraint and seclusion. He draws on survey data to ascertain whether there is a link between a lack of autism awareness and provision in education settings for young people, and an increased likelihood of criminal behaviour later in life. This book looks at the type of offences that young people with autism are commonly arrested for, and the contributing autistic traits that are related to them, which can be termed 'risk factors'. Criminal offences including stalking, arson, and cyber-dependent crimes are examined in detail, and this book also considers how individuals with ASD are treated by the criminal justice system.

This volume is ideal for students, researchers, and practitioners in the fields of forensic psychology, criminology, special educational needs, and social work.

Dr Neil Alexander-Passe is a school leader, a former SENDCO (Special educational needs and disabilities co-ordinator) and Assistant Head for primary and secondary schools in London. He is an 'Inclusion Expert' at the Department of Education (UK), and the author of 15 books focused on dyslexia and neurodiversity from a lived-experience, trauma perspective and has published 12 peer-reviewed papers. He is on the academic boards of dyslexia charities in Australia, and on the editorial board of a dyslexia-based academic peer-reviewed journal in Singapore.

Autism Awareness and Crime

Investigating the School-to-Prison Pipeline

Neil Alexander-Passe

Routledge
Taylor & Francis Group

LONDON AND NEW YORK

Cover image: ©Feodora Chiosea

First published 2026
by Routledge
4 Park Square, Milton Park, Abingdon, Oxon OX14 4RN

and by Routledge
605 Third Avenue, New York, NY 10158

Routledge is an imprint of the Taylor & Francis Group, an informa business

© 2026 Neil Alexander-Passe

The right of Neil Alexander-Passe to be identified as author[/s] of this work
has been asserted in accordance with sections 77 and 78 of the Copyright,
Designs and Patents Act 1988.

British Library Cataloguing-in-Publication Data
A catalogue record for this book is available from the British Library

ISBN: 978-1-041-01264-1 (hbk)
ISBN: 978-1-041-01378-5 (pbk)
ISBN: 978-1-003-61443-2 (ebk)

DOI: 10.4324/9781003614432

Typeset in Times New Roman
by codeMantra

Contents

Illustrations

Figures

Tables

Foreword

Amanda Kirby

This book serves as a critical exploration of how schools, societal systems, and punitive justice policies contribute to the 'school-to-prison pipeline' for autistic individuals, shedding light on an often-overlooked group. This book is a valuable resource for educators, law enforcement, policymakers, and advocates seeking to create systemic change and improve outcomes for autistic individuals.

This book opens with a comprehensive explanation of autism, emphasising the importance of adopting a social rather than medical model of disability. It critiques interventions such as Applied Behavioural Analysis (ABA) that aimed too much at trying to 'fix' autistic behaviours instead of advocating for societal change to accommodate and support neurodivergent individuals. This foundational perspective frames this book's exploration of systemic barriers.

The author takes a wide perspective and highlights how primary schools may offer some understanding of autism, but the transition to secondary school often introduces rigid behaviour policies, sensory overload, and insufficient teacher training. This combination frequently leads to anxiety, masking, and the escalation of unmet needs. The discussion on how mainstream education fails to provide appropriate support for autistic students is both insightful and troubling.

One of the chapters examines the victimisation of autistic individuals, including 'mate crime', where trust and immaturity are exploited. This segment is vital for raising awareness about the risks autistic individuals face in social and institutional environments, offering a much-needed lens into safeguarding. The detailed explanation of different 'behaviours' seen such as meltdowns and shutdowns provide clarity on behaviours often misunderstood by educators and law enforcement.

The discussion on punitive measures such as exclusion, restraint, and seclusion underscore the need for alternative, empathetic approaches that have also been highlighted in the media and emphasise the urgent need for reform.

Autism and Crime is a thought-provoking and essential read that illuminates the systemic barriers faced by autistic individuals in education, society, and the criminal justice system. With its blend of research, lived experiences, and actionable recommendations, it is a vital resource for anyone committed to equity, understanding, and reform. This book doesn't just educate; it challenges readers to rethink their assumptions and act to dismantle the school-to-prison pipeline for autistic individuals. Lessons learned can be applied more widely in the criminal justice system for vulnerable groups.

Professor Amanda Kirby MBBS MRCGP PhD FCGI

Amanda Kirby is the founder and CEO of Do-IT Solutions, a tech-for-good company providing neurodiversity screening and support tools for education and employment. A medical doctor and Emeritus Professor at the University of South Wales, an Honorary Professor at Cardiff University, and a Visiting Professor at Trinity College, Dublin. Amanda has a PhD in neurodiversity and emerging adulthood.

She founded and led a clinical and research team for 20 years and has authored 10 books and over 100 research papers, including Neurodiversity at Work, which won the 2022 Business Book Awards for EDI. Amanda was a former chair of the ADHD Foundation, sits on a number of advisory boards and contributed to BSI's Design for the Mind guidelines. She has worked in the field of neurodiversity and justice for nearly 20 years and has published key papers recognising the cumulative complexity of adversity and neurodiversity.

In 2023, Amanda co-authored the Neurodiversity Index Report, was named a LinkedIn Top Voice, and inspired over 149,000 followers with her Neurodiversity 101 newsletter. With lived experience of neurodiversity, she is passionate about improving equity in education and work globally.

Foreword

Clare Allely

Autistic individuals are no more violent or more likely to engage in offending behaviour compared to the general population. This is a critical point to recognise right from the offset. It is becoming increasingly recognised, both in the academic literature and in clinical practice, that autistic individuals are actually *less* likely to engage in offending behaviour overall when compared to non-autistic individuals. It is also important to be aware that autism by itself is neither a sufficient nor necessary condition to propel an individual to engage in any type of offending behaviour. Importantly, rather than being the perpetrators of offending, an increasing number of studies show that autistic individuals are more likely to be the victims of crime.

Nevertheless, there is a small subset of autistic individuals who do engage in offending behaviour, and we know that it statistically tends to be certain types of offending such as sexual offending, arson, computer offences, stalking, and violent offences. It has previously been highlighted that there is a need to explore the relationship between autism and stalking. To date, there have been no empirical studies exploring this. However, there is an increasing amount of anecdotal evidence of young autistic people who engage in stalking behaviour when seeking friendships or an intimate relationship. Autistic individuals may also find it difficult to understand why the individual they are pursuing is not responding to them in the way they want. Or the young autistic person may be in a romantic relationship where the other person breaks up with them and they cannot understand why and continue to try and pursue a relationship with that person who no longer wants to be with them. In some cases, an autistic individual may mistake a person's social niceties as an indication of romantic interest which may result in the pursuit of unwanted romantic relationships.

It is, therefore, vital that there is an increased understanding and awareness of how certain features of autism spectrum disorder or autism spectrum condition may provide the context of vulnerability to engaging in offending behaviours for the purposes of prevention and timely intervention.

Studies have found that a number of parents of teenagers with autism described their son's feelings towards a girl as a problem given the behaviours they consequently engage in (e.g., intrusive following of the girl) or their impaired understanding of why their feelings are not reciprocated by the target of their affections. Stalking can be due to the tendency of some autistic individuals to obsess and fixate upon individuals who become objects of their interest. The literature also describes the situation where two autistic boys became so obsessed with a girl in their school that they would follow the girl around. For instance, going to her locker, or meeting her after a class in the hallway. In both of these cases, the girl who was the target of the unwanted attention had attempted to talk to the boys herself as did the parents and teachers in the school. However, both boys could not appreciate and understand the girl's feeling of being stalked. From the literature (and anecdotal experience) that has been carried out there are certain features of autism that may provide the context of vulnerability to engaging in stalking behaviours at least in some cases. These include features such as a lack of awareness of social norms; restrictive preoccupations and interests; an inability to understand the viewpoint of others (impaired Theory of Mind); an inability to attend to or recognise other's social cues; lack of appropriate skills and knowledge and a developmental lag. It is also well-established that autistic young people receive, overall, much less learning regarding romantic skills from either their parents, siblings, observation, the media, sex education, or peers. This is all important to understand and consider when working with young autistic people.

There is also a very real need for the identification and understanding of how the innate vulnerabilities which are associated with autism can provide the context of vulnerability to both offline and online sexual offending. In 2010, Nick Dubin, at the age of 33 years, was arrested for the possession of child sexual abuse material (CSAM). In this book, *The Autism Spectrum, Sexuality and the Law: What every parent and professional needs to know* which he co-authored with Isabelle Hénault and Tony Attwood, Nick provides a detailed and personal account of his experiences of the criminal justice system and growing up. Nick was diagnosed with Asperger's syndrome in 2004. In this book, Nick discusses how various features of his ASD (in Nick's case Asperger's) provided the context of vulnerability to engaging in the viewing of indecent child imagery. Some examples of these features include the inability to appreciate the consequences and implications of viewing of images of minors and literal thinking, impacting on the ability to appreciate that something that is so freely available can actually be illegal.

The understanding of the association between autism and engaging in the viewing of CSAM is not well recognised and understood which needs to be addressed. Some of the factors which can contribute to an autistic individual engaging in the viewing of CSAM include: unbridled curiosity of ASD individuals; autistic individuals' interest is not necessarily deviant – 'counterfeit deviance'; CSAM's mere existence on the internet sends the message of legality to the autistic teen or young adult; autism individuals' inability or impaired ability to intuit social mores and legal rules; empathic impairments (but note that autistic individuals do have empathy when told that the children in the images are victims and are in distress, etc.); unless explicitly explained, autistic individuals fail to see the harm in merely viewing or receiving CSAM and the fact that the distinction between of-age and underage females is intentionally blurred by the media and pop culture and legal 'adult' porn.

In this book the author, recognising the importance of these issues, expertly guides the reader into how young people and adults with autism may get drawn into crimes. It also investigates whether autism is misunderstood in schools, and by the police, and what can be done to improve the outcomes of autistic young people. The difficulties and challenges that autistic children face in school are also discussed in detail. There are useful case study examples throughout this book to provide the reader with some useful context to the theory and issues being discussed.

This book will be particularly invaluable to educators, teachers, and any professional working with young autistic people. It focuses on increasing our understanding of young autistic people. It is also driven by the critical recognition of ways in which a subgroup of young autistic people may go from school to prison and outlines in an accessible way how this can be prevented through appropriate support, understanding, and timely intervention.

Professor Clare Allely

Clare Allely is a Professor of Forensic Psychology at the University of Salford in England and is an affiliate member of the Gillberg Neuropsychiatry Centre at Gothenburg University, Sweden. Clare is an Honorary Research Fellow in the College of Medical, Veterinary and Life Sciences affiliated to the Institute of Health and Wellbeing at the University of Glasgow. She is also an Associate of The Children's and Young People's Centre for Justice (CYCJ) at the University of Strathclyde. Clare is a Chartered Member of British Psychological Society (CPsychol since 2013) and Associate Fellow of British Psychological Society (AFBPsS since 2013).

Clare's research expertise covers two key areas. First, exploring how certain features of autism spectrum disorder may provide the context of vulnerability to engaging in a wide range of offending behaviours including: lone-actor terrorism, extremism, the viewing of indecent child imagery, mass shootings, school shootings, sexual offending, cybercrime, stalking, violence, zoophilia, and arson. She has published in the field of autism spectrum disorder and the features of autism that may provide the context of vulnerability to being radicalised, engaging in extremist online material and engaging in terroristic behaviours. She has also published research focused on autism in the courtroom, prison, and secure care. Clare's second area of research expertise is in exploring the pathway to intended violence in the perpetrators of extreme acts of violence including lone-actor terrorism, school shooting, mass shooting, and serial homicide.

Clare acts as an expert witness in criminal cases involving defendants with autism spectrum disorder and contributes to the evidence base used in the courts on psychology and legal issues through her published work. She is the author of the books The Psychology of Extreme Violence: A Case Study Approach to Serial Homicide, Mass Shooting, School Shooting and Lone-actor Terrorism, published by Routledge in 2020 and Autism Spectrum Disorder in the Criminal Justice System: A Guide to Understanding Suspects, Defendants and Offenders with Autism, published by Routledge in 2022.

Foreword

Matthew Graham

Dr Neil Alexander-Passe continues his important thematic exploration of neurodivergence and the criminal justice system through the lens of the 'school-to-prison pipeline' in this detailed consideration of Autism and Crime. Never has the topic been more important.

As a solicitor and advocate in the criminal justice system for over 20 years supporting the autistic community, I have seen with withering frequency the consequences of our collective failures to understand and adapt to the strengths and weaknesses of autistic people. Those consequences can be described by the prevalence of autism in prison, the number of young autistic people we criminalise, or the terrible number of autistic victims and their families trying to navigate a bewildering police and court system. Those statistics count, but behind each is a person, a human, their family and carers being let down, being traumatised, and too often being denied justice.

Neil's book recognises, vitally, that our understanding of autism, or the potential lack of it, is at the root of these injustices. His experience as a frontline Special Educational Needs and Disability school practitioner means he is well placed to take this perspective, seeing those children being funnelled down a pipeline, as he describes it, towards criminalisation. Ever-strained public resources make the provision of widespread specialist education for the autistic community a pipedream perhaps, but this does not mean we cannot do better. Neil highlights, as but one example, the importance of appropriately focussed sex education for autistic pupils if they are to achieve, safe, healthy relationships, helping prevent harm before an autistic adolescent collides with the reality of dating.

Managing autism in today's online world is rightly given focus here. Those involved in supporting the autistic community should be ever more concerned with online safety. Online spaces simultaneously present a rich opportunity for exploring interests, learning and development whilst being almost entirely unregulated and ripe for exploitation. The risks are ever-present. Striking a balance between those healthy opportunities and unhealthy risks is our 21st-century reality, virtual or otherwise, but criminalisation may be only a knockaway.

As a solicitor going to police stations and courts week in, week out for decades I know that the dichotomy between what should happen and what happens is wider than ever. There has without doubt been real progress in resources available, legislation, guidance, and best practice. In writing, the system may appear marvellous. Yet, as Neil's chapters on being failed by the criminal justice system carefully describe, the reality as reflected through research and experience can be very different. I echo that and then some, routinely seeing and hearing casual ignorance, prejudice, myths, and stereotyping. As I travel around the country dealing with cases and delivering training, attending conferences, and listening to the community I see and hear ever more examples of this chasm between what should or could occur, and what happens on the ground.

Whilst this reality is undoubtedly exhausting, there exists enough good practice, changed initiatives and increasing awareness to offer real hope and optimism. Well-researched guidance to police on dealing with suspects in custody is beginning to cut through. The topic of interviewing and questioning autistic witnesses and suspects is advancing again year on year. Judicial College guidance has caught up and has a growing influence. There are pockets of outstanding best practice in some police forces and more professionals than ever have received specific autism training. Yet the criminal justice system cannot operate in isolation from our communities, and progress in schools, colleges, children's services, employment, and beyond will ultimately make the difference.

We can all play our part, and Neil's book is a very welcome and timely addition to the resources available, drawing together with his characteristic expertise and thoroughness in both research and lived experience.

Matthew Graham, Partner at Stone King LLP

Matthew is a criminal justice specialist, having practised in courts and police stations nationally for over 20 years. He works with individuals and organisations across the criminal justice system to improve outcomes, improve safeguarding and improve experiences of all who participate in the criminal justice system. Matthew has a particular interest in working with the neurodiverse community, in particular with those of complex need, both with respect to criminal law issues and legal services more generally. His practice is top-ranked by both Legal 500 and Chambers and Partners, and Matthew is described as having 'exceptional knowledge' with 'excellent strategic insight' and one of the most 'meticulous solicitors'.

1   Introduction

This book aims to investigate why many young people and adults with autism get drawn into crimes, due to their autistic traits and symptoms. It will also investigate whether autism is misunderstood in schools, and by the police, and what can be done to improve the outcomes of autistic young people.

This is the third book in a series on 'the school-to-prison pipeline'. The first, entitled 'Dyslexia, Neurodiversity, and Crime', was published in 2023, and the second, 'ADHD and Crime', was published in 2024. This third book aims to investigate a much-misunderstood group in both schools and society, given autism does not magically disappear as soon as a young person leaves school.

Chapter 1 takes the reader through a journey from understanding autism, to how it manifests and is diagnosed. I am reluctant to talk about treatment; however, some see Applied Behaviour Analysis as a suitable treatment to teach those with autism how they should act in society, taking a medical model approach, that a person with autism needs to be fixed. I prefer the social mode of disability perspective, that society needs to better understand autism and how it affects those with autism. I choose my words carefully, as society places barriers on those with autism, and those in authority (doctors, teachers, and sometimes parents) have a huge impact on how those with autism live.

Schools have a huge part to play in how a young autistic person interacts with the world, and whilst primary schools may be more understanding of how autism manifests, secondary schools tend not to be, due to many factors, such as more formalised educational environments, strict behaviour policies, and less autism awareness among staff.

Whilst autistic boys tend to be diagnosed from three years old at nursery/school, many girls mask their autistic symptoms and may remain undiagnosed as adults. The diagnosis was once the gateway to gaining the correct support in schools; however, these days it's not, and an application for an 'Education Health Care Plan-EHCP' in the UK is needed to gain ring-fenced funding for support. Sadly, an EHCP is not enough to gain the right level and type of support, and due to a national shortage of specialist schools, most with autism are taught in mainstream classrooms of 30+ young people. This can be a recipe for disaster, firstly due to the lack of intensive autism teacher training, and secondly the physical space. 30+

DOI: 10.4324/9781003614432-1

students in each classroom in large mainstream schools will be too much for the majority of young people with autism to manage, causing sensory overload.

Chapter 2 looks at anxiety. In essence, the result of not being able to cope in mainstream education will cause anxiety with possible fight, flight, freeze, or fawn responses. This chapter aims to educate the reader about the many stressors in schools and society that those with autism struggle with, which are many. It's their reactions to these stress factors (fight, flight, freeze, or fawn) that can make the young autistic person vulnerable.

Chapter 3 looks at school bullying and victimisation, and the many dangers a person with autism may encounter at school and in society. The perceived immaturity in those with autism makes them easy victims, and this chapter looks at 'mate crime', in which a person with autism can be taken advantage of by others.

Chapter 4 looks at the anger and anger management of individuals with autism. This chapter starts by looking at what might cause anger in those with autism, the triggers, such as sensory overload, communication difficulties, and changes in routine. Anger is mentioned a lot when it comes to those with autism, sometimes violent outbursts, which is why public perception regarding autism can be disproportionately negative. Treatment, such as cognitive behavioural therapy, can be useful in this regard, to understand the triggers and to change a person's resulting behaviours (anger and violence). Medication options are discussed, but again this, I argue, is essentially treating the manifestation and not the cause.

Chapter 4 offers reasoning as to why those with autism may have anger outbursts. Meltdowns and shutdowns are discussed which gives a name to the anger and why. A meltdown is the culmination of events, not just the single event which comes before the anger/violence. Public perception of a severe overreaction to one event, for example, throwing a chair or table after being told something they don't like, but it's the culmination of several events, and the Spoon theory is discussed to try to explain the build-up and exhaustion.

Some with autism, more so girls, will have a 'shutdown', which is like a meltdown, an unconscious reaction to a series of events, but a shutdown can vary widely from lying down on the floor and not moving, or stopping communicating for a while. After each meltdown or shutdown, there is a period when the body resets so that it can return to normal function, which can be a few hours.

Restraint and seclusion have been recommended by medical professionals based on the 'medical model of disability'; however, only hospitals and residential homes need to record their use. Schools fall outside the legal guidelines, and in Scotland, there has been a movement to change this. The Calum's law initiative was created by a mother after her son was restrained at school, restrained until he passed out.

As autistic meltdowns are often misunderstood by many, the triggers can be unrecognised/dismissed. Sadly, as a result, many with autism have been sectioned under the UK's Mental Health Act, placing them in residential hospitals or assessment units. They may be heavily drugged and restrained until they are deemed 'fit' for society release. In some cases, young people become institutionalised and trapped. It may take huge efforts by their families to secure release and avoid them being held for many years, in some cases 20+ years.

Chapter 6 looks at the impact of meltdowns, namely suspensions and exclusions from mainstream schools, which highlights the lack of autism awareness and punitive behaviour policies, in the same schools that believe they are inclusive. An investigation into the impact of exclusions on young people with autism reflects the negative result of such policies.

Chapter 7 looks at criminal behaviours, the type of offences that young people with autism are commonly arrested for, and the contributing autistic traits that are related to them which can be termed 'risk factors'. Many criminal offences are examined: violence, sexual crimes, stalking, child pornography, arson, and cyber-dependent crimes.

Chapter 8 is an examination of the criminal justice system and how those with autism are treated by the police and in court. Their capacity to commit the crime is needed to ascribe culpability, and criminal law relies on two fundamental elements: the 'actus reus' (guilty act) and the 'mens rea' (guilty mind). These are discussed.

Chapter 9 looks at the two online surveys related to this book, looking at the effects of meltdowns, criminal offences committed, and involvement with the police. Parents of young people with autism and adults with autism were surveyed and then were offered to be interviewed for the study.

Chapters 10 and 11 are the discussion and conclusion chapters which aim to pull many themes together to offer meaning to the book.

I'm forever grateful to my wife Andrea and hugely blessed to have her in my life. She enables me to have it all, my research, my writing, and my family. Also, to Stuart Chatterton, for again supporting my writing endeavours with proofreading and suggested amendments.

2   What is Autism?

Autism is defined as a neurological difference affecting how individuals process and cope with their environment, characterised by core difficulties in:

- Social interaction and communication
- Restricted and repetitive patterns of behaviour.

Those with autism tend to see their differences as an integral part of their identity, often preferring to be called an 'autistic person'. This can be compared to others with (learning) differences who often see it as only one part of who they are, so preferring to be called, for example, a 'person with dyslexia', being a person first and dyslexic second. Those with autism often see themselves as being autistic first, with their autism being the foundation of their personality and identity.

What most of the population perceives as 'normal life' is quite the opposite for a growing section of society. Autistic people can find everyday interactions, frightening, confusing, and extremely stressful as described by an autistic person "To me the outside world is a baffling incomprehensible mayhem which terrifies me. It is a meaningless mass of sights and sounds, noises and movement, coming from nowhere, going nowhere". Another stated, "I feel like an alien visiting a world I don't understand and that doesn't understand me, everything is unpredictable, random and frightening" (Archer, 2024).

Autism is a lifelong developmental condition/disability that affects how people perceive, communicate, and interact with others, although it is important to recognise that there are differing opinions on this, and not all autistic people see themselves as disabled. With an estimated 700,000 autistic adults and children in the UK, approximately 1% of the population, most people probably know someone who is autistic. In addition, there are an estimated 3 million family members and carers of autistic people in the UK (National Autistic Society, 2023).

Autism spectrum disorder (ASD) is one of the most common childhood-onset neurodevelopmental disorders. In the UK, the estimated prevalence in adults is about 1.1%, with relative consistency across studies (NCCMH, 2023). Comparing this estimated prevalence of autism in adults with that of children (1%–2 %), researchers suggest that autism is underdiagnosed amongst adults (Huang et al., 2020; O'Nions et al., 2023). The proportion of males to females diagnosed with

DOI: 10.4324/9781003614432-2

autism varies across studies but always indicates a greater proportion of males to females, mostly ranging from 3:1 to 5:1 (NCCWCH, 2022; BMJ Best Practice, 2023). Studies of autism in adults have shown that up to 80% of people have experienced difficulties in obtaining a diagnosis, and many adults will not have received a formal diagnosis (NCCMH, 2023).

Neurodiversity

Autism is one of a range of conditions which have been named 'neurodiversity' or being 'neurodivergent', with 'neuro' meaning brain and 'diverse' or 'divergent' meaning different, so different brains, which develop or work differently. So talking about individuals who are 'neuro-typical' (not with neurodiverse differences) and 'neuro-diverse' as a person with neurodiversity.

Neurodiverse conditions include those with:

- Autism (Autism Spectrum Disorder/Condition)
- ADHD (Attention-Deficit Hyperactivity Disorder)
- Down syndrome
- Dyslexia (also known as a Specific Learning Difficulty)
- Dyspraxia (also known as Developmental Coordination Disorder)
- Dyscalculia
- Intellectual disabilities
- Mental health conditions, e.g., bipolar disorder, obsessive-compulsive disorder, etc.
- Prader-Willi syndrome
- Tourette's syndrome
- Williams syndrome
- Traumatic brain injury
- FASD (Foetal Alcohol Spectrum Disorder).

It is argued that those with neurodivergent conditions see, process, and work differently, and can be more creative as a result as they have different skills and abilities to bring to problems. It is argued that they can feel less restrained by societal norms and, therefore, may consider unusual or unconventional combinations of factors to solve a problem (see Figure 2.1).

With technological advances, constraints of the past may become obsolete, such as the introduction of electric or hydrogen cars. Yet, many still will not challenge 'conventional' thinking. Many of the world's most important entrepreneurs are known to be neurodiverse, and many have more than one neurodiverse condition, e.g., autism and ADHD, dyslexia and ADHD, or autism and Tourette's syndrome. Martin (2023) gives a flavour of some of these individuals:

Martin (2023), Leicestershire Partnership NHS Trust (2024), and Behaviour Interventions (2024) give a flavour of some of these individuals:

- Sir Richard Branson – Founder of the Virgin Group. Branson, has ADHD and dyslexia, and credits these conditions with his business success.

- Charles Schwab – Charles Schwab Corporation. The founder of the eponymous multi-billion-dollar investment services provider is also dyslexic, although he was only diagnosed with his condition when he reached the age of 40. He has been clear on how dyslexia has been a challenge.
- Barbara Corcoran – Corcoran Group. Corcoran faced challenges at school in her case, her grades suffered due to challenges related to dyslexia. But her mother apparently drummed into her that her 'disability' was a gift, not an impairment, and would enable her to solve problems by using her imagination to fill in the blanks.
- Ingvar Kamprad – IKEA. Kamprad was a Swedish business magnate and the founder of IKEA, Kamprad was diagnosed with both dyslexia and ADHD. It was his difficulties remembering product codes that led to IKEA's famously creative furniture names – chairs and desks have men's names and garden furniture uses names of Swedish islands.
- David Neeleman – JetBlue. Neeleman founded JetBlue Airlines and is now CEO of Azul. He is seen as a poster boy of ADHD entrepreneurship.
- Elon Musk – Space X. Musk in 2022 announced that he is on the autistic spectrum. As an entrepreneur, billionaire, and business icon, his announcement sparked many conversations about neurodiversity globally.
- Anthony Hopkins – Actor. Hopkins is an award-winning actor. He was diagnosed with Asperger's syndrome as a child. Some of his traits of autism include obsessive thinking, difficulty maintaining friendships, and looking at people with a unique perspective.
- Jerry Seinfeld – Comedian. Seinfeld is thought to be one of the most popular comedians of all time. He openly recognises himself as having ASD due to his history of social challenges and unique way of thinking literally.
- Satoshi Tajiri – Creator of Pokémon. Tajiri has stated that he is on the high-functioning end of the autism spectrum. He has confirmed on more than one occasion that he has Asperger's syndrome.
- Chris Packham – Naturalist, conservationist. A TV presenter including programmes on autism, such as reflections on how autism has affected his thinking and behaviour.

The list is quite long of those with autism who have been successful, and also include:

- Anthony Ianni – Basketball champion, USA
- Clay Marzo – Surfer
- Courtney Love – Musician
- Dan Ackroyd – Actor
- Dan Harman – Musician, aka Owl City
- Dani Bowman – Animator, autistic advocate/speaker
- Daryl Hannah – Actor
- Dr. Devon Price – Social psychologist, blogger and author of books such as: 'Unmasking Autism – The Power of Embracing our Hidden Neurodiversity'; 'Laziness Does Not Exist'
- Dr Temple Grandin – Professor of animal science, autistic writer and advocate/ speaker

- Eminem – Musician
- Greta Thunberg – Political activist
- Hannah Gadsby – Comedian
- Marty Balin – Musician: Jefferson Airplane
- Naoki Higashida – Non-speaking author of 'The Reason I Jump' – which is now also a Netflix film.
- Tony Del Blois – Musician – autistic and blind
- Wentworth Miller – Actor

The reason for listing so many people is to importantly convey that autism does not relate to low intelligence and that you can have autism and be very successful in a very broad range of fields.

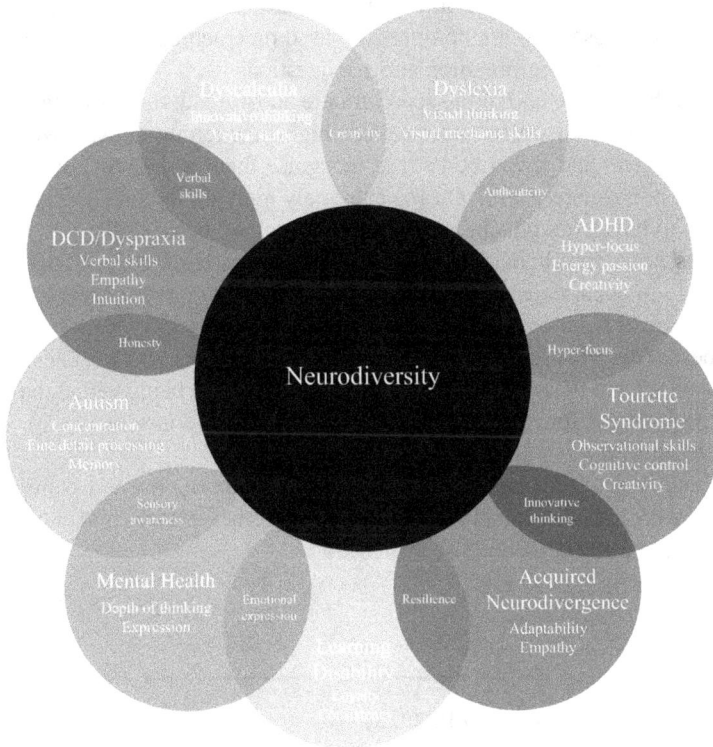

Figure 2.1 Neurodiverse skills (*Weinberg & Doyle, 2017*).

The Autistic spectrum

It is said, "when you meet one person with autism, you have met one person with autism". This is why the terms 'Autism Spectrum Disorder' or 'Autism Spectrum Condition' are used. The first uses the medical model and calls autism a disorder, whereas more modern thinking prefers to call it a condition, which aims to move it towards the social model of disability, that disability is a social construct, and it is a society which disables autistic individuals, in how it acts towards them.

Whilst diagnosis is possible from three years old, the National Autistic Society (2019) found most first concerns by parents/teachers happen in secondary school, peaking at 13–15 years old, resulting in late diagnosis. Ten to 12-year-olds were the second most prevalent age group.

Whilst many traits of autism are commonly seen, as a spectrum disorder, no two people with autism will have the same traits, so a personalised approach is argued to be best. As a spectrum disorder/condition, there is a very broad range of how it affects individuals.

On the one severe end, it affects the ability to speak/communicate, so these individuals do not develop the skills to speak, so will communicate with sign language and visual signs, e.g., Makaton is a sign language commonly used by those with non-verbal forms of autism. Picture Exchange Communication (PECs) is also used by those who are non-verbal, based on teaching the use of images to form sentences to read information and ask questions.

On the other severe end of the spectrum are autistic individuals once known as having 'Asperger's disorder', now called 'high-functioning autism' who can be highly intelligent, and it can be hard to recognise them as having autism as they mask (hide it) extremely well. On the extremely high ability side are those called savants, who have strengths in one area but lack many basic skills, e.g., a famous savant was flown in a helicopter around Manhattan in New York for 30 minutes, he was able to accurately draw the skyline of Manhattan in fine detail, however, lacked the social skills to talk about what he saw and drew.

It is best to describe the autism profile as having strengths and weaknesses. Most with autism tend to be in the middle range of the spectrum being verbal, having the ability to speak and function in society. They can function in society with varying degrees of ability.

It is important to recognise that as a spectrum condition, it's across the average range of intellect, so one should not consider a non-verbal autistic child as having low intelligence, as a recent media case demonstrates.

Case study (Brinkhurst-Cuff, 2023)

Jason Arday believes in destiny. The University of Cambridge's youngest Black professor, he joined its faculty of education in March 2023, at 37. Before then, he had been a professor at Glasgow and Durham universities; published three books of academic work, mainly focusing on race and education. All of this he has squeezed into a time period where he was learning to navigate the world with neurodivergence; Arday didn't speak until he was 11 and couldn't read or write until the age of 18. Diagnosed with autism and global developmental delay when he was three, he was taught sign language when he was four. When he was 11, after "thousands of hours" of speech therapy and support from his mother, who used music and lyrics to help him understand how words flowed and fit together, something clicked one day. "The experts made some pretty bleak diagnoses about how I would have to be in assisted living," he says. "But on that fateful day, I said hello." He stopped using sign language shortly after.

Autistic traits

Autistic traits can be as follows according to the UK's National Health Service (2024a).

Generic traits in all ages/genders

- Not understanding social 'rules', such as not talking over people
- Avoiding eye contact
- Getting too close to other people, or getting very upset if someone touches or gets too close to you
- Noticing small details, patterns, smells, or sounds that others do not
- Having a very keen interest in certain subjects or activities
- Liking to plan things carefully before doing them

In children

- Not responding to their name
- Avoiding eye contact
- Not smiling when you smile at them
- Getting very upset if they do not like a certain taste, smell, or sound
- Repetitive movements, such as flapping their hands, flicking their fingers, or rocking their body
- Not talking as much as other children
- Not doing as much pretend play
- Repeating the same phrases

In young people/teenagers

- Not seeming to understand what others are thinking or feeling
- Unusual speech, such as repeating phrases and talking 'at' others
- Liking a strict daily routine and getting very upset if it changes
- Having a very keen interest in certain subjects or activities
- Getting very upset if you ask them to do something
- Finding it hard to make friends or preferring to be on their own

- Taking things very literally – for example, they may not understand phrases like 'break a leg'
- Finding it hard to say how they feel

In girls

Autism can be harder to spot in girls, autistic girls may:

- Hide some signs of autism by copying how other children behave and play
- Withdraw in situations they find difficult
- Appear to cope better with social situations
- Show fewer signs of repetitive behaviours

In adults

Common signs of autism in adults include (National Health Service, 2024b):

- Finding it hard to understand what others are thinking or feeling
- Getting very anxious about social situations
- Finding it hard to make friends or preferring to be on your own
- Seeming blunt, rude, or not interested in others without meaning to
- Finding it hard to say how you feel
- Taking things very literally – for example, you may not understand sarcasm or phrases like "break a leg"
- Having the same routine every day and getting very anxious if it changes

In women

Autistic women tend to be harder to identify and may struggle to gain a diagnosis, they may be more likely to:

- Have learned to hide signs of autism to 'fit in' – by copying people who do not have autism
- Be quieter and hide their feelings
- Appear to cope better with social situations
- Show fewer signs of repetitive behaviours

Understanding language (verbal and non-verbal)

As we form relationships with families, friends, and others, there are several things non-autistic people/neurotypicals take for granted, to detect mood and appreciate that using a particular tone of voice has implied meaning. For individuals with autism, this can be a complicated process, struggling with subtle clues/differences.

Jackson (2002) describes how difficult it can be to understand what is required, when an emphasis on just one word in a sentence can alter its meaning quite dramatically, for example,

- *I* can't do that… implies I can't but maybe someone else can

- I *can't* do that… implies it is not possible
- I can't do *that*… implies I can't do that but may be able to do something else

Our mood is often reflected in our body language. A frown and eyes down can mean we are unhappy without having to use words. If we are listening to someone with autism talking about a topic of particular interest and we are bored or frustrated by reacting with a loss of eye contact, huffing, puffing, and moving away, however, those will not end the conversation, as individuals with autism can often miss subtle body signals.

Idioms are used regularly by us in everyday language, for example, 'Let's paint the town red', 'I am going to knock some sense into you', or 'It's raining cats and dogs'. Phrases such as these can be highly confusing and illogical to individuals with autism who take things very literally and may lead to troublesome and unexpected consequences. In a Welsh Assembly report (2010), they noted a prisoner with autism who took a sarcastic comment made by an officer seriously, who told him 'Why don't you go and ask everybody'; so he did! Staff said he was 'refusing to listen' and was 'annoying staff by repeating the same question to everybody' which they construed as an attempt at manipulative behaviour rather than a literal interpretation of a throw-away line by an officer.

Causes and diagnosis

Evidence suggests that autism may be genetic. However, scientists have struggled to identify which genes might be implicated in autism. It is thought that autism is likely to have multiple genes responsible, rather than a single gene, it is estimated 200–1,000 genes impact autism susceptibility (Bell, 2024). However, it is not caused by emotional deprivation or the way a person has been brought up. There is no link between autism and vaccines, even though there have been many scares in the last few decades about the measles, mumps, and rubella vaccine (Hviid et al., 2019).

It is known that autism is hereditary and therefore does run in families. A majority (around 80%) of autism cases can be linked to inherited genetic mutations, the remaining cases likely stem from non-inherited mutations. Noting there is no evidence that children can develop autism after early foetal development because of exposure to vaccines or postnatal toxins. "Everything known to cause autism occurs during early brain development" according to Professor Daniel Geschwind, an award-winning autism researcher (Bell, 2024). Whilst in the 1970–80s theories believed autism was caused by bad parenting, his research into the genetic underpinning of autism has led to a greater understanding of its genetic basis.

Diagnosis routes can vary according to gender and age. Boys-men with autism tend to manifest in more traditional-behavioural-external ways, so it is easier to see, and therefore earlier diagnosis tends to happen, commonly from three years old. Girls can manifest in very different and more passive-internal ways, so is much harder to identify and begin the diagnosis journey. Girls will also tend to manifest with emotional and social secondary traits which are the result of non-diagnosis/support.

It is now believed that there are two subsets of autism, one externally manifesting and the other internally. Boys sometimes present with internal manifestations, and likewise, girls sometimes manifest with exernal manifestations, but it is less common.

Research points to high levels of non-diagnosis for females, and this is reflected in girls in school. Agnew-Blais's (2023) paper on delayed ADHD diagnosis amongst girls and women uses the term 'hidden in plain sight'. Kirby et al. (2020) discuss the low assessment of females in one Scottish prison, they conclude current systems do not appear to identify women with functional difficulties or other adversity adequately. Greater use of interdisciplinary working and shared training is indicated. This reflects their exhibiting subtler symptoms and often being adept at camouflaging their struggles, manifesting anxiety, eating disorders, and self-harm. Saporito (2022) and Antezana et al. (2019) amongst others also highlight under-diagnosis, pointing to a gender bias understanding amongst teachers and professionals, noting a missed diagnosis can result in the development of mental and physical health issues and greater impairment across domains and a patient's lifespan. They may struggle to 'share' friends and become overly possessive as if their friends belong to them. They may want friends but not know how to get them. Often, they observe and imitate, or 'mask' to try to fit in, and are more likely than autistic males to be able to understand and interpret the behaviour and emotions of others so that they can imitate.

Case study (this author)

In one secondary school, where I was the SENDCo, special needs manager. There were 15-year-old non-identical twins, one a boy, the other a girl. The boy had severe autism diagnosed when he was very young and was awarded an EHCP (Educational Health and Care Plan). In the UK, such children gain additional government funding to support their needs up to the age of 25. The girl twin was perceived not to have autism. However, as puberty hit and she entered her mid-teenage years, she began to develop social and emotional difficulties, including a severe eating disorder and anxiety. She was being treated for her eating disorders, but no one had questioned the cause. It was only through my insistence to investigate 'female presentation of autism', that she was finally diagnosed with autism. Diagnostic teams have been slow to recognise that autism in girls and boys can manifest in very different ways, and they can be blinkered by secondary manifestations.

In the United Kingdom (UK), diagnosis normally starts with identification by an adult, or a teacher but can also be a parent. The teacher will contact the parent for a chat and then if consent is given a referral is made to the SENDCo (Special Needs and Disability Coordinator) in the young person's school. Parents can also go to their doctor for a referral to CAMHS, but without the screeners being used to support such a referral there is a higher chance it would be rejected by triage teams.

A battery of screeners is commonly completed by both the parents and a teacher who knows the child well. The SENDCo then meets with the parents to review the two sets of screeners before completing a CAMHS referral form (CAMHS stands for 'Child and Adolescent Mental Health Service', part of the UK's National Health Service). CAMHS will then triage the referral and if agreed will add the child to an assessment pathway. The UK government has set a 12-week (3 months) target for young people to be seen by a psychiatrist; however, sadly this is never the case. In the best-resourced areas, this commonly may take 12–24 months (1–2 years); however, many more in the UK wait for up to 60 months (5 years).

CAMHS is perceived to be the gold standard in the UK, where they will meet twice with the child and a parent. The first meeting is to take a long health and behaviour history with an observation, followed by more screeners, diagnostic measures, an educational questionnaire sent to the parent and the child's school, and a blood test offered. The final meeting will review the results and take additional observations. If the child meets the DSM-V (fifth edition) criteria, then a diagnosis will be made (CDC, 2024). In some cases, more than one diagnosis is recognised; however, due to budget restrictions, many are then added to another diagnosis pathway and waiting list to gain any secondary diagnosis, for example, commonly ADHD.

There are, however, some cases where a child manifests many autistic traits but falls short of formal diagnosis criteria; this can create difficulties for parents and schools as they are unsure of the best strategies to use. The lack of a formal autism diagnosis can mean certain services and provisions are not open to the young person. I know of several cases where this happened when the child was young, and parents have struggled to access provision for their child. I have made new CAMHS referrals to reassess when they are in secondary school, as teenagers can have more clearly defined autistic traits.

The alternative is to bypass CAMHS and opt for a private diagnosis. Whilst this is a lot faster (1–3 months) it can be very expensive (up to UK£3000 for a pure autism diagnosis in 2024), and if ADHD is also present, then this additional diagnosis can cost extra (up to UK£2000 in 2024 prices). The quality of assessment can vary greatly, depending on if the diagnosing psychiatrist also works for CAMHS. Some reports can be extremely short in detail without measures used to support their findings, and without blood tests, many are based on an online assessment and only one assessment meeting with no input from schools. During the COVID-19 pandemic online assessments began to be offered and have grown in use.

Parents can be short-changed by trying to bypass CAMHS, spending a lot of money for an assessment which may be less robust, and may be rejected by schools and local authorities as the basis for an EHCP application.

In the UK, many severely affected young people with learning difficulties/ disabilities, such as autism and ADHD, can apply for government funding, an EHCP, which will give guaranteed funding for a young person until they turn 25 years old (or if they leave education or go to university). This can fund extra in-class in classrooms, specialist teachers, and subject to severity and available places, entry to special schools.

Diagnostic criteria

According to the American 'Centers for Disease Control and Prevention-CDC' (2024), to meet diagnostic criteria for autism according to Diagnostic and Statistical Manual of Mental Disorders fifth Edition, known as DSM-5 (American Psychiatric Association, 2022), a child must have persistent deficits in each of three areas of social communication and interaction (see A below) plus at least two of four types of restricted, repetitive behaviours (see B below).

- **(A) Persistent deficits in social communication and social interaction across multiple contexts, as manifested by the following, currently or by history (examples are illustrative, not exhaustive):**

  - Deficits in social-emotional reciprocity, ranging, for example, from abnormal social approach and failure of normal back-and-forth conversation; to reduced sharing of interests, emotions, or affect; to failure to initiate or respond to social interactions
  - Deficits in non-verbal communicative behaviours used for social interaction, ranging, for example, from poorly integrated verbal and non-verbal communication; to abnormalities in eye contact and body language or deficits in understanding and use of gestures; to a total lack of facial expressions and non-verbal communication
  - Deficits in developing, maintaining, and understanding relationships, ranging, for example, from difficulties adjusting behaviour to suit various social contexts; to difficulties in sharing imaginative play or in making friends; to absence of interest in peers
  - Severity is based on social communication impairments and restricted, repetitive patterns of behaviour. For either criterion, severity is described in three levels.

    - Level 3 – Requires very substantial support
    - Level 2 – Requires substantial support
    - Level 1 – Requires support

- **(B) Restricted, repetitive patterns of behaviour, interests, or activities, as manifested by at least two of the following, currently or by history (examples are illustrative, not exhaustive):**

  - Stereotyped or repetitive motor movements, use of objects, or speech (e.g., simple motor stereotypes, lining up toys or flipping objects, echolalia, idiosyncratic phrases).
  - Insistence on sameness, inflexible adherence to routines, or ritualised patterns of verbal or non-verbal behaviour (e.g., extreme distress at small changes, difficulties with transitions, rigid thinking patterns, greeting rituals, need to take same route or eat same food every day).

- Highly restricted, fixated interests that are abnormal in intensity or focus (e.g., strong attachment to or preoccupation with unusual objects, excessively circumscribed or perseverative interests).
- Hyper- or hyperreactivity to sensory input or unusual interest in sensory aspects of the environment (e.g., apparent indifference to pain/temperature, adverse response to specific sounds or textures, excessive smelling or touching of objects, visual fascination with lights or movement).
  Specify current severity:
- Severity is based on social communication impairments and restricted, repetitive patterns of behaviour. For either criterion, severity is described in three levels.
  - Level 3 – Requires very substantial support
  - Level 2 – Requires substantial support
  - Level 1 – Requires support

Autistic symptoms must be present in the early developmental period (but may not become fully manifest until social demands exceed limited capacities or may be masked by learned strategies in later life). Symptoms must indicate clinically significant impairment in social, occupational, or other important areas of current functioning.

Importantly, these behaviours should not be better explained by another intellectual disability (intellectual developmental disorder) or global developmental delay. As Intellectual disability and ASD frequently co-occur, comorbid diagnoses of ASD and intellectual disability should be investigated. Overall, social communication skills should be below the age-expected developmental level.

The alternative to the DSM-V is the ICD-11 (World Health Organization, 2024), and each is valid for diagnostic use.

Levels of autism

Diagnosis tends to be made to three levels of autism (ASD), as I-autism (2025) details:

- **Level 1: Requires Support** – Level 1 ASD describes people who do not need a lot of support. They may have a hard time communicating with neurotypical people, including their peers, for example, they may not say the right thing at the right time or be able to read social cues and body language.
- **Level 2: Requires Substantial Support** – People diagnosed with Level 2 ASD have a harder time masking than those diagnosed with Level 1 and may find it hard to communicate or socialise in ways that are accepted or understood by neurotypical society. Likewise, they will find it harder to change focus or shift from one activity to the next.
- **Level 3: Requires Very Substantial Support** – People with Level 3 diagnoses need the most support and are subsequently at very high risk for neglect, abuse, and discrimination. Those in this category will have many of the same traits as those with Levels 1 and 2 diagnoses but are entirely unable to mask and have very high burdens of self-regulation.

Problems gaining a diagnosis

Many parents explain there are delays to gaining a diagnosis, not just with the National Health Service-CAMHS, but also with schools and doctors not taking the likelihood of autism seriously. As mentioned before, it was very difficult for a female student of mine manifesting self-harm to be considered for an autism assessment. The following case studies illustrate the lengths some may go to for assessment.

National Autistic Society (2022) reports on difficulties gaining an assessment, and despite asking the NHS and local doctors to assess and asking for why, are denied a reason. In the many cases highlighted, they got themselves arrested to be put in front of a judge to gain a recommendation that they should be assessed. This extreme behaviour, such as making threats and attempting suicide, reflects their desperation for their human right to be offered an autism diagnostic assessment when feel ignored. To be clear, such behaviour was not caused by their autism but by their autism being overlooked.

Treatment

There is no known 'cure' for autism. However, there are many fake cures and potentially harmful interventions found on the internet. Many people believe that autism does not require a 'cure' and should be seen more as a difference, not a disadvantage. This does not mean that autistic people do not face challenges, but with the right support in place, most are capable of living fulfilling and happy lives. Many with autism work, gain successful careers, get married, and have families.

Applied behaviour analysis

Some parents believe in treatments such as 'Applied Behaviour Analysis (ABA)' (Autism Speaks, 2024), but this is considered controversial by many with autism, as it treats autism as something 'wrong' and in need of fixing (medical model of disability), rather than a difference that can bring a range of strengths as well as challenges (social model of disability).

A very interesting recent post on Facebook resonated with the above. 'We spend years teaching our autistic young people to cope in the outside world, but we rarely teach the outside world to cope with our autistic young people'. Meaning, why should those with autism have to fit into someone else's environment? If one relates this to the deaf community, such people may not all see themselves as 'hearing impaired' as that would imply that they are *faulty* or *broken*. They may see themselves as a unique and gifted group in society, the deaf community.

Positive reinforcement

Positive reinforcement is one of the main strategies used in ABA. When a behaviour is followed by something that is valued (a reward), a person is more likely to repeat that behaviour. Over time, this encourages positive behaviour change. First, the therapist identifies a goal behaviour. Each time the person uses the behaviour or skill successfully; they get a reward. The reward must be meaningful to the individual – examples include praise, a toy or book, watching a video, access to a playground or other locations, and more. Positive rewards encourage the person to continue using the skill. Over time this leads to meaningful behaviour change.

Antecedent, behaviour, consequence

Understanding antecedents (what happens before a behaviour occurs) and consequences (what happens after the behaviour) is another important part of any ABA programme. The following three steps – the 'A-B-Cs' – help us teach and understand behaviour:

- An antecedent: This is what occurs right before the target behaviour. It can be verbal, such as a command or request. It can also be physical, such a toy or object, or a light, sound, or something else in the environment. An antecedent may come from the environment, from another person, or be internal (such as a thought or feeling).
- A resulting behaviour: This is the person's response or lack of response to the antecedent. It can be an action, a verbal response, or something else.
- A consequence: This is what comes directly after the behaviour. It can include positive reinforcement of the desired behaviour, or no reaction for incorrect/inappropriate responses.

Looking at 'A-B-Cs' helps us understand:

- Why a behaviour may be happening. How different consequences could affect whether the behaviour is likely to happen again
- Example: Antecedent: The teacher says "It's time to clean up your toys" at the end of the day.
- Behaviour: The student yells "no!"
- Consequence: The teacher removes the toys and says "Okay, toys are all done."

How could ABA help the student learn a more appropriate behaviour in this situation?

- Antecedent: The teacher says "time to clean up" at the end of the day.
- Behaviour: The student is reminded to ask, "Can I have 5 more minutes?"
- Consequence: The teacher says, "Of course you can have 5 more minutes!"

It is argued that with continued practice, the young person will be able to replace the inappropriate behaviour with one that is more helpful and constructive, and which may illicit more positive responses from others.

Support in schools

Support in schools can greatly vary according to the location of the school and the level of funding a school receives for special educational needs (SEN). Some UK head teachers do not use their special needs funding for additional and targeted provision, as they believe that all teachers should be teachers of special needs students and deliver inclusive teaching.

The reality is somewhat different, teachers of 30+ mixed-ability students in a classroom without additional adult support will often struggle to offer inclusive teaching to all students, especially those with autism.

Most local educational authorities have dedicated and disability (SEND) team, and many also have specialist advisory staff for autism, who can offer help and advice to teachers, schools, and parents. However, a referral is normally required for their service, and this may not always be easy to achieve due to their own priority criteria.

In some locations, until a referral is made to, and accepted by, CAMHS for an autism diagnosis, autism advisory teams will not offer support. Most schools offer autism training every few years. However, this may not be from trained staff and may only cover the basics.

As initial teacher training does not cover many SEND topics such as autism, new teachers and many existing teachers may have very little experience and skills to offer autistic students in their classrooms. As the class teacher, it will be their responsibility through their observations to highlight if a young person may have autism and refer for more investigation. As you can begin to see, if they have little or no knowledge and experience of autism this will not happen, causing those with autism to go undiagnosed for many years, maybe for their whole school education.

This will also mean that without understanding the needs of the young people in their classroom they may use well-meaning but inappropriate strategies to engage them. Whilst their best intentions may be to support the students, they are likely to misunderstand the causes of dysregulation and meltdowns, and treat any behaviour negatively, resulting in blame and further meltdowns. These meltdowns can be more pronounced in boys, resulting in labelling of girls as merely quiet and reserved. It also means that many young people will feel misunderstood and their needs left uncatered for.

The Children's Commissioner (2022b) report found autistic children want support to help them do well, but they often experience a system which is more interested in asking 'what is wrong with you?' than 'how can we help?'. Some children said that they didn't feel listened to by the adults around them, for example, their teachers or social workers. Children want to be understood without stigmatising labels which can be marginalising and isolating. Children told the Commissioner team that adults should know the things that can make a difference to them in their learning (e.g., class size, fidgeting toys, and proper breaks), and implement these things consistently when they have been agreed. It was felt vital that children's wishes and feelings are a central part of the process, and whenever a child does not have a parent to support them in being heard, high-quality independent advocacy is available.

She did a 'brilliant' job of masking everything she found hard. From the school's perspective, she was a very polite child who followed all the rules, who did as she was told, who was keen... she didn't stick her head above

the parapet in any way, so when I was saying she's coming home absolutely
overwhelmed and utterly distraught, they just couldn't see it.
- Parent of an autistic child
(Children's Commissioner, 2022b)

There are over 180,000 autistic pupils in England, 73% of whom are in mainstream schools. But the Commissioner's research reveals that autistic children and young people are being failed by a woeful lack of appropriate school places and teachers are unequipped to meet autistic students' needs. The research suggests only 26% of autistic pupils feel happy at school. 74% of parents or carers said their child's school place did not fully meet their needs, and 26% of parents waited over three years to receive support for their child.

The Commissioner found that whilst 87% of teachers surveyed felt confident or very confident supporting autistic pupils in the classroom, findings from their 2021 report show that 70% of autistic children and young people said school would be better if more teachers understood autism, and 54% of autistic students said that having teachers who don't understand them is the worst thing about school. There is clearly a disconnect between teachers' confidence in supporting children, and how well supported those young people feel.

Training is key to this, with their finding that only 39% of teachers surveyed had received more than half a day's autism training and for secondary school teachers alone this figure was just 14%, based on training over their teaching career (so maybe a 5–20-year span).

The Children's Commissioner (2022b) advocates the UK Government to urgently address this growing problem of a lack of appropriate school places by launching an autism school places taskforce, to address the needs of autistic pupils and make sure there are the right school places to meet demand.

Young people with SEND commonly face exclusion in some schools because it has been decided by the senior leadership team that their care couldn't be managed within their mainstream setting. As one young person spoke to said, "Why is it straight away exclusion, exclusion?" Boy, 15, attending a special school (The Children's Commissioner, 2022b). This sends a clear message of rejection to young people and their families.

The Children's Commissioner concluded that autistic students were disproportionately over-represented in UK government data relating to formal exclusions. However, even more concerning was the number of stories of informal exclusions, where children are sent home and asked not to come in. These are illegal and not officially recorded. In their 2021 parent survey, 20% of parents reported their child had been informally excluded in the last two years.

My previous school was not good, the consequence room with booths where
kids would sit from 9am to 2:30pm, not allowed to go to the toilet, get a drink,
anything, no work to do. For kids like me with a disability it just doesn't help.
Boy, 15, now attending a special school
(The Children's Commissioner, 2022b).

The headteacher of a special school in Oxfordshire remarked that it was all too common that a child would develop challenging behaviour due to a late SEND diagnosis in mainstream education. When these children do finally have access to a special school and/or specialist support, teachers spend too much time focussing on behaviour management rather than teaching and managing their trauma from their time in mainstream education. It was only once the child had their support needs met (emotional and academic), could they begin to re-engage with learning properly. This resulted in lost learning time, making outcomes harder to reach. The headteacher concluded that mainstream class teachers need to be looking for signs, such as poor attendance or persistent absence, behavioural needs, that a child might need additional support, and be using these triggers for early intervention.

Beyond school, government figures suggest only 29% of autistic people are in any form of employment, compared to around 80% of adults in the general UK population. Suggesting schools are not preparing them for the workplace.

The views of autistic students in the Children's Commissioner's (2022b) report

Many autistic students reported that they do not feel their peers understand enough about autism, whilst just 8% of respondents said they think their peers do understand enough about autism. In this report:

- We heard that autistic students were hiding their diagnosis from their classmates, for fear it would be misunderstood and be a trigger for bullying.
- Only 26% of autistic children felt happy at school.
- 70% of autistic students and young people said school would be better if more teachers understood autism.
- 54% said they don't have a quiet place to go to at school.
- 54% of autistic students said that having teachers who don't understand them is the worst thing about school.

In another study, parent–child views were (National Autistic Society, 2019):

- Fewer than half of students and young people on the autism spectrum said they were happy at school.
- 42% of parents said their child was refused an assessment of their SEN the first time it was requested.
- 50% of parents said their child waited more than a year for support to be provided at school.
- 40% of parents said their child's school place did not fully meet their needs.
- Fewer than 5 in 10 teachers said they were confident about supporting a student on the autism spectrum.
- 60% of young people said that the main thing that would make school better for them was having a teacher who would understand autism.

It is very evident from the Children's Commissioner (2022b) report that the needs of autistic young people are not being met in mainstream education, placing such young people in large noisy classrooms, and creating random events that can cause dysregulation and meltdowns, resulting in sometimes explosive and aggressive behaviour reactions which tend to be viewed negatively by both teachers and other students, leading to ostracisation.

She was on the receiving end of some really horrible bullying (...) She'd come home to me and say, 'Mummy, why would you? Why does someone talk about a birthday party in front of someone that they know isn't invited?' She literally couldn't understand why people would do these sorts of things... it was very difficult for her... And she lost those friends. So her experience also is not to trust people.

Parent of an autistic child
(The Children's Commissioner, 2022b).

I just think the impact on the mental wellbeing for some kids... [I] don't think they quite understand the trauma experienced by sitting in a classroom of that size.

Parent of an autistic child
(The Children's Commissioner, 2022b).

A caretaker would come and do a fire alarm test in the morning... that triggered something for her and she would get quite anxious and want to leave, go out into the playground rather than be inside the school.

Parent of an autistic child
(The Children's Commissioner, 2022b).

Applying for an Educational Health Care Plan (EHCP)

In the UK, schools are expected to initially provide young people with special educational needs and disabilities (SEND) with extra support for their studies. The SEND Code of Practice (Department of Education, 2015) is the guidance given to schools. Schools are required to spend up to the first £6000 (GBP) of any extra SEND support for each young person of school age. Where a young person needs more than UK£6000 worth of support, parents/carers can apply for an EHCP, which would recognise the young person as having severe needs, and secure individual funding for them until they reach 25 years old.

The first stage is to apply for an EHC assessment, and for this, the application by the parent, supported by the school must satisfy two legal requirements:

- Whether the child or young person 'has or may have' SEN; and
- Whether they 'may' need special educational provision to be made through an EHC plan.

If the answer to both questions is yes, then the LA must carry out an EHC needs assessment. This assessment normally includes an assessment by an educational psychologist, and other relevant professionals, for example, a speech, language, and communication therapist, an autism specialist teacher, an occupational or physiotherapist, etc.

There is a statutory 20-week (5-month) timetable from the point of an initial application to an EHCP being written. Most local authorities abide by this timeframe; however, many do not, which places them in a problematic legal position.

From my own experience, over the last ten years with many local authorities in London and the Southeast of English, even the most extensive EHCP application can be refused, and many local authorities rely on delaying tactics to safeguard their limited higher needs budget. Once refused a parent has the option to go to mediation or apply for the case to be heard by a special need's tribunal. Such unnecessary delays can be due to additional information they wish to have such as evidence of provision to date and its effectiveness, and how much the school has spent to date on the young person's additional needs. These are not legally required and cannot be enforced.

There is a 30-day deadline for the local authority and parents to meet for a mediation meeting, and it is hoped the local authority will, once a case has been made, agree to an EHC assessment. A parent can choose not to go through the mediation process and instead ask for a 'medication certificate' to support a tribunal application. The waiting list for Tribunals is very long, and it may take over a year for a case to be heard. Many local authorities have extensive legal teams, and even if they know they will lose, saving one year's EHCP funding can range from UK£15 to UK£50,000 for a single young person can be a considerable saving, especially when multiplied by tens and hundreds of applications they receive each year.

UK government statistics indicate that the number of appeals in 2022–23 rose by 2,600 (24%) from 2021 to 2022. Since 2014, the number of appeals has increased every year. These appeals represent children and families who are unable to get the support they need, the vast majority of whom are then successful in challenging a local authority's decision. However, the appeal process can take up to 18 months. The proportion of cases found at least in part in favour of the appellant also reached a record high of 98%, up from 96% in both 2021–22 and 2020–21 (Children's Commissioner, 2024).

Adams (2024) highlights that only 1.2% or 36 of the 10,000 tribunal appeals in 2022–23 were successful for local authorities and that councils were wasting £100 million per year on such appeals. In 2023–24, this has increased to 21,000, a 55% year-on-year increase. Adams reports that experts comment that the surging numbers of appeals and mounting costs were evidence that special education provision was becoming an adversarial battle between cash-strapped councils and desperate families, with the National Audit Office amongst those recommending that 'wholesale reform' was needed. Also noting the Independent Provider of Special Education Advice, a charity providing free legal support to families, commented:

> It's hard to avoid the conclusion that local authorities must calculate, at some level, that it costs them less to contest tribunal appeals, even if they lose, than to provide every child and young person with what the law entitles them to as a matter of course – because the majority of families don't [or] can't appeal.

Arooj Shah, the chair of the Local Government Association's children and young people board (in Adams, 2024), commented that

Councils fully recognise the right of families to take appeals to tribunals. However, the fact a significant number of cases are being taken to a tribunal hearing is symptomatic of a system that is failing for families, and councils too, who want to provide the very best for every child, in spite of the rising need for support and financial pressures.

Shah concludes "These show that reform of special educational needs and disabilities [SEND] services is urgent and essential."

28% of appeals were against refusals by local authorities to conduct an education, health and care assessment, which is the necessary first step towards getting an EHCP. Despite only 32% of pupils with EHCPs having autism, almost half (45%) of appeals were related to autistic children and young people – suggesting that autistic children may find accessing support particularly challenging.

The Children's Commissioner (2022b) report also found too many young people are failing to gain an EHCP because they are waiting for a formal diagnosis of a special need or disability from a doctor or medical professional. Such delays to EHCPs were viewed to be unacceptable. Autism is the most common type of SEND for children with EHCPs: 103,429 students in the UK have autism as their primary need.

"The most disappointing thing is that we still don't have an EHCP, I don't know how to get it or any support. I feel like we've just fallen off a cliff." Mother of girl, aged 12 with autism, attending mainstream school (Children's Commissioner, 2022b).

"Teachers aren't trained to help us." Girl, 13, attending a mainstream school with an EHCP. This suggests even with an EHCP the support is not given, due to teachers lacking autism training (Children's Commissioner, 2022b).

The Autistic child

Dealing with anxiety

Anxiety affects a lot of autistic children and adults. It can be caused by not being able to make sense of the world around them and feeling misunderstood or unaccepted by others. It might be because of (NHS, 2024a,b):

- A change in routine, such as a change of class at school
- Difficulty identifying, understanding or managing their feelings
- A noisy or brightly coloured room

Behaviours

Some autistic children may manifest (NHS, 2024):

- Stimming – a kind of repetitive behaviour as a coping/calming strategy (such as flapping their hands or flicking their fingers)

- Meltdowns–acompletelossofcontrolcausedbybeingoverwhelmed-dysregulated

Eating difficulties

Autistic children may struggle due to sensory difficulties (NHS, 2024):

- Only wanting to eat foods of a certain colour or texture
- Not eating enough or eating too much
- Eating things which are not food (called pica)
- Having problems with coughing or choking whilst eating
- Be constipated, so they feel full even when they have not eaten a lot of food

It may help to keep a food diary, including what, where, and when your child eats. This can help you notice any common issues your child has.

Problems sleeping

Many autistic children also find it hard to get to sleep or wake up several times during the night. This may be because of (NHS, 2024):

- Anxiety
- Sensitivity to the light from smartphones or tablets used before bed
- Problems with the sleep hormone melatonin
- Issues such as hyperactivity or a health condition that affects sleep

You can help your child by:

- Keeping a sleep diary of how your child sleeps to help you notice any common issues
- Following the same bedtime routine even at weekends and during school holidays
- Making sure their bedroom is dark and quiet
- Letting them wear ear plugs if it helps
- Talking to a doctor about how to manage health conditions that make sleep difficult, such as food sensitivity or breathing problem

At home and socially

A young child with autism will struggle to make sense of the world, it seems not only illogical but also too loud and nothing much makes sense. Their parents would have recognised early on that they do not 'need' others, may not have cried as a baby, and preferred to be by themselves, rather than play with other children. They may have fascinations, so may play with the same toy all the time, or develop a passion for trains or another topic, and consume large amounts of knowledge about them. In some cases, they can be extremely intelligent and teach themselves other languages.

At school

School can be very hard for a child with autism. Boys will tend to manifest more outwardly noticeable traits which may be, for example, struggling to cope with noise and smells. These will quickly become dysregulated by anything that could be seen as change, for example, not having their usual teacher, not being able to sit in their usual seat in class or in the dinner hall, not having the right-coloured lunch tray, or forgetting their PE kits. Children with autism crave and need order to remain calm (self-regulate) and to be able to learn. Many use stimming strategies to remain calm, being highly repetitive, for example, aligning objects, staring at spots, blinking rapidly, playing with a favourite toy or fidget toy, clenching and unclenching fists, repeating phases, and repetitive movements (see Appendix 1 for a very long list of Stimming strategies).

Reactions to dysregulation can be severe, and I have seen a young child with autism react violently to a school fire alarm, like how someone could react to being stabbed with a knife. This is why boys may be referred for diagnosis at a very young age (in nursery). Sadly, teachers see a need to restrain autistic young people due to how they react, misunderstanding why they have acted in that way, and perceiving the autistic person to be a threat to themselves and others. This will be discussed in later chapters of this book.

They may manifest hypersensitivity to noise, smell, and change. They will struggle to be creative but will be very good at copying things. They will work best with a set of instructions but will be lost without them. They will struggle to understand jokes and humour and will take all language use in a very literal way. Where there is combined autism with ADHD, the challenges manifest in size, as the child will struggle to sit down to learn, always be on the go, and have problems with attention/focus.

Some autistic children may also find it hard to make friends due to misunderstanding social rules, which will affect their ability to feel included, luckily many prefer to play by themselves, which adults find hard to understand. Interestingly the stress placed by adults on an autistic child making friends, as the 'normal' thing to do, can cause unnecessary anxiety to the autistic young person. They tend to be the last to be chosen for team games as they tend to have poor social networks at school and are less popular.

Autistic girls

When the autistic child is a girl, they will tend to be very quiet, have few friends, be seen as lonely, will copy/mimic other behaviour by girls to fit in (called 'masking'), be passive, may also rely on other girls to speak for then (seen as quiet, shy, or a dreamer), and will struggle to regulate their emotions. They will mask very well and remain under the radar for much of their schooling. The frustrations need to be expressed, but sadly they are internalised without any outlet. To cope with such struggles many girls choose various means to regain control of their lives and environments, choosing self-harm and anorexia as a result, with anxiety disorders. This makes the diagnosis of any core difficulties, such as autism, very hard, as psychiatrists and mental health teams will treat the perceived more important secondary manifestations (self-harm, anorexia, and anxiety) instead. Various studies suggest that the ratio of autistic males to females ranges from 2:1 to 16:1. With the most up-to-date estimate of 3:1 (National Autistic Society, 2019).

Whilst boys will tend to externally manifest their dysregulation, girls will tend to internalise and can develop emotional and mental health difficulties as a result. This is now being perceived as two subsets of autism, one external and the other internal in its manifestation, rather than male and female in presentation.

The Autistic Teenager

At home

Teenage years, along with puberty, tend to be times when social networks are very important; however, for the teenager with autism it's the complete opposite. It's a time for exploration, to use their intellect, memory, and language skills to develop huge amounts of knowledge about topics that fascinate them, for example, cars, trains, aircraft, wars and history. They will have by now trained their parents to understand how they like things to be done, their obsessive-compulsive disorder (OCD) traits, and their need to impose order where there is none. This form of control allows them to manage their life, and keep themselves calm and regulated; however, this need for control can be very powerful and parents can feel they are always 'walking on eggshells' as a result. The lack of control, or their perceived lack of control, can cause meltdowns due to dysregulation.

At school

At school, the autistic teenager will struggle, even with additional classroom support (e.g., having an EHCP). Being in a mainstream school in a classroom of 25–30 teenagers, many of whom are not interested in learning, can be a recipe for disaster, and so the challenge of school is to regulate oneself and to shut out all the sensory information bombarding them – too many people, noise, constant change, smells, and teachers who do not understand them. Having so many teachers means that many of them do not have the time to get to know them and understand their needs. Ignorance that they struggle in classroom settings, and ignorance that they lack the skills to make friends and to choose who they should work with when a teacher shouts out 'right class pair up to work on the problem set'.

Some with autism can have conflicting 'inside voices'; however, they do not share these with others, for fear of being seen as freaks, or disturbed. These voices can tell them to run to safety, but in a school, there may seem to be no obvious areas of safety. It's conflicting advice. It's a daily or hourly challenge to self-regulate.

Socially with friends

The autistic teenager knows they don't need friends but understands that everyone else thinks they do. They lack the skills to make friends, so rely on stock answers of phases to say, and it's easier to cosy up to a group who are the least annoying, and at some point, they will accept them. The need to be popular is bizarre to them, but they understand others, especially their parents see this as something to aim for. At the weekend and during school holidays they prefer to be alone or with their family, it's safer and more predictable. They can make friends online, gaming or on other platforms, where they can find people who are like-minded. However, they are naive to the dangers of such friendships, and that some of the people they are talking to online are adults, who might take advantage of their vulnerability and naivety.

Girls with autism tend to be loners at school, with very few friends. They struggle socially and this makes them feel anxious. Life outside of the safety of their home is wearing a mask, doing the right things, and saying the right things, but internally they are struggling and lack control of themselves. At home they can be very erratic with meltdowns-shutdowns after keeping it together during the day at school. Sadly, many turn to controlling their bodies through anorexia and others forms of self-harm, for example, cutting. It's about control in a world they cannot control. It's also about feeling alive and escaping a world that they feel alien in.

The concept of being an 'alien' is two-way. Many with autism see themselves in a world they struggle to understand. Likewise, for a young generation, in the TV shows, *The Big Bang Theory* and *Young Sheldon*, the character of Sheldon is autistic but not specifically mentioned. Whilst many with autism see themselves as being superior and above others, with a higher IQ, many who are not autistic can seem like aliens: uncaring, unemotional, and more like a robot. The struggle of the autistic person is that the world around them seems illogical and hard to read or understand.

Frustrations

The world is very frustrating to autistic teenagers, it's chaotic and unordered. Adults want them to do things they don't want to do, which makes no sense. Others seem to know the rules of how to act and do things, but no one has told them the rules of the game so they can't play it, which is highly frustrating. When they try and make order through OCD and stimming repetitive tendencies (see Appendix 1), they are told they are weird, but it's the world around them that 'they' perceive as weird. Autistic people believe they can fix the world and make it right again if others would allow them.

The Autistic adult

Many adults have undiagnosed autism, surviving a childhood of being blamed for not being normal, but no one helping them to understand what normal is. They have tried their best to do and say the right thing, and many have survived school, got into university, and hopefully into a paying job through their academic, rather than emotional intelligence. Being able to do things that many around them can't or are not intelligent enough to do, so many find careers, such as coding and programming, or using their maths skills, allowing them to excel in careers where they are left alone. It's okay to be a bit geeky in those professions; however, most with autism don't realise how geeky they really can be.

Lacking social skills, and being undiagnosed, they lack many of the skills needed to make friends and, therefore, are likely to be single. Unless they find another autistic-like themselves, they are likely to spend evenings and weekends alone. Most autistic adults will not socialise at or after work.

Some autistic adults struggle to regulate themselves and without support from their parents are perceived to need to be in supported living accommodation. Whilst higher functioning autistics go to university and have careers, many more struggle at school and go to college, and then into lower-paid professions. Such autistic adults may need support throughout their lives to function in society, e.g., live independently, pay bills, and go shopping.

Teaching a child/young person with Autism

Burton-Hughes (2019) amongst other educators suggest the following are good strategies to use for those with autism at school. As autism is a spectrum difference a tailored approach is needed; however, the following can be a guide:

- **Establish a routine with them.** The world is often a confusing and anxiety-inducing place for autistic children. This is why they find great comfort in a predictable and stable routine. Fortunately, the structured nature of school is perfect for this, but one needs to find a way to make its daily routine clear to them. Visual timetables can be effective and are widely used by schools. This involves adding images and simple words to a timetable, to describe the activities and transitions in the child's day. Having this visual aid can give the autistic child a sense of security, whilst also acting as a reminder for those who support them.
- **Consider the learning environment.** Many children with autism can experience sensory sensitivity, causing them to have intense positive or negative reactions to sensory stimulation. So, a useful and simple step is making the classroom environment less overwhelming for them. As every autistic child is different, teachers will have to learn what their sensitivities are, and how they react to hearing certain sounds or touching certain fabrics, parents or carers can offer input for this. Then try to remove or reduce any stimuli in the environment that causes them anxiety. For example, if the school bell is distressing, then allow them to wear noise-cancelling headphones five minutes before it goes off.
- **Manage changes and transitions.** Because an autistic child's routine is crucial to their comfort, changes and transitions can be incredibly overwhelming for them. Changes are often unavoidable and even necessary in school, but you can alleviate their anxiety by preparing the autistic child beforehand. For example, if a change of classrooms, then take the child to view it a few days in advance. Show and give them pictures of it for them to look at until the day of the change. Giving some predictability to any unexpected task can help it feel less daunting for the child and give them time to prepare themselves.
- **Communicate clearly.** Whilst autism varies, it can impact a child's ability to communicate and interpret meaning. Careful consideration should be made to

the words and sentences used. Avoid complicating metaphors and rhetorical questions. Keep them simple and direct is best. For instance, "Tim, can you please start packing up your pencils and tidy them away into drawers please?" A much clearer instruction for them is: "Tim, put pencils away." You could also point to the place they need to store the pencils.

- **Integrate their interests.** One of the many things that make autistic children unique is how they develop highly focused interests. Whether it's trains, electronics, unicorns, or a certain period in history, these interests can all be used as gateways to learning. For example, if you know that their interest is trains, then integrate words and pictures related to them in maths problems and spelling exercises. Doing so can make a big difference in how engaged the autistic child can be.
- **Work with their parents/carers.** Parents and carers are the true experts on their autistic children, impacting how they are at home and school. Teachers should coordinate and share knowledge with them, suggest interventions that have worked at home or in school for the child and integrate these into their routine. Not only will building a working relationship benefit the autistic child, but it will also help the parents/carers feel more relaxed and confident about their child's education.
- **Build your resilience.** Even when you think you're doing everything right, teaching an autistic child can still be challenging. The child and their parents are counting on you to do your best though, so it's important to learn how to be resilient from those difficult days. Building a relationship with autistic children is not something that happens overnight, it takes time, dedication, and patience. You won't always get things right to start with, and ultimately, autistic children are still children, who can be challenging even at the best of times. Remember, autistic children are not difficult on purpose, they are doing the best they can with their worldview and the support they have available.

So, on those days when you have an autistic child disrupting class and you feel like giving up, just remember that they are likely acting out for a reason. It's usually because of a need that isn't being met, once teachers learn what their needs are, they may find things become so much easier. That sense of accomplishment one gains from supporting them will one day outweigh any stress felt in the past.

References

Adams, R. (2024). £100m spent in England on failed efforts to block children's send support. *The Guardian online.* 22 December 2024. Retrieved 08/01/2025. www.theguardian.com/uk-news/2024/dec/22/100m-spent-in-england-on-failed-efforts-to-block-childrens-send-support

Agnew-Blais, J.C. (2024). Hidden in plain sight: Delayed ADHD diagnosis among girls and women – A commentary on Skoglund et al. (2023). *Journal of Child Psychology and Psychiatry.* 2024 October, *65*(10), 1398–1400. https://doi.org/10.1111/jcpp.14023. Epub 2024 May 26. PMID: 38798101.

American Psychiatric Association (Ed.). (2022). *Diagnostic and statistical manual of mental disorders* (5th ed.), Text Revision (DSM-5-TR). Washington, DC: American Psychiatric Publishing. ISBN 978-0-89042-575-6.

Antezana, L., Factor, R.S., Condy, E.E., Strege, M.V., Scarpa, A., & Richey, J.A. (2019). Gender differences in restricted and repetitive behaviors and interests in youth with autism. *Autism Research*. 2019 February, *12*(2), 274–283. https://doi.org/10.1002/aur.2049. Epub 2018 Dec 17. PMID: 30561911.

Archer, N. (2024). When two different worlds collide (autism spectrum conditions and the criminal justice system). *Autism West Midlands*. Retrieved 05/07/2024. https://livingautism.com/two-different-worlds-collide-autism-spectrum-conditions-criminal-justice-system/

Autism Speaks (2024). Applied Behaviour Analysis (ABA). Retrieved 01/07/2024. https://www.autismspeaks.org/applied-behavior-analysis

Behaviour Interventions (2024). 20 Famous people with autism spectrum disorder (ASD). Retrieved 14/08/2024. https://behavioral-innovations.com/blog/20-famous-people-with-autism-spectrum-disorder-asd/

Bell, A. (2024). What causes autism? Is autism genetic or environmental? 10 April 2024. Retrieved 28/10/2024. https://medschool.ucla.edu/news-article/is-autism-genetic

BMJ Best Practice (2023). Autism spectrum disorder. *13 Jun 2023. British Medical Journal (*BMJ). Retrieved 06/05/2025. bestpractice.bmj.com/topics/en-gb/379

Brinkhurst-Cuff, C. (2023). Jason Arday: He learned to talk at 11 and read at 18 – Then became Cambridge's youngest Black professor. *The Guardian Newspaper Group*. Tue 11 July 2023 10.00 BST. Retrieved 01/07/2024. https://www.theguardian.com/society/2023/jul/11/jason-arday-cambridge-university-youngest-black-professor

Burton-Hughes, L. (2019). How to support a child with autism in the classroom. *High Speed Training*. Retrieved 19/06/2024. https://www.highspeedtraining.co.uk/hub/how-to-support-a-child-with-autism-in-the-classroom/

Centers for Disease Control and Prevention-CDC (2024). Clinical testing and diagnosis for autism spectrum disorder. 16 May 2024. Retrieved 01/07/2024. https://www.cdc.gov/autism/hcp/diagnosis/index.html

Children's Commissioner (2022b). Beyond the labels: A SEND system which works for every child, every time. November 2022. Retrieved 14/07/2024. https://assets.childrens commissioner.gov.uk/wpuploads/2022/11/cc-beyond-the-labels-a-send-system-which-works-for-every-child-every-time.pdf

Children's Commissioner (2024). New statistics on Education, Health and Care Plans (EHCP) for children with special educational needs. 29 January 2024. Retrieved 22/07/2024. https://www.childrenscommissioner.gov.uk/blog/new-statistics-on-education-health-and-care-plans-ehcp-for-children-with-special-educational-needs/

Department of Education (2015). SEND code of practice. January 2015. Retrieved 14/08/2024. https://www.gov.uk/government/publications/send-code-of-practice-0-to-25

Huang, Y., Arnold, S.R., Foley, K.R., & Trollor, J.N. (2020). Diagnosis of autism in adulthood: A scoping review. *Autism*, *24*(6), 1311–1327.

Hviid, A., Hansen, J.V., Frisch, M., Melbye, M. (2019). Measles, mumps, rubella vaccination and autism: A nationwide cohort study. *Annals of Internal Medicine, 170*, 513–520. https://doi.org/10.7326/M18-2101. Epub 2019 March 5.

I-autism (2025). *Understanding the 3 Levels of Autism*. Retrieved 14/05/25. i-autism.com/the-3-levels-of-autism/

Jackson, L. (2002). *Freeks, geeks and Asperger syndrome*. London: Jessica Kingsley Publishers.

Kirby, A., Williams, W., Clasby, B., Hughes, N., & Cleaton, M. (2020). Understanding the complexity of neurodevelopmental profiles of females in prison. *International*

Journal of Prisoner Health. Published on 18 December 2020. https://doi.org/10.1108/IJPH-12-2019-0067

Leicestershire Partnership NHS Trust (2024). Autistic people in the public eye. Retrieved 28/10/2024.

Martin, H. (2023). Six famous entrepreneurs who turned their neurodiversity into their secret weapon. Updated 22 June 2023. Retrieved 01/07/2024. https://www.talentedladiesclub.com/articles/six-famous-entrepreneurs-who-turned-their-neurodiversity-into-their-secret-weapon/

National Autistic Society (2019). The Autism Act, 10 years on: A report from the All Party Parliamentary Group on Autism on understanding, services and support for autistic people and their families in England. Retrieved 09/07/2024. https://pearsfoundation.org.uk/wp-content/uploads/2019/09/APPGA-Autism-Act-Inquiry-Report.pdf

National Autistic Society (2022). Youth justice report. 6 October 2022. Retrieved 14/07/2024. https://www.autism.org.uk/what-we-do/news/youth-justice-report

National Autistic Society (2023). Education report 2023. 30 May 2023. Retrieved 14/07/2024. https://dy55nndrxke1w.cloudfront.net/file/24/asDKIN9asAvgMtEas6gIatOcB5H/NAS_Education%20Report%202023.pdf

National Health Service – NHS (2024a). Signs of autism in children. Retrieved 17/07/2024. https://www.nhs.uk/conditions/autism/signs/children/

National Health Service – NHS (2024b). Signs of autism in adults. Retrieved 17/07/2024. https://www.nhs.uk/conditions/autism/signs/adults/#:~:text=Autism%20in%20women&text=have%20learned%20to%20hide%20signs,fewer%20signs%20of%20repetitive%20behaviours

NCCMH (2023). Recognition, referral, diagnosis and management of adults on the autism spectrum. *National Collaborating Centre for Mental Health (NCCMH)*. https://www.nice.org.uk

NCCWCH (2022). Autism: Recognition, referral and diagnosis of children and young people on the autism spectrum. *National Collaborating Centre for Women's and Children's Health (NCCWCH)*. https://www.nice.org.uk

O'Nions, E., McKechnie, D.G., Long, C., Mandy, W., & Stott, J. (2023). How can autistic adults be supported in primary care? *British Journal of General Practice*, *73*(736), 518–521.

Saporito, K. (2022). Why autism has been underdiagnosed in girls and women: Better-informed perspectives are changing the field. 3 February 2022. Retrieved 29/01/2025. www.psychologytoday.com/us/blog/understanding-the-diversity-in-neurodiversity/202202/why-autism-has-been-underdiagnosed-in#:~:text=Autistic%20females%20are%20underdiagnosed%2C%20particularly%20in%20individuals%20without,for%20females%2C%20later%20diagnoses%2C%20missed%20diagnoses%2C%20and%20misdiagnoses.?msockid=2bbbb20fceec64fe23c2a6eecf736524

Weinberg, A., & Doyle, N. (2017). *Psychology at work: Improving wellbeing and productivity in the workplace* (L.M. Coulthard, Ed.). London: British Psychological Society. ISBN 978-1-85433-754-2

Welsh Assembly (2010). Autistic spectrum disorders a guide for criminal justice system practitioners in Wales. December 2010. Welsh Assembly.

World Health Organization – WHO (2024). International statistical classification of diseases and related health problems 11th revision (ICD-11)-WHO version for; ICD-11 for mortality and morbidity statistics. Retrieved 17/07/2024. https://icd.who.int/browse/2024-01/mms/en

3   Anxiety

Causes of anxiety for those with autism

Most people experience frustration, stress, or anxiety as part of everyday life situations. Some people learn how to cope so well, that stress or anxiety has little impact on them. But for others, including individuals with autism, stress and anxiety can cripple them to varying degrees. So, situations that create anxiety in one individual may not be for another.

Dave Nelson, director of The Community School in Decatur, Georgia, a junior high and high school for adolescents with autism (Davis, 2012), comments,

> *Every single one of my students has anxiety almost every day. What is so interesting, however, is how different the manifestations of that condition can be. Some students begin asking constant questions; some interrupt constantly; some retreat or run away; and some get rude or provoking. Everyone (adults included) has their special way of showing when they're anxious, from biting fingernails to getting headaches to talking a lot.*

Louise Page, an autism therapist and mother of an individual with autism comments

> *You may observe them, for example, looking down at their feet, or wringing their hands or their hands may be set flat against their thighs, looking fearful or frozen to the spot, or outwardly distressed (e.g. behaviour outburst) and so on. Also, their fight or flight response may be exaggerated, and efforts to return their state to a relative calm may be very difficult.*

Flight, fight, freeze, and fawn

Researchers have identified how individuals cope with anxiety and stress, understood as four strategies to cope:

- **Fight**: facing any perceived threat aggressively
- **Flight**: running away from danger
- **Freeze**: unable to move or act against a threat

DOI: 10.4324/9781003614432-3

- **Fawn**: immediately acting to try to please to avoid any conflict

So, when we talk about how autistic people cope with stress and anxiety, the above helps us to frame the responses. 'Fight' is the only combative strategy, whereas 'flight' and 'fawn' are avoidance strategies, with 'freeze' being seen as a passive strategy. The following helps to better understand each strategy (Guy-Evans, 2023).

Fight response

When you feel in danger and believe you can overpower the threat, you are in fight mode. Your brain sends signals throughout your body to rapidly prepare for the physical demands of fighting, seen as:

- Tighten the jaw or grinding of the teeth
- An urge to punch someone or something
- Feeling intense anger or killing someone, even yourself
- A desire to stomp or kick
- Crying
- Glaring at people, conserving angrily
- An upset stomach, feels like knots or burning
- Attacking the source of the danger

Flight response

This is believing you can defeat the danger by running away. In some cases, running away is the best decision. Take a burning building as an example. Unless you are a firefighter, it is best to get out of there as fast as you can. The following emotional and physical responses signify you are in flight mode:

- Excessively exercising
- Feeling fidgety, tense or trapped
- Constantly moving legs, feet, and arms
- Restless body that will not stop moving
- Sensation of numbness in extremities
- Dilated eyes, darting eyes

Freeze response

When one feels neither like fighting nor fighting, freezing is an option. This list of responses lets you know you are in freeze mode:

- Pale skin
- Sense of dread
- Feeling stiff, heavy, cold, numb

- Loud, pounding heart
- Decreasing in heart rate
- Sensing tolerated stress

Fawn response

Fawning is an important modern-day survival instinct and can be a response to complex trauma, it could be called a coping or survival strategy, or even masking, as young autistic children learn that submission and appeasement are effective ways to avoid harm or conflict. It can be defined as (Inclusive Teach, 2024; Ryder, 2022):

- Abandoning the self (what you want or need) to attend to the needs, wishes, and demands of others
- It's a process where we take care of others by suppressing our emotions, needs, or identity
- Fawning is both a trauma response and an attempt to maintain safety. It can also be an expected social behaviour in Western cultures
- We often perform prosocial behaviours even when our internal state doesn't align with them

Examples may be:

- Adapting behaviour to avoid conflict, rejection, or exclusion. It's akin to wearing a social mask—a camouflage that conceals authentic responses.
- A response characterised by submissive and appeasing behaviour, where individuals seek to please or comply with the person or situation causing the threat to reduce the risk of harm.
- Masking—a close cousin of fawning—is our social chameleon act. Masking involves adapting our behaviour to fit in with our surroundings. We adjust the hue of our personalities to match the backdrop, concealing our authentic selves.
- Neurodiverse individuals often engage in masking. They suppress stimming behaviours so as not to annoy people or appear 'different'. They attempt to repress or tolerate sensory sensitivities even if they are desperate to push back against them, and unique ways of processing the world. Why? To be accepted, to blend seamlessly, and to avoid standing out.
- But beneath the mask lies a delicate balance. How much authenticity do we sacrifice? How much energy do we expend to fit the mould?

In a classroom setting, fawning (masking) may look like this:

- People-pleasing behaviour: A student exhibiting a fawn response may try to please the teacher or other students excessively, even at the expense of their own needs or boundaries. They may agree with everything the teacher says, even if they don't fully understand or agree with it, to avoid conflict or disapproval.
- Camouflage: Observing and mimicking others for social camouflage. Developing a repertoire of rehearsed responses or questions.

- Eye contact: Forcing eye contact and social conversation to maintain social convention.
- Excessive compliance: They may follow instructions or rules to an extreme degree, even if the instructions are unreasonable or harmful to themselves. They may not advocate for their own needs or question authority figures.
- Flattery or ingratiation: A student exhibiting a fawn response may excessively compliment or flatter the teacher or other students, even if the praise is not entirely genuine. This behaviour is aimed at gaining approval or avoiding conflict.
- Minimising their own needs or concerns: They may downplay their struggles, needs, or concerns to avoid causing trouble or being seen as a burden, bottling these up at the cost of their well-being.
- Difficulty setting boundaries: They may have trouble saying 'no' or setting healthy boundaries with others, leading to overcommitment, or being taken advantage of.
- Chameleon-like behaviour: They may adapt their behaviour, opinions, or personality to match what they perceive is expected or desired by others, rather than expressing their authentic selves.

It could be argued that fawn (masking) responses cause the most internal struggles in autistic young people as they spend so much effort in 'survival' mode that all they want to be is to be left alone.

Unstructured times

Davis (2012) suggests an unstructured time that has no specific rules or activity which creates boundaries or limits can be very challenging for those with autism. These may include:

- Waiting for and/or riding the school bus
- Before and after school time
- Transitions throughout the day (place to place, person to person, topic to topic)
- Lunch/cafeteria
- Recess
- Physical education

Academic situations

Other everyday activities at school can anxiety, including:

- Understanding what to do and how to do it
- Breaking down tasks
- Writing
- Reading
- Organisation of your books or work
- Grades, receiving marks and feedback

- Presentations in class
- Answering aloud in class
- Tests

One student of mine was happy doing classwork but struggled severely with his work being marked and feedback. He would get highly dysregulated and helplessly lie on the classroom floor. This indicated very high levels of stress and anxiety from receiving grades and judgement from others.

Sensory issues

Sensory issues can be triggered almost any time or anywhere daily (Davis, 2012). Whether the individual is experiencing an anxious moment or not, sensory integration challenges can overpower a person's ability to control him- or herself. Sensory situations that may provoke anxiety can include:

- Crowds – school assemblies, concerts, field trips, grocery stores, etc.
- Space – too large, too crowded, too bright, too loud, too smelly, etc.
- Sounds/noise, e.g., a fire alarm
- Natural disasters/events, e.g., torrential rain, hail, snow
- Smells – cafeteria, restrooms, cleaning materials, markers, paints, colognes
- Food – sight, texture, taste, smell, sound when eating
- Haircuts
- Dental or medical issues
- Showers, bathing (some individuals have shared that showers 'hurt' their bodies)
- Clothing – too tight, scratchy
- Brushing teeth

Social situations

Social situations are already challenging for individuals with autism, and anxiety can increase in the moment or even in anticipation of an upcoming event (Davis, 2012). Some examples include:

- Novel events – unplanned and unannounced
- Changes in plans – daily school routine interrupted, or family plans changed
- Adjusting personal interests with class or family plans
- Outdoor activities – concerts, picnics, recess
- Large gatherings – school assemblies, family gatherings
- Young children (who are unpredictable in many ways)
- Initiating a conversation with a peer
- Routines – After a day at school where the child was able to maintain body control, listen, complete activities, and appear composed, going home and having even more expectations including typical routines, can increase anxiety and agitation. Routines such as:
  - Doing homework

- Chores
- Meal, bath, bedtime routines
- Getting ready for school

Challenging behaviour and why it happens?

Challenging behaviour is behaviour that has negative effects on autistic children and teenagers, and other people around them (Davis, 2012), for example, autistic children and teenagers might:

- Refuse requests or ignore instructions, which makes it hard for their family to get things done
- Leave the classroom or hide under a table, which might affect their learning
- Take their clothes off in public or invade people's personal space, which might be unsafe for them and others
- Behave aggressively or hurt themselves

It's important to understand why your autistic child is behaving in challenging ways. When you understand why, you can work out how to respond. Your child might behave in challenging ways because they:

- Don't understand other people's social cues or expectations
- Have trouble with classroom learning
- Feel overwhelmed by sensory input
- Have trouble with changes in routine or transitions between activities
- Find it hard to understand or talk about their feelings
- Find it hard to manage their reactions when things happen around them
- Can't do a certain routine or ritual, or things don't go to plan
- Are tired or don't feel well.

References

Davis, K. (2012). Anxiety and panic struggles. Retrieved 19/06/2024. https://www.iidc.indiana.edu/irca/articles/what-triggers-anxiety-for-an-individual-with-autism.html

Guy-Evans, O. (2023). Fight, flight, freeze, or fawn: How we respond to threats. 9 November 2023. Retrieved 31/07/2024. https://www.simplypsychology.org/fight-flight-freeze-fawn.html

Inclusive Teach (2024). Fawning and autism: Unmasking the hidden survival instincts. 13 March 2024. Retrieved 31/07/2024. https://inclusiveteach.com/2024/03/13/fawning-and-autism-unmasking-the-hidden-survival-instincts/

Ryder, G. (2022). The fawn response: How trauma can lead to people-pleasing. 10 January 2022. Retrieved 31/07/2024. https://psychcentral.com/health/fawn-response#definition

4   Bullying and Victimisation

Interpersonal victimisation refers to violence and abuse that occur within close personal relationships, committed by people such as friends, family members, or carers (Pearson et al., 2022). It can involve sexual and financial exploitation (e.g., forcing someone into unwanted sexual activity with oneself or others, someone forcing you to give them money), physical, psychological, or emotional abuse, and humiliation/cruelty. Studies suggest between 49% and 80% of autistic adults have been victimised by someone they know.

Pearson et al. (2022) argue that it is important to understand the nuance between interpersonal victimisation and other forms of peer victimisation such as bullying, despite some overlap between the two, as research suggests that autistic people are often bullied. Both interpersonal victimisation and bullying/peer victimisation can include physical, emotional, and psychological harm against one another, and have a negative impact on well-being outcomes for autistic people. However, unlike bullying, interpersonal victimisation is defined by the presence of an interpersonal relationship, therefore 'trust', between the perpetrator and victim. Acknowledgement of the role that social relationships can play in providing the context for interpersonal victimisation to occur is crucial, given the mistaken belief that autistic people neither desire nor value social relationships. Many seek them out to please parents and others, however, struggle with understanding them, which makes them easily preyed upon.

Forster and Pearson (2020) asked autistic adults about their experiences of relationships and understanding of Mate Crime, which is a form of interpersonal victimisation by those considered to be friends ('mate' is a British slang term for a friend). Participants outlined the challenges that they faced building genuine, reciprocal relationships and their experiences of victimisation. They also spoke about their difficulties identifying unreasonable behaviour from others, and their raised need for social compliance. These findings were consistent with previous research into relationship and peer victimisation among autistic adults.

The perception of autistic people being vulnerable is developed in society by the stereotype of autistic people being 'child-like'. Research suggests autistic people are more likely to experience situational vulnerabilities (e.g., underemployment, poverty, isolation, and lack of social support) that might place them at a higher risk of victimisation. However, situational vulnerabilities are often underpinned

DOI: 10.4324/9781003614432-4

by stigma and marginalisation that autistic people experience routinely in both academic and public spheres.

Starting at school, the autistic child can be bullied

Researchers suggest victimisation starts at school, Park et al. (2020) investigated the prevalence of risks and factors associated with bullying involvement (victimisation, perpetrator, and perpetrator-victimisation) among students with autism. From 34 studies they found prevalence estimates for victimisation (67%). The risk of victimisation in students with autism was found to be significantly higher than that in typically developing students and students with other disabilities. Furthermore, deficits in social interaction and communication, externalising symptoms, internalising symptoms, and integrated inclusive school settings were related to higher victimisation, and externalising symptoms were related to higher cases of bullying of young people with autism. They conclude the need for bullying intervention for students with autism, especially those who are younger, are in an inclusive school setting, and have higher social difficulties and externalising/ internalising symptoms. They found students with autism appear to be particularly vulnerable to bullying involvement due to their deficits in social communication, and difficulties with empathy.

Interestingly, and not good for inclusive school initiatives, they found a positive effect for victimisation and the inclusive school setting, this meant that students with autism who were integrated into the inclusive school setting experienced more severe victimisation than those who were not. Bullying occurs in the presence of a power imbalance between bullies and victims. An inherent power imbalance exists between students with autism and typically developing peers due to impairments in social communication, social skills, and comorbid conditions in students with autism. Their findings indicate that simply exposing students with autism to inclusive school settings, without appropriate preparation, not only fails to promote the acquisition of social skills and development of peer relationships for students with autism but also poses harm to students with autism by increasing their risks for peer victimisation. For successful outcomes in inclusive education for students with autism, suggest peer-mediated interventions against bullying; disability awareness education for students, families and school staff; supervision during recess time; and firm and consistent disciplinary methods for bullying across various settings, including homes, schools, and communities. They also found that victimisation in verbal and relational bullying types was more frequent in younger students with autism (5–12 years) than in adolescents with autism (13–22 years). Also, students with autism were significantly more likely to be targets of physical-victimisation when schooled in a mixed school setting (inclusive setting and segregated setting) than in an inclusive school setting.

Neurodivergent Rebel (2022) helps to explain what this might look like

What the other kids would do to me was pick on me, when the teacher wasn't looking, and they would constantly pick at me, picking at me, pick at me, picking at me. Maybe it was throwing spitballs at me, or poking me in the back, or just doing some constant little thing, every time the teacher wasn't looking... until I couldn't take it anymore. Eventually, I would get boiling mad, like a volcano, and the pressure would build up, and I would turn around and scream at them, or have a reaction.

When this happened, I would be the one who would get in trouble, not the other kid, who was constantly throwing things at me, or smacking me, or poking me, or taking my things, when the teacher wasn't looking.

Interestingly she notes "once I went to one of my teachers and told them that I was being bullied and picked on. The teacher's response was 'If you would just act normal, the other kids would leave you alone'". This lack of understanding by teachers is reflected in their students, hence the bullying noted above.

Haigh (2023) reported in the national UK press the case of Charlie Michael Baker, a 16-year-old boy with autism, who was bullied so badly that he was left suicidal. He chose to write a book as he was always made to feel different, after 'ruthless bullying over many years' and developed an eating disorder as a result. He said, "It was a really dark, dark, dark time for me. I didn't talk to anyone about it, not even my parents knew". In Year 7, bullying by other students in his class became so bad that teachers decided to remove him from the classroom altogether and place him on his own in a room with glass walls – instead of tackling the problem. He says, "It's always easier to take the victim away. You can either punish one person or 20. They are not going to exclude 20 children. They can't do anything to the whole year [group]".

Research by Altomare et al. (2017) argues students with special education needs, including autism, often possess low social status within school settings, making them particularly susceptible to peer victimisation. Conversation challenges and a lack of awareness of social cues, in addition to their rigid and/ or repetitive behaviours, may be perceived as odd by their typically developing peers. Suggesting the social naivete of such students can lead to increased social vulnerability and the potential for manipulation by other, more socially savvy students. They note that students with autism experience high rates of victimisation and are four times more likely than typically developing students to report being bullied (Wainscot et al., 2008). Self-reported rates of peer victimisation of students with autism are between 57% and 75% (Kowalski & Fedina, 2011), while parent-reported rates range from 46% to 77% (Cappadocia et al., 2012). These rates are higher than those students with cystic fibrosis (14.3%), learning disability (24.2%), attention-deficit/hyperactivity disorder (29.2%) or typically developing students (8.5%; Twyman et al., 2010).

Altomare et al. (2017) concluded after a study of 38 autistic children, 8–13 years old, that they coped by:

- Telling a teacher or another adult – the most common response. Some participants reported that they would first try to solve the situation on their own, and if unsuccessful, would then tell an adult. Others indicated that telling someone would make them feel better, while acknowledging that it would not change the situation.

- Stand up/say something – Another common response was to stand up to the bully. However, some of the students stated that their 'comebacks' had the potential to further entice the bully to continue bullying.
- Problem-solving – Only seven students suggested problem-solving techniques when faced with peer victimisation. Responses within this subtheme indicated some degree of resilience and entailed efforts to maintain the peace with creative and mature ways to befriend the bully.
- Externalising behaviour – Eleven students suggested externalising strategies (e.g., getting angry, physical aggression, and/or revenge). Interestingly, some students suggested unrealistic and vengeful responses.
- Ignoring – Fifteen participants suggested ignoring as a strategy, suggesting that ignoring is effective when it is a one-time occurrence, but not necessarily if it occurs repeatedly.
- Walk away/stay away – Twelve participants suggested walking away from or avoiding the bully, either as an initial response or after other strategies were ineffective.
- Barriers to strategies – Eleven participants reflected barriers to certain strategies and the challenge of determining a straightforward solution, as bullying may persist despite telling a teacher, suggesting that simply telling an adult or someone in authority may not effectively address the situation.
- Uncertainty – Eleven participants reported uncertainty. Some responses indicated hesitation, frustration, and an inability to provide an idea for what to do when faced with bullying.

The autistic young person is the bully

The preceding section regarding bullying suggests that of the strategies noted by Altomare et al. (2017), many were uncertain of the effectiveness of interventions by others such as teachers. One of the strategies noted was externalised behaviour: physical aggression and revenge. Walton (2012) and Anderson (2012) help to understand why some with autism bully back after being bullied themselves. From a study of 1,167 children with ASD, ages 6–15, almost two-thirds of autistic children had been bullied at some point in their lives, and they were three times more likely than neurotypical kids to be bullied in the past three months. This was even true for home-schooled autistic children, who were sometimes educated at home precisely because of the bullying issue. The three most common types of bullying were verbal, or, in other words, psychological: "being teased, picked on, or made fun of" (73%); "being ignored or left out of things on purpose" (51%); and "being called bad names" (47%). But almost a third of autistic children also experienced physical bullying – being shoved, pushed, slapped, hit, or kicked.

The study also goes on to highlight that those with autism are also more likely to bully others, as a result. According to the report, many of these kids may be both bullies and victims, which is somewhat more common in children with developmental or emotional problems. Children with autism who bully may do it unintentionally. "My son doesn't realise he is bullying," said one parent. "He is trying to get other kids to pay attention to him so he does it by grabbing their ball away from them or getting 'in their face' when they say to stop." Another parent said, "Our boy... may take an object from another child or scream when unhappy but any purposeful cruelty, he would never do". Autistic children who are being bullied and then bully in return, may not have the social skills to avoid or to get themselves out of the situation. According to Anderson (2012), "Unlike victims who are more passive, bully-victims insult their tormentors or otherwise try to fight back in a way that only makes the situation worse." Other bullying researchers have noticed that children with behavioural, emotional, or developmental issues may behave as both bully and victim (Van Cleave & Davis, 2006), suggesting that unlike victims who are more passive, bully victims insult their tormentors or otherwise try to fight back in a way that only makes the situation worse. They are often "disruptive and impulsive, with poor social and problem-solving skills."

Considering the deficits in social understanding that children with autism have, it may be that their 'bullying' is different than that manifested by typical children who, generally use aggression to increase and maintain social status in the peer group. Some parents whose children had 'bullied' noted that the motivation behind the behaviour had nothing to do with becoming top-dog, a power play.

One problem some parents reported was social misunderstanding. For example, a child with autism might believe a peer who had bumped into them by accident had done so on purpose and then lash out. Some noted that children would begin to bully only after having been bullied first.

Hwang et al.'s study (2018) investigated autism and school bullying: Who is the Victim? Who is the Perpetrator? They discussed behaviours in bullying are characterised by the perpetrators' intention to cause mental and/or physical suffering to others (Olweus, 1994). Perpetrators generally determine what will cause pain and/or discomfort for their victims and then act accordingly. They argue that young people with autism will be likely to have considerable difficulty conducting this level of social analysis and execution, due to their difficulty in understanding and using the subtle and not-so-subtle social rules and cues, as well as their general inability to take the perspective of others. However, they remark that children with autism may have potentially more aggressive behaviour than typical children due to various comorbidities. However, their findings indicate that children with autism are more likely to be the *victims* of bullying and less likely to bully others when compared with typically developing children. Park et al. (2020) also found young people with autism acting as perpetrators.

Whilst those with autism may bully, Hwang et al. (2018) suggest the following should be considered:

- Young people with autism have limited insight into social processes (Frith & Hill, 2004; van Roekel et al., 2010), and they may not be aware of the consequences of their own behaviours/words, for example, they may say brutally frank but accurate, things regarding characteristics of their peers causing seemingly purposeful offence.

- Young people with autism may have increased levels of aggressive behaviours, especially if routines are disrupted or they are exposed to irritating sensory stimuli; thus, those with autism with increased levels of aggression could be labelled as bullies, even in the absence of social intention (van Roekel et al., 2010).
- The high level of comorbidity in children with autism can contribute to aggressive behaviour or irritable effect, which, in turn, can be perceived as perpetrating behaviour.
- Studies suggest perpetrating, bullying behaviours of children with autism are only related to comorbidity with disruptive behaviour disorder (conduct disorders and ODD) and to emotional regulation difficulties (Zablotsky et al., 2013).

Van Roekel et al. (2009) discuss the perception of bullying and victimisation consists of two main parts: first, one must perceive that the action is aggressive, and second, one has to perceive that this aggression is directed towards a person who is relatively weaker than the aggressor(s), which refers to an imbalance of power. Although it can be expected that bullying and victimisation are related to autism, an important question is whether adolescents with autism can perceive bullying or victimisation when it occurs. Studies suggest those with autism commonly have a deficit in the understanding of the minds and mental states of other people (State of Mind), and consequently also in understanding the intentions of others, making the act of bullying challenging.

One parent helps to explain that those with autism can plan and inflict revenge or punishment on others, in her case, herself as a parent when they are perceived to be wronged (NAS85258, 2022).

> *He likes giving me kisses before he goes to bed. A few nights ago, I did the bedtime routine and he fell asleep before he could give me some kisses. In the morning, he came into my room to 'punish' me as this was revenge for his not being able to kiss me before he fell asleep. He came in calmly and proceeded to attack me in the morning as he said this was my punishment. This is just one example. Another time, he got upset over something I did and I locked myself in my room as he was attacking me. He convinced me in a calm voice that he would not attack me as long as I unlocked the door. As soon as I unlocked the door he then attacked me.*

This can be explained by the known autistic trait of having a strong sense of justice, and when those with autism feel unfairly treated they will strongly protest, and in this and other cases take revenge.

It could be argued that young people with autism who choose the external behaviour and revenge pathway may lack the social awareness that their actions may be criminal and this places them in scope for police intervention. Whilst they may argue that they have been wronged (bullied or victimised), it will be their actions that are judged if they are criminal in nature. So bullying in young people with autism may be linked to revenge after being wronged, rather than the need to improve social standing, which is where traditional bullying is based on.

Cycles of victimisation

The following quotes are from an in-depth study of 'Autism, Victimisation and Mate Crime' (Forster & Pearson, 2020):

- "Bullied at school, ganged up on, bullied at work, stolen from, my natural generosity exploited." (woman, 54)
- "Taken advantage off by male mates when incapacitated. Stalked by ex. Abused by friend I wouldn't date. Suspect friend stole from me." (woman, 40)
- "I was bullied a lot growing up and victimised during my teenage years by people I thought of then as friends" (woman, 46).
- "A male friend raped me and sexually assaulted me for over four hours and he kept trying to pull my hearing aids…My mam has mentally emotionally and financially abused me throughout the years…My brother regularly took his anger out on me in many ways such as mentally emotionally and physically… I have been bullied throughout growing up and was even cyber bullied at college." (woman, 36)

The most reported forms of interpersonal victimisation were intimate partner violence and abuse from family members (e.g., sister or mother); however, participants also wrote about experiences with (ex) friends and colleagues. Some participants wrote about how they had gone on to form good relationships after multiple experiences of abuse. However, this was not the case for everyone, and the experience of polyvictimisation (having experienced multiple victimisations such as sexual abuse, physical abuse, bullying, and exposure to family violence) had led others to see themselves as the problem "I believe there is something wrong in the way I introduce myself to friendship which makes people feel I am worth nothing beyond physical resources" (woman, 30). The perception that the autistic person saw that they were the problem allowed them to legitimise the abuse and led to further abuse taking place in some cases.

Problems with trust

In Pearson et al. (2022), many of their autistic participants identified personal difficulties around trust, which was not surprising given the range of negative experiences in interpersonal experiences to date. However, problems with trust manifested in several different ways, some participants worried about how being too trusting could be taken advantage of by perpetrators, while still wanting to see the best in others "Having my trust misused and abused where I am actually giving people the benefit of the doubt" (man, 54).

Others felt like they could not trust themselves or their judgement about other people's behaviour, understanding their difficulties recognising manipulation which placed them in danger "I take things literally and miss so much of some people's manipulative behaviour, I'm oblivious" (woman, 54).

Others found the problem was not the identification itself, but trusting their judgement "I end up rationalising their behaviour when they themselves are vulnerable, which leads to me excusing thing I probably shouldn't" (woman, 30). This was also indicative of the difficulties involved in identifying victimisation when the perpetrator also experiences vulnerability.

In some cases, previous abuse had made them distrustful, particularly of people in authority, such as parents.

> *My parents were very verbally abusive and manipulative...I felt I couldn't trust adult figures which was further compounded...I didn't feel safe with authority figures, nor did I trust they actually meant it when they said I could reach out to them for help.*
>
> (non-binary, 25)

The difficulties for autistic young people/adults in recognising victimisation and being over trusting of others have led some to be gaslighted to believe they were in the wrong.

- "Some of these incidents have been overt—such as a friend underhandedly stealing my jewellery...and then denying all knowledge, which I have tended to believe at the time. Other examples have been less clear, for example though coercion, elaborate lies, guilt tripping..." (woman, 30).
- "...both of them essentially lecturing me about how I was 'too sensitive' and that I was being selfish and that this was just how this friendship worked... 'being honest' with me 'for my own good'. This leads to me thinking I was a horrible person for questioning them...they gaslit me several times" (man, 26).

'I had to', the role of compliance

Compliance was highlighted by many participants as playing an important role in their experiences (Pearson et al., 2022). Some of the participants spoke of a need to please others, or 'go along' with their manipulations "(I) have been pressured into doing things that I wasn't comfortable with to try to please others who I thought were friends" (woman, 45). However, compliance reasons were not uniform across participants. Some desired to avoid confrontation.

> *Friends would ask me to buy them stuff when I was in town and then would just not mention paying me when coming to collect and knew I would find the conversation too awkward to directly ask for the money.*
>
> (Man, 36)

Some recognised the danger of the situation that they were in, and compliance was described as self-preservation "I knew I had to do what they told me and be their 'friend' or else they would make my life hell" (woman, 28). Others complied out of a desire not to get others 'into trouble', particularly in situations where an uneven power dynamic with the perpetrator was present, "I was like their personal bank account, and I got into serious debt as a result. I managed to pay it off, but it took nearly 10 years to do so" (woman, 33).

Other participants in Pearson et al. (2022) said that they struggled to spot negative social intentions and identify abusive behaviour, or trust their judgement about other people, which is consistent with other researchers in the field. Some of the participants seemed to blame themselves for not 'spotting' the abuse while it occurred, labelling themselves as oblivious. One participant who did recognise that they were being manipulated during the situation itself also said it made them feel naïve and therefore helpless.

Spotting these signals for autistic people can also rely on not taking people at 'face value' and engaging in continuing reflection on what someone has said or done. For an autistic person who tends to be straightforward in their communication style and who says what they mean, it might not occur that someone they are interacting with is being disingenuous (untruthful). However, the nature of autism can mean they can play on situations and their consequences continuously to an intensity that is both unhealthy and can lead to stalking to try to fix situations.

Interestingly, participants felt they needed to appease perpetrators or avoid confrontation, themes indicated by other researchers. Others complied out of recognition that it was the only way to maintain a semblance of safety within risky situations, for example, having to comply with the demands of others to avoid physical harm.

Mate crime

Mate crime is a word for someone deliberately befriending a person with autism so they can take advantage of them. Sometimes people 'pretend' to be friends with autistic people to use for things, like money or a place to stay.

> *Sometimes people with autism get given independent accommodation and a 'mate' has pretended to be their friend, so they have a free place to stay. They then invite friends around to hang out which can intimidate autistic people as they don't feel able to say no.*
> (Andy Buchan, a police officer in Ambitious About Autism, 2024)

Another common problem is these supposed friends asking you for money, saying things to you like "Can you lend me some money until I get paid?" This 'mate' then refuses to pay back the money and often threatens victims for more cash.

"Autistic people may get benefits paid to them and spend relatively little so it appears that they have lots of cash lying around," says Andy Buchan. He's also keen to point out that people with autism can be perpetrators of this, not just victims.

Why is this happening to people with autism?

Often people with autism can find it more difficult to make friends and feel isolated from the rest of society. This means sometimes you can be so desperate for friendship, that they accept even aggressive people or people who degrade them.

"Friendships for autistic people can be confusing and sporadic," says Andy Buchan. "So, if someone shows an interest in them or their passions, this can seem like the greatest thing in the world. So, they'll often turn a blind eye to the deficient parts of the relationship" (Ambitious About Autism, 2024).

References

Altomare, A.A., McCrimmon, A.W., Cappadocia, M.C., Weiss, J.A., Beran, T.N., & Smith-Demers, A.D. (2017). When push comes to shove: How are students with autism spectrum disorder coping with bullying? *Canadian Journal of School Psychology*, *32*(3–4), 209–227. https://doi.org/10.1177/0829573516683068

Ambitious About Autism (2024). Mate crime. Retrieved 29/07/2024. https://www.ambitiousaboutautism.org.uk/about-us/media-centre/blog/mate-crime

Anderson, C. (2012) IAN research report: Bullying and children with ASD. 26 March 2012. Retrieved 30/01/2025. www.kennedykrieger.org/stories/interactive-autism-network-ian/ian_research_report_bullying

Cappadocia, M.C., Weiss, J.A., & Pepler, D. (2012). Bullying experiences among children and youth with autism spectrum disorders. *Journal of Autism and Developmental Disorders*, *42*, 266–277.

Forster, S., & Pearson, A. (2020). "Bullies tend to be obvious": Autistic adult's perceptions of friendship and the concept of 'mate crime'. *Disability & Society*, *35*(7), 1103–1123. https://doi.org/10.1080/09687599.2019.1680347

Frith, U., & Hill, E. (2004). *Autism: Mind and brain*. New York: Oxford University Press.

Haigh, E. (2023). I was bullied for being 'different': Brave teenager's brutally honest account of his 'dark time' growing up with autism that was so bad it left him suicidal. 13 August 2023. Retrieved 30/01/2025.

Hwang, S., Kim, Y.S., Koh, Y.J., & Leventhal, B.L. (2018). Autism spectrum disorder and school bullying: Who is the victim? Who is the perpetrator? *Journal of Autism and Developmental Disorders*. 2018 January, *48*(1), 225–238. https://doi.org/10.1007/s10803-017-3285-z. PMID: 28936640; PMCID: PMC5886362.

Kowalski, R.M., & Fedina C. (2011). Cyber bullying in ADHD and Asperger syndrome populations. *Research in Autism Spectrum Disorders*, *5*, 1201–1208.

NAS85258 (2022). Revenge and planning. *National Autistic Society: Community Pages*. Retrieved 30/01/2025. community.autism.org.uk/f/parents-and-carers/30722/revenge-and-planning

Neurodivergent Rebel (2022). Autism, ADHD, and bullying – My NeuroDivergent autistic/ADHD (AutDHD) experience. 19 October 2022. Retrieved 30/01/2025. https://neurodivergentrebel.com/2022/10/19/autism-adhd-and-bullying-my-neurodivergent-autistic-adhd-autdhd-experience/

Olweus, D. (1994). Bullying at school: Basic facts and effects of a school based intervention program. *Journal of Child Psychology and Psychiatry*, *35*(7), 1171–1190. https://doi.org/10.1111/j.1469-7610.1994.tb01229.x

Park, I., Gong, J., Lyons, G.L., Hirota, T., Takahashi, M., Kim, B., Lee, S.Y., Kim, Y.S., Lee, J., & Leventhal, B.L. (2020). Prevalence of and factors associated with school bullying in students with autism spectrum disorder: A cross-cultural meta-analysis. *Yonsei Medical Journal*. 2020 November, *61*(11), 909–922. https://doi.org/10.3349/ymj.2020.61.11.909. PMID: 33107234; PMCID: PMC7593096.

Pearson, A., Rees, J., & Forster, S. (2022). This was just how this friendship worked. https://doi.org/10.1089/aut.2021.0035. Epub 2022 Jun 9. PMID: 36605970; PMCID: PMC9645672. Experiences of interpersonal victimisation among autistic adults. *Autism Adulthood*. 2022 Jun 1, *4*(2), 141–150.

Twyman, K.A., Saylor, C.F., Saia, D., Macias, M.M., Taylor, L.A., & Spratt, E. (2010). Bullying and ostracism experiences in children with special health care needs. *Journal of Developmental & Behavioral Pediatrics*, *31*, 1–8.

Van Cleave, J., & Davis, M.M. (2006). Bullying and peer victimisation among children with special health care needs. *Pediatrics*, *118*(4), e1212–e1219.

van Roekel, E., Scholte, R.H., & Didden, R. (2009). Bullying among adolescents with autism spectrum disorders: Prevalence and perception. *Journal of Autism and Developmental Disorders*. 2010 Jan, *40*(1), 63–73. https://doi.org/10.1007/s10803-009-0832-2. Epub 2009 Aug 8. PMID: 19669402; PMCID: PMC2809311.

van Roekel, E., Scholte, R.H.J., & Didden, R. (2010). Bullying among adolescents with autism spectrum disorders: Prevalence and perception. *Journal of Autism and Develomental Disorders*, *40*, 63–73. https://doi.org/10.1007/s10803-009-0832-2

Wainscot, J.J., Naylor, P., Sutcliffe, P., Tantam, D., & Williams, J.V. (2008). Relationships with peers and use of the school environment of mainstream secondary school pupils with Asperger syndrome (high-functioning autism): A case-control study. *International Journal of Psychology and Psychological Therapy*, *8*, 25–38.

Walton, A. (2012). Why autistic children are bullied more – And bully in return. *Forbes*. 24 April 2012. Retrieved 30/01/2025. www.forbes.com/sites/alicegwalton/2012/04/24/why-autistic-children-are-bullied-more/

Zablotsky, B., Bradshaw, C.P., Anderson, C., & Law, P.A. (2013). The association between bullying and the psychological functioning of children with autism spectrum disorders. *Journal of Developmental & Behavioral Pediatrics*, *34*(1), 1–8. https://doi.org/10.1097/DBP.0b013e31827a7c3a. [doi] 00004703-201301000-00001

5   Anger and Anger Management

Research suggests those diagnosed with autism are prone to anger outbursts. An 'on-off' quality during which individuals may be calm one second and then have an autistic outburst in the next is common. Family members and significant others may grow resentful over time due to misunderstanding this behaviour.

Many parents of young children, from three to four years old, may struggle with a child experiencing huge mood swings, mainly in boys, which drives early diagnosis. However, if such outbursts are meltdowns, then it becomes easier to understand that what seems like random outbursts are the culmination of many stresses during the day.

On the National Autism Society's chat room, Secretsock (2024) offers a window into the autistic experience.

> I'm at my wits end and really need some advice. My 19-year-old daughter has high-ability autism (Asperger's). She has been living in a residential place for just over a year and is making excellent progress with independent living skills. She has lots of potential but the main thing that holds her back is her violent outbursts when she has a meltdown. These happen less than they used to but she is still totally out of control when the red mist descends. She's physically violent, verbally abusive, and destroys things.

She goes on to note

> Most of the time these outbursts can be avoided. The problem is that there is a very high turnover of staff, and they are so short-staffed, that they must take on agency people who are not trained. As a result, they are not aware of my daughter's triggers... being interrupted, being hurried, being touched. Last week all 3 triggers happened, and the meltdown was so bad that the two staff on duty (one who'd been there a week, the other was on her 2nd day) had to barricade themselves into the staff room and call the police.

The girl was relieved to be arrested because (afterwards) she said she felt safer at the police station. Whilst being arrested for assault (for punching both members of staff) and criminal damage (she smashed some plates and damaged walls), the

DOI: 10.4324/9781003614432-5

unit didn't want to press charges, but despite this, she still received a criminal caution.

Conflict can be handled properly by helping the affected individual and immediate family members understand the causes of this anger. According to Pasadena Villa (2013), there are six common causes of anger in relation autism:

- Being swamped by multiple tasks or sensory stimulation: Multitasking has become more common in today's on-the-move society. People expect others to be able to do more than one task at a time. But what may seem minimal to some can be extremely stressful to an individual on the spectrum, resulting in autism mood swings.
- Other people's behaviour: A person with autism may take great offence to insensitive or sarcastic comments that most may understand as light humour. Being ignored, whether on purpose or by accident, is a prevalent trigger as well.
- Having routine and order disrupted: Autism causes individuals to function differently and many subconsciously cope with stress by following strict daily regimes. Disrupting a routine means disrupting a coping mechanism.
- Difficulties with school, employment, and relationships: Many individuals on the spectrum report feeling like their talents and capabilities are often overlooked and unappreciated. For example, teachers and employers may be unaware of their autism and needs, being it may not be diagnosed yet, or are aware of common autistic traits might dismiss their attempts at friendship or communication, which can lead at times to bullying and alienation.
- Intolerance of imperfections in others: Both physically and mentally, the individual may have stressors indirectly caused by people. For example, high-pitched voices or people who speak too fast may be stressors. Allowing them to express these aggravations may result in a further understanding of their autism mood swings.
- Build-up of stress: Everything previously listed can potentially add up to a build-up of stress. Individuals who haven't taken steps towards managing anger can have a hard time dealing with built-up stress. Many individuals on the spectrum need support when it comes to processing their stress and emotions.

Schiller (2023) suggests several factors can contribute to anger in individuals with autism, including:

- Sensory overload: Individuals with autism may be more sensitive to sensory input, such as loud noises, bright lights, or certain textures. When they are exposed to too much sensory input, it can be overwhelming and lead to feelings of frustration and anger.
- Communication difficulties: Communication is often a challenge for individuals with autism. When they are unable to express their needs or feelings, it can lead to frustration and anger.
- Changes in routine: Individuals with autism often thrive on routine and predictability. When their routine is disrupted or changed, it can be stressful and lead to feelings of anxiety and anger.

Treatments

Many believe that autism is merely a difference and any treatment is controversial, being an incorrect approach to 'correcting' them. Treatments such as cognitive behavioural therapy (CBT) suggest autistic young people/children can be trained to modify their behaviour, into something like neurotypical.

Cognitive behavioural therapy options for anger management in autism

CBT is an evidence-based approach to managing anger that may be effective for individuals with autism. CBT is a type of therapy that focuses on changing negative thought patterns and behaviours. It can help individuals with autism learn how to recognise triggers for their anger, identify negative thoughts and beliefs that contribute to their anger, and develop strategies for coping with difficult situations.

According to Schiller (2023), using CBT, individuals with autism work one-on-one with a therapist to develop personalised strategies for managing their anger. These strategies might include relaxation techniques, such as deep breathing or progressive muscle relaxation, cognitive restructuring, which involves identifying and challenging negative thoughts, and problem-solving skills. Research has shown that CBT can be effective in reducing anger and other challenging behaviours in individuals with autism. One study found that children who received CBT showed significant improvements in their ability to manage their emotions compared to those who did not receive therapy. However, CBT may not be appropriate or effective for all individuals with autism who struggle with anger. It's important to work closely with a qualified therapist to determine if CBT is the right approach and to develop a personalised treatment plan.

It is argued by some that CBT offers a promising approach for managing anger in individuals with autism. By learning new skills and strategies for coping with difficult situations, individuals with autism can improve their emotional regulation and quality of life.

Questions could be asked as to why the focus is on those with autism modifying their behaviour, which is a reaction to their environment. Wouldn't it be better to modify their environment (e.g., noise, room lighting, avoidance of crowds, etc.) so that they don't get dysregulated in the first place and manifest in anger? A saying comes to mind, we spend years training an autistic person to cope in society, but no time training those in society to cope with autistic people.

Social skills training for anger management in autism

Like CBT, social skills training can be an effective tool for managing anger in individuals with autism (Schiller, 2023). Social skills training focuses on teaching individuals with autism how to communicate more effectively and navigate social situations with greater ease. It is argued that by improving their social skills, individuals with autism can reduce frustration and anxiety that can lead to anger outbursts. Social skills training can also help individuals with autism develop greater self-awareness and empathy for others, which can improve their ability to understand and manage their emotions.

Social skills training may involve one-on-one coaching or group therapy sessions, depending on the individual's needs and preferences. Some common goals of social skills training include:

• Learning how to read nonverbal cues, such as facial expressions and body language
• Practicing conversational skills, such as taking turns speaking and asking appropriate questions
• Developing problem-solving skills for social situations
• Improving emotional regulation by identifying triggers for anger and developing coping strategies

Research has shown that social skills training can be effective in improving communication, reducing challenging behaviours, and increasing the overall quality of life in individuals with autism. It's important to work closely with a qualified therapist or behaviour analyst to develop a personalised treatment plan that meets the individual's unique needs. Overall, incorporating social skills training into a comprehensive treatment plan for managing anger in individuals with autism can be an effective way of reducing frustration and improving communication abilities.

Medication options for anger management in autism

In addition to therapy and mindfulness techniques, medication can also be an option for managing anger in individuals with autism. However, it's important to note that medication should not be the first line of treatment and should only be used under the guidance of a qualified healthcare professional.

Several types of medications may be used to manage anger in individuals with autism, according to Schiller (2023); these can include:

• Anti-depressants: Some anti-depressants are effective in reducing irritability and aggression in individuals with autism. However, these medications can have side effects such as drowsiness and decreased appetite.
• Anti-psychotics: Anti-psychotic medications may also be used to manage anger and aggression in individuals with autism. These medications can help reduce symptoms such as hallucinations and delusions but can also have side effects such as weight gain and movement disorders.
• Mood stabilisers: Mood stabilisers are another type of medication that may be used to manage anger in individuals with autism. These medications can help regulate mood swings and reduce impulsivity but can also have side effects such as tremors and dizziness.

References

Pasadena Villa (2013). Six most common causes of anger in relation to autism disorders. 22 May 2013. Retrieved 20/06/2024. https://pasadenavilla.com/resources/blog/common-causes-of-anger-autism/

Schiller, J. (2023). High-functioning autism and anger: What you should know. 10 August 2023. Retrieved 19/06/2024. https://www.thetreetop.com/aba-therapy/autism-and-anger

Secretsock (2024). Asperger's daughter arrested. The autistic community chat room. *National Autistic Society.* Retrieved 01/07/2024. https://community.autism.org.uk/f/miscellaneous-and-chat/5015/aspergers-daughter-arrested

6 Autism and Meltdowns/ Shutdowns

Many autistic people have meltdowns. The public often finds it hard to tell autism meltdowns and temper tantrums apart, but they are very different things. This chapter will help to explain what a meltdown is, how to anticipate it, identify its causes, and minimise its frequency.

What is a meltdown?

A 'meltdown' is an intense response to an overwhelming situation. It happens when someone becomes completely overwhelmed by their current situation and temporarily loses control of their behaviour. This loss of control can be expressed verbally (e.g., shouting, screaming, crying), physically (e.g., kicking, lashing out, biting), or in both ways.

Meltdown should not be confused with tantrums (Ntiamoah, 2024). There are essential differences between the two. Children who have tantrums are typically clever and able to avoid doing what they are told. Children who meltdown often cannot help themselves when they meltdown. Some children with the most severe behaviours cannot control their outbursts, and there may be no way to predict when or how long a meltdown will go once it begins.

When a person is completely overwhelmed, and their condition means it is difficult to express that in another way, the result can be a meltdown. A temper tantrum is when a person does not get what they want, for example, a toy, and by giving the toy the tantrum stops. In the case of a meltdown, it's uncontrolled and will not stop no matter what you do for the autistic person. Meltdowns stop when the body has run out of steam, followed by a recovery process which may take another 20–40 minutes in some cases.

Meltdowns are not the only way an autistic person may express feeling overwhelmed. They may also 'shut down' by refusing to communicate, interact, withdrawing from situations they find challenging or avoiding them altogether.

According to research by Phung et al. (2021), autistic individuals describe feeling out of control and feeling this with their entire body. They describe having blurry vision, muscles getting hot, cheeks getting warm, and shoulders bunched up. They have a diminished ability to think and sometimes difficulty finding words

DOI: 10.4324/9781003614432-6

or remembering basic things. Autistics describes feeling completely out of control like everything is fuzzy.

Phung et al. (2021) also describe a stage called burnout, which can proceed to a meltdown, in which the autistic person begins to feel fatigued, overwhelmed, slowed down, and has difficulty with cognition. This is a period where continued pressure and overwhelming sensory and emotional stress begin to erode the autistic person's ability to function and perform daily tasks. Encouraging autistic people to decrease emotional and sensory pressure at this point can prevent meltdowns.

What is a shutdown?

Most would see a 'meltdown' as exploding and a very physical manifestation of their intense dysregulation. For others, they may 'implode' or 'shutdown' by shutting down, by not talking or communicating. In one school I saw a teenage boy with autism completely shut down, they lay in the middle of a busy school corridor and would not move or communicate, oblivious to what was going on around them. They needed 30–45 minutes in that same position to re-regulate themselves, I had to assign staff to be a guard, so no one stepped on him.

A person having a shutdown might (Leicestershire Partnership NHS Trust, 2024)

- Find it difficult to speak or might not talk at all
- Want to hide away somewhere dark and alone or curl up in bed
- Feel like they suddenly have no energy at all and want to sleep or find it difficult to move
- Have less patience and difficulty regulating emotions
- Increased stimming
- Making decisions becomes impossible
- Difficulty regulating temperature
- Masking more than usual

Interestingly, there is a discussion regarding shutdowns and absence/silent seizures, as the two can look very similar. An absence/silent seizure tends to last between 10 and 30 seconds, and an atypical absence seizure lasts longer, up to 20 seconds or more. Whereas an autistic shutdown can last much longer.

Rosen (2020) has researched autism and epilepsy and notes a comorbidity of 30% having both conditions. The high rate of comorbidity is thought to be caused by genetic and microstructural brain differences which feature in both conditions.

What a meltdown feels like

Lewis and Stevens (2023) describe that meltdowns (shutdowns) hold different meanings to different people. From a study of 32 autistic adults, they concluded that during a meltdown, most autistics described feeling overwhelmed by information, senses, and social and emotional stress. They often felt extreme emotions, such as anger, sadness, and fear, and had trouble with thinking and memory during the meltdown.

Participants described trying to stay in control of themselves, often feeling like they were not themselves during meltdowns. They described the meltdown as a way of letting go of or releasing the extreme emotions they felt. They tried to stay away from things or people that might trigger a meltdown or tried to make sure they were alone if they felt a meltdown may be coming as a way of avoiding harm, including harm to their bodies, their emotions, and their relationships. These findings offer an important look into what it is like for autistic adults to have meltdowns from their point of view. It is interesting to note that those in the study tried to avoid meltdowns, hearing a recent podcast on Meltdowns the presenters said when anxious, they knew that if they didn't use stimming strategies (see Appendix 5) they were likely to fall into a meltdown – having a sense when a meltdown was possibly coming.

A meltdown may look like this (Reframing Autism, 2024):

- Crying, wailing, sobbing
- Screaming
- Throwing objects, breaking objects
- Flapping or pacing
- Withdrawing or shutting down
- Clenching or grinding teeth
- Zoning out or dissociating
- Running away (eloping)
- Hitting, punching, biting, kicking, or pushing (objects, oneself, or others)
- Intense stimming (e.g., rocking, vocal stims, muscle tensing, joint cracking)

Autistic meltdowns can last from ten minutes to an hour or longer, but often last at least 20–30 minutes after the removal of the initial trigger (potentially longer if the trigger is not removed or resolved). It's important to note that a meltdown is never a contrived or pre-meditated act, and an individual often has little to no control over the behaviours that may manifest during the height of a meltdown.

Reframing Autism (2024) offers an example to explain how a meltdown can occur: A child is in the toy store with their parent. The child is feeling dizzy from the fluorescent lights and the loud beeping sounds of some musical toys. The parent notices the child displaying increasingly anxious behaviours. The parent tries to distract the child by showing them a toy, but the stressful stimuli persist, and so the child becomes dysregulated. The child begins involuntarily flapping, crying, and fidgeting and is having trouble expressing themselves. Their behaviour becomes increasingly panicked and distressing leading to a meltdown.

What to do

If someone is having a meltdown or not responding to you, then don't judge them. This can make a world of difference to an autistic person and their carers. The following may help:

- Give them some time – it can take a while to recover from information or sensory overload.
- Calmly ask them (or their parent or friend) if they are ok but bear in mind, they'll need more time to respond than you might expect.
- Make space – try to create a quiet, safe space as best you can. Ask people to move along and not stare, turn off loud music, and turn down bright lights – whatever you can think of to reduce the information overload, try it.

The following may also be helpful (Leicestershire Partnership NHS Trust, 2024):

- When responding to a meltdown try and match your energy to the person, so if they are shouting and lashing out, then it could be best to approach with a firm voice and some level of energy in your body language; if they are very quiet and not moving much, then it will be best for you to use a calm, quiet voice and be quite still.
- Give them time. It can take a while to recover from sensory overload or situation overwhelm.
- Try to create a quiet, safe space as best you can. Remove any objects/people/ sounds that are creating sensory overload if possible.
- For helping a person to calm down from a meltdown try giving them a rolled-up towel (or coat or something strong and made of fabric) and get them to give it a very big twist – then let go, twist again, repeat. You can model this and join in. You can also encourage them to practise this when they are calmer so that it is easier to remember when they are not so calm.
- Breathing techniques can also help. For example: breathe in for a count of 3, hold for 3, and breath out for 6…. This can help to reset the mind and body.

What NOT to do in a meltdown? Attwood and Garnett (2024) suggest not to:

- Talk about punishment, consequences, damage, and cost of any damage caused
- Use reason when the person is too emotional to be reasonable
- Interrogate, that is ask for an explanation as to why the person is so agitated or distressed
- Encroach on personal space
- Turn the situation into a lesson
- Make sudden movements
- Correct agitated behaviours
- Match the person's mood with your speech

- Criticise the person for being overly dramatic or selfish
- Use physical restraint
- Make critical, demeaning, or patronising comments

Aggressive behaviour during meltdowns

Parents worry about an autistic child's aggressive behaviour during meltdowns since it tends to lead the child to hurt themselves. Patnam et al. (2017) with Yalim and Mohamed (2023) found that children with autism tend to self-harm physically during a meltdown rather than hurting others. Bernard (2015) also noted that these aggressive actions can be repetitive. According to Patnam et al. (2017), common behaviours during meltdowns are: rocking, wrist biting, self-scratching, kicking, banging their heads, or even lashing out violently have been identified as self-harm. However, Bernard (2015) recognises an association between self-injurious behaviour and the severity of autism, where meltdowns tend to happen more frequently in a child with severe autism.

Meltdowns by autistic individuals can also involve anger, hostility, and sudden-onset violent outbursts including self-harm and rage 'episodes'. According to Thinking Autism (2021), up to 20% of individuals with autism exhibit such violent behaviours. In many cases, aggression involves the destruction of property and direct violence towards other people including carers, causing them bodily harm. In the case of Charlie, 13 years old with autism autistic (in Phil, 2023), recent meltdowns became very extreme and violent both physically and verbally, smashing up his home and trying to hurt his family. His family is normally quite good at not letting him get too wound up before it's too late, but on some occasions unfortunately he gets past the point of no return. They are unsure why the neighbours haven't called the police! Charlie when calm can be loving and polite, but when he loses his temper, he can be the complete opposite.

Anticipating a meltdown/shutdown

Many autistic people will show signs of distress before having a meltdown, which Reframing Autism (2024) refers to as the 'rumble stage'. They may start to exhibit signs of anxiety such as pacing, seeking reassurance through repetitive questioning, or physical signs such as rocking or becoming very still. At this stage, there may still be a chance to prevent a meltdown/shutdown. Strategies to consider include distraction, diversion, and helping the person use calming strategies such as fiddling with toys or listening to music, removing any potential triggers, and staying calm.

Reframing Autism (2024) suggests some ideas to help calm a person experiencing a meltdown/shutdown:

- A drink of water
- Soft toys or cushions to hold

- Something to rock on
- Noise-cancelling headphones
- Comforting smells
- Calm music (or upbeat music that they enjoy, if that is their preference)
- Singing, humming
- A weighted blanket or vest
- Space
- Peace and quiet
- Turning the lights off
- A cool compress for the head

Reframing Autism (2024) offers an example to explain how one can avoid a meltdown, an Autistic person in a grocery store is getting overwhelmed by the food smells, bright lights, and loud beeping from the checkouts. They start to become agitated and start fidgeting and pacing. Their anxiety is increasing the longer they're exposed to the trigger. If given the option to leave the store, or to put on some sunglasses and noise-cancelling headphones, then they may be able to take the edge off the dysregulation and bring themselves down from that heightened nervous system state. However, if they're left without coping tools, and are required to continue feeling distressed, then a meltdown is much more likely.

Identifying the causes

A meltdown/shutdown is a reaction to an overwhelming experience. If your family member or the person you support has meltdowns, then attempt to identify what is overwhelming for them. To help achieve this, complete a diary over some time, recording what happened before, during, and after each meltdown/shutdown. Patterns may emerge, and you may find that meltdowns/shutdowns occur at times, in particular places, or when something has happened. Possible causes identified by Reframing Autism (2024) may include:

- Sensory dysregulation: too much or too little sensory input – is one of the most common causes behind a meltdown. Sounds, textures, smells, light, movement or lack of them can become so overwhelming, that an autistic person's mind can be thrown off balance.
- Social situations (e.g., social anxiety or misunderstandings)
- Experiencing changes and unpredictable things, so changes in routine and other sources of anxiety, like social interactions or anticipating high-stress events, can also be triggers.
- Meltdowns are common too in situations when communication is challenging, and it is difficult to express needs to others and get support.
- Basic needs (e.g., being overtired, hungry, thirsty, or in pain)
- Very emotional situations
- Sometimes a meltdown is the only way a person must express that something is wrong.

Minimising triggers

Once you have a clearer idea of what may be triggering meltdowns, think about ways you might minimise that trigger. Every autistic person is different, but sensory differences, changes in routine, anxiety and communication difficulties are common triggers.

Sensory considerations

Many autistic people have sensory differences. They may be over-sensitive to some senses, under-sensitive to others and often a combination of both. One example of this may be a person who is over-sensitive to touch and sound, people brushing past them, so a loud announcement at a train station could cause pain and sensory overload, leading to a meltdown. In this situation, it could be helpful to listen to calming music on headphones to block out loud noises and to wait until everyone has got off the train before approaching the platform to avoid crowds of people. In other situations, consider creating a low arousal environment (e.g., remove bright lights) or use sensory equipment (e.g., glasses with dark or coloured lenses, ear defenders, a weighted blanket).

In a previous research project, this author interviewed an autistic academic who had to share an office with other researchers. She knew that the bright lights were a problem and asked for the lighting to be changed, which was refused as it would have affected the others in the room. This caused her to work elsewhere to prevent meltdowns, and resulted in a decreased mental well-being, as she felt she had been refused reasonable accommodations in her workplace (Reframing Autism, 2024).

Change in routine

Consistent, predictable routines and structure are very important for autistic people and a change to routine can be very distressing. A good example of this is having to go a different route to school or work due to roadworks could cause feelings of anxiety that may trigger a meltdown. In this case, clear visual support giving notice of the change, explaining the change, reassurance that the rest of the routine remains the same, and adding extra support such as a calming/comforting activity to do in the car or bus could help.

For an unexpected change to routine, a parent/teacher could plan for them using:

• A picture symbol to explain the change
• Reinforcement that the rest of the day will be the same (if that's the case)
• Offering a chance to express any frustration appropriately (such as hitting a pillow or ripping paper) followed by an activity that is known to calm the person such as taking deep breaths, listening to calming music, going for a walk, or squeezing a stress ball.
• An increase of structure around ordinary transitions, helping the person to navigate the change from one activity to another throughout the day. Using a clear timetable

explaining when the transitions will be, using timers to count down to transitions, and using a favourite toy or character to be part of the transition, can all help.

- Use of a sensory aid such as a weighted blanket.

Anxiety

With its unwritten rules and unpredictable nature, the world can be an extremely challenging environment for autistic people causing many to experience anxiety. Without tools and strategies to help manage their feelings of anxiety, those with autism may experience a meltdown as a result. Have a plan beforehand of what to do if the person you are supporting feels anxious, such as a calming music playlist to listen to or a stress ball in their pocket.

Build relaxation time into their routine; this will help with general emotional well-being and help them to better able to manage when something that could trigger a meltdown occurs. Strategies can vary from person to person and may consist of quiet activities, for example, taking a walk, listening to music, playing a computer game, reading, doing puzzles, using fiddle toys, or more strenuous activities, for example, jumping on a trampoline or going to the gym (Reframing Autism, 2024).

In the case of more strenuous activities, observe whether the activity really does calm them down. If it doesn't, but is just an activity they really enjoy, still build in time for that activity but also try and find one that does genuinely calm them down and make time for that as well.

Communication difficulties

Autistic people can find it difficult to express their wants and needs, from a non-verbal child struggling to express their need for a drink, a teenager finding it hard to express their emotions, to an adult trying to explain why they are overwhelmed. This can result in overwhelming feelings, such as anger and frustration, leading to a meltdown (Reframing Autism, 2024).

Support the person to find ways to understand and express their emotions appropriately before they get overwhelmed and find ways to make your own communication more easily understandable. Some autistic people may find verbal communication difficult due to misunderstanding body language, tone of voice, irony, and sarcasm from others.

Coyle (2023) reports on a police complaint, after an autistic girl was arrested for saying a female officer "looked like her lesbian nana". The incident was filmed and posted on the internet. The West Yorkshire Police spokesman confirmed a 16-year-old had been arrested on suspicion of a homophobic public order offence; six officers were used to arrest her. Although her mother told them her daughter was autistic, this was ignored. Her mother said, "My daughter was having panic attacks from being touched by them and they continued to manhandle her. Her nana is a lesbian, she's married to a woman". The force added that the girl was subsequently interviewed with an appropriate adult and was released on bail pending further inquiries. The arresting officer was sent for further training as a result.

Case study (Amato, 2022)

Ryley, 16 years old, is technically non-verbal. He was visiting his grandparents at the time, as reported by his parents. He told them he was going to go to the 'swings' behind their home between dinner and dessert. The boy often goes to that park by himself, and his parents say there have never been any issues before. As Ryley is technically non-verbal, but his family explain that he does speak some words and can answer questions; it just takes him extra time to respond. They described him as a very timid and empathetic person. RCMP (local police) said Ryley was unable to identify himself, so he was arrested for 'his safety and that of the public'. The Alberta Serious Incident Response Team said a 911 caller reported a 'younger male' that was in his 'early 20s' who may have had 'some severe handicap' or be on drugs. Whilst in custody the boy began to be dysregulated, self-harmed and was removed to a hospital for his own safety. The family learned where Ryley was only after calling 911 to report that he was missing.

Howard (2017), a reporter for CNN, discusses John Haygood, a ten-year-old boy with autism. He was arrested at a school in Florida; in a video, his hands are cuffed as two officers escort him to the back seat of a police car. He was arrested at the school last week for felony battery against a paraprofessional (learning support assistant), allegedly punching and kicking his paraprofessional (learning support assistant), which left scratches and marks. The police report noted it was not the first time this paraprofessional had been assaulted by this child, which he had reported internally, but the boy had 'been given many opportunities to change his behaviour but he had not', but now the paraprofessional wanted to pursue criminal charges. Previously John had allegedly made threats to kill the paraprofessional. The arresting officer asked John whether he would be willing to walk to the patrol car, and John replied, "Don't touch me. I don't like to be touched", according to the incident report. He can be heard making similar comments in the video. John was then handcuffed and transported to a juvenile detention centre, where he spent the night.

The case study of John suggests that rather than the school knowing he was autistic and making reasonable allowances for him, the lack of these caused dysregulation and meltdowns. To then blame John for these meltdowns seems unfair and discriminative. Could John have changed his autism, no. Could the school and paraprofessional have changed how they supported John knowing his autistic needs, yes.

Meltdowns which may lead to school suspensions and police arrest

If you take a closer look at the traits of autism, it is easy to see why these may be misunderstood by others, and their vulnerabilities taken advantage of.

> **Case Study (this author)**
>
> *Sensory sensitivities leading to dysregulation. A 14-year-old male student in a mainstream class was asked to move seats in the lesson, no pre-warning was given nor reason, and in a noisy room of 25 other teenagers, he got dys regulated. The teacher was raising her voice to say that he must move immediately. He was now highly dysregulated and in a blind rage, seeing a red midst, threw his books off his table. Unfortunately, the teacher was standing by him, was pushed back by his rage, and she fell and hit her head hit a nearby table. He says he has no recollection of the event, and it was not his intention to hurt the teacher. He is a very sweet and naïve boy with a love of trains. He was suspended, and as this was his second such 'assault' on a teacher when dysregulated the school wanted to expel him. He was sent to a pupil referral unit for six weeks so that he could calm down whilst the school could do the paperwork to exclude him permanently. The special needs manager (SENDCO) made a very strong case that he was highly dysregulated, and the teacher was not putting in place the strategies suggested for him. The boy was allowed to return to the school after a four-day internal suspension and then allowed to return to normal classes. This could have easily meant he was placed in an unsuitable provision/school due to his violence, away from his friends who helped him stay regulated at school.*

Aggression in autism can involve severe tantrums, anger, hostility, and sudden-onset violent outbursts including self-harm and rage 'episodes'. According to Thinking Autism (2021), up to 20% of individuals with autism exhibit such violent behaviours. In many cases, aggression involves the destruction of property and direct violence towards other people including carers, causing them bodily harm. The aggressive episodes are part of uncontrolled anger as part of meltdowns, caused by other people's actions and unplanned events.

Such aggressive behaviours can have very negative effects on the daily functioning and quality of life of people with autism and their caregivers and further, add to stress and social isolation due to how others react to autistic people after experiencing their meltdowns, for example, with fear. Research suggests that aggression in autism causes carers and teachers greater stress than the core features of autism. Aggression is associated with more negative outcomes for children with autism and their caregivers, including decreased quality of life, increased stress levels, and reduced availability of educational and social support. Studies suggest individuals with autism and aggressive behaviour also have lower educational and employment opportunities, their aggressive behaviours can lead to involvement with the criminal justice system.

One needs to remember that when an individual acts aggressively and destructively towards other people, things, or themselves, hitting, smashing, tearing, biting, etc., the possible reasons and triggers for such behaviours are numerous. Listening to a recent podcast about autistic meltdowns, the adult presenters with autism said that they preferred to hit and bite themselves, then cause property damage or hurt others, as dealing with the consequences of such actions could cause subsequent meltdowns, for example, having to answer the many why questions and possible questioning by the police.

Phillips and Hines (2017) for a UK BBC television programme reported on the following case studies.

Elliot, 12 years old, with autism and learning difficulties meaning he is unable to speak. His condition requires round-the-clock care, and he does not understand the effects of his actions. Ian and Lucy say their son became violent and aggressive from the age of five. "He's still only violent 5% of the time - but the consequences of that violence are getting worse and worse". "I'm scared of him. You live on a knife edge. You don't know what's coming next". His parents have had to put bars across the window in Elliot's bedroom and locks on the door to help keep him – and their other children – safe. "You kind of get used to your child's bedroom looking like a cell of some kind", his father says. Elliot attends a special school, but the couple thought they did not get enough specialist support from their local council. "You have to get to the point where one of you is hospitalised or you've had to call the police out [for help to arrive]".

Phillips and Hines (2017) also discuss Cameron, 19 years old, autistic, who from the age of three years his parents did not know how he would react. His siblings must lock themselves in the room because they are so scared. Life at home has become very difficult, and his parents are currently looking for a residential care home for him. His mother, Hannah, says the family can no longer manage Cameron's behaviour. "It's really upsetting because I love him so much", she says "I don't want people to be scared of him, because his nature is gentle. I feel sorry for him because he's frustrated, and he can't tell me or other people why".

The biggest problems have been with schools not being properly educated in autism. Our son was being bullied at his academy [school] and was physically beaten up, but the school did very little [to help]. He finally broke down one day and exploded and was expelled. He damaged property and the school tried to [get the police to] charge him. Sadly, he would come home and damage our house and was violent towards family members.

A family member in our survey
(National Autistic Society, 2024)

What we've found is that those with autism are vulnerable within the educational context because they don't read the situation very well. They're also getting in trouble in schools, then they become excluded and then they get placed in an inappropriate provision, because they've been seen as having a behaviour problem, and before you know it, a stigma would be placed upon them.

Educational psychologist
(National Autistic Society, 2024)

Victimisation at school

S, an autistic adult in National Autistic Society (2024), recounts the difficulties she had at school both from other pupils and the teachers and how this contributed to her getting into trouble, noting

> *I didn't have many friends and the friends I did have used to befriend me and just basically take what they could out of me and then turn on me because they were actually onside with the bullies... I was getting tortured in school constantly not only by pupils, it was by teachers also that didn't understand me. I didn't trust anybody.*

KE, an autistic adult, told us about how difficult he found school and how teachers would often misinterpret his behaviour because they didn't understand autism. He says he spent more time in isolation than he did in classrooms (National Autistic Society, 2024).

Victimisation can come from both teachers and fellow students, from the misunderstanding why they, autistic young people, are having a meltdown, reacting in certain ways, and when they see a meltdown, a violent meltdown, to label them as 'trouble' and 'unsound' and 'dangerous'. This closes any hope of making friendships, leading them to feel isolated and blamed for their autism. Classmates steer clear of them, and teachers label them as 'trouble', and this label sticks to them for their whole school career.

Peers would bully, both physically and name calling which can be very hurtful, making other peers, sympathetic ones, wary of being friends with them for fear of becoming associated with a stigmatised person.

References

Amato, S. (2022). 'Police hurts': Autistic Alberta teen living in fear after RCMP arrest, family says. *Edmonton News*. 28 October 2022. Retrieved 19/06/2024. https://edmonton.ctvnews.ca/police-hurts-autistic-alberta-teen-living-in-fear-after-rcmp-arrest-family-says-1.6128520

Attwood, T., & Garnett, M. (2024). Managing an autistic meltdown. Retrieved 17/06/2024. https://attwoodandgarnettevents.com/managing-an-autistic-meltdown-by-prof-tony-attwood-and-dr-michelle-garnett/

Bernard, M.F. (2015). Responses towards tantrum behavior in children with autism spectrum disorder. Lafayette, Louisiana: ProQuest LLC. 1–11.

Coyle, H. (2023). Police face complaint over arrest of autistic Leeds teenager. *PA Media and BBC News*. 10 August 2023. Retrieved 19/06/2024. https://www.bbc.co.uk/news/uk-england-leeds-66462895

Howard, J. (2017). 10-Year-old with autism arrested at Florida school. *CNN News*. Mon 24 April 2017. Retrieved 19/06/2024. https://edition.cnn.com/2017/04/21/health/autism-florida-10-year-old-arrested-bn/index.html

Leicestershire Partnership NHS Trust (2024). Meltdowns and shutdowns. Retrieved 17/06/2024. https://www.leicspart.nhs.uk/autism-space/health-and-lifestyle/meltdowns-and-shutdowns/

Lewis, L.F., & Stevens, K. (2023). The lived experience of meltdowns for autistic adults. *Autism*. 2023 August, *27*(6), 1817–1825. https://doi.org/10.1177/13623613221145783. Epub 2023 Jan 11. PMID: 36632658.

National Autistic Society (2024). Meltdowns – A guide for all audiences. Retrieved 19/06/2024. https://www.autism.org.uk/advice-and-guidance/topics/behaviour/meltdowns/all-audiences

Ntiamoah, J. (2024). Tantrums and meltdowns in children with autism spectrum disorder: A literature review. May 2024. https://www.researchgate.net/publication/380605613_Ntiamoah_Joseph_Tantrums_and_Meltdowns_in_Children_with_Autism_Spectrum_Disorder_A_Literature_Review

Patnam, V.S.P., George, F.T., George, K., & Verma, A. (2017). *Deep learning based recognition of meltdown in autistic kids*. 2017 IEEE International Conference on Healthcare Informatics (ICHI), Park City, UT, 2017, pp. 391–396. https://doi.org/10.1109/ICHI.2017.35

Phil (2023). Teenage meltdowns. The autism community pages. National Autism Society. Retrieved 18/06/2024. https://community.autism.org.uk/f/parents-and-carers/30364/teenage-meltdowns

Phillips, N., & Hines, T. (2017). I'm scared of my own autistic child. *BBC Website.* 30 October 2017. Retrieved 18/06/2024. https://www.bbc.co.uk/news/education-41597815

Phung, J., Penner, M., Pirlot, C., & Welch, C. (2021). What I wish you knew: Insights on burnout, inertia, meltdown, and shutdown from autistic youth. *Frontiers in Psychology*. 2021 November 3, *12*, 741421. https://doi.org/10.3389/fpsyg.2021.741421. PMID: 34803822; PMCID: PMC8595127.

Reframing Autism (2024). All about autistic meltdowns: A guide for allies. Retrieved 17/06/2024. https://reframingautism.org.au/all-about-autistic-meltdowns-a-guide-for-allies/

Rosen, A.R. (2020). Because autism is increasingly prevalent and frequently comorbid with epilepsy, children with epilepsy should have autism screening. *Epilepsy and Autism*. October 2020, 40–43. Retrieved 05/08/2024. https://practicalneurology.com/articles/2020-oct/epilepsy-and-autism

Thinking Autism (2021). Aggression in autism – One simple cause. *Autism Science and Research News*. 24 July 2021. Retrieved 18/06/2024. https://www.thinkingautism.org.uk/aggression-in-autism-one-simple-cause/

Yalim, T., & Mohamed, S. (2023). Meltdown in autism: Challenges and support needed for parents of children with autism. *International Journal of Academic Research in Progressive Education and Development*, *12*(1), 850–876.

7   Restraint and Seclusion

Restraint is emerging as a hot topic among autistic self-advocates and parents. People on both sides feel their position is correct. Either restraint leads to abuse and should be banned, or restraint is necessary for the safety of the public, and those who deny it are idealistic.

Whenever people are restrained against their will, there is always a risk of abuse and cruelty. The sad truth is that many staff working with developmentally challenged (neurodivergent) people are poorly trained and poorly paid, a bad combination that can and has led to horrific outcomes. The condemnation of such incidents is deserved. Unfortunately, known incidents may be just the tip of the iceberg, as much abuse involving restraint may never be reported.

Many, if not most, autistic individuals who are restrained cannot talk freely about their experience. Either their disability precludes free public communication, or they are under guardianship and not free to speak publicly when caregivers control social or internet communication opportunities. There is a risk that those people will be mistreated and have no voice to seek justice. Such a thing is awful to contemplate, yet, I believe, all too real.

Critics of restraint feel that caregivers, teachers, and support staff should have more specific autism training to de-escalate situations before they escalate. For them, restraint should be the last resort, to be employed rarely, if at all. Some schools employ restraint more often, and for them, it can be a slippery slope into abuse.

Schools may say, "We never use restraint as a punishment; we only restrain to prevent injury," yet the availability of restraint means staff may employ it in ways that management would not condone. The unrulier the students, and the more overloaded the staff, the greater the risk (Robison, 2018).

Advocates point out that potentially dangerous behaviours that trigger restraint can be managed better. For example, a person who bangs his head repeatedly might wear a helmet. Another person may be overloaded by sensory stimuli or tormented by school bullies. Remove the torment/bullying, and you can commonly avoid any meltdowns?

Many of us look back on our childhoods and consider that our teachers did their best yet failed to understand us fully. In the case of young people with autism, teachers may have been unaware that lights, sounds, and smells drove them

DOI: 10.4324/9781003614432-7

crazy. They didn't see the taunts in the schoolyard. They didn't understand when their teaching methods were incompatible with their individual learning style. Our knowledge has improved somewhat, but misunderstandings in the teaching profession remain rife. I have seen this as a teacher, SENDCo and school leader.

Robison (2018) argues that parents, staff, and teachers in their study all justified restraining kids to prevent them from harming themselves or others. Parents spoke of expecting schools to protect their child, and that includes preventing them from harming themselves and others. Some opponents of restraint suggest we should be allowed to harm ourselves if that's our choice. No matter how adults feel about that for themselves, there is little chance minors will be allowed to self-destruct in present-day society. Mainstream society rightfully does not support harming oneself (self-harm) or others, and that is sometimes a factor in using restraint.

In the end, restraint may happen when all else fails. We can and should strive to avoid getting into such an extreme position, but if we are realists, we must recognise that it may inevitably happen. When it does, we have just three choices (Robison, 2018):

- Use staff to restrain the person and unwind the situation.
- Isolate the person so no one else is harmed and let them work it out themselves.
- Call the police and allow them to manage the situation.

In May 2009, the US Government Accountability Office completed its nationwide investigation into the use of restraint and seclusion in public schools (McIlwain, 2015). They concluded that no federal laws were in place to keep educators from using dangerous and abusive methods to restrain or seclude a student. This is especially troubling for students with special needs, particularly for those with communication challenges such as autism. In the United Kingdom (UK) in 2024, there is a similar situation; there is only guidance to schools and educators, and no need to record when restraint is used. However, hospitals and residential homes are legally required to record when restraint is used.

Students with disabilities are 2.71 times more likely to be subject to restraint procedures compared with typically developing students (Marques & Barnard-Brak, 2023). Research has found that individuals at the highest risk of the use of restrictive interventions are those who exhibit self-injurious behaviours, aggression, and destruction (Webber et al., 2011). McGill et al. (2009) found that 90% of individuals with autism, with or without cognitive impairments, in their sample were physically restrained at least monthly, sometimes weekly, more than individuals with other disabilities and disorders. Individuals with a hearing, physical, neurological, communication, or visual impairment or autism were more likely to be subjected to mechanical restraint than individuals with other disabilities and disorders (Webber et al., 2019). In another study, thirty-six percent of individuals with autism, with or without cognitive impairments, were subject to seclusion at least monthly, almost weekly (McGill et al., 2009). Considering these findings, individuals with autism seem more likely to be subjected to physical and restrictive interventions. The question is why, and is this the best intervention? Maybe it's due to the lack of knowledge or interventions that restraint is commonly used by default.

The UK's Committee of the Rights of the Child (2016) in Hodgkiss and Harding (2023) suggests that physical restraint should only be used on a child or young person as a last resort (Cabinet Secretary for Education and Skills, 2022). In the UK, national guidelines recommend using physical restraint to protect a pupil or member of staff from harm, but also to prevent 'disruptive behaviour' or 'remove disruptive children from the classroom where they have refused to follow an instruction to do so' (Department for Education, 2013). A survey by the Challenging Behaviour Foundation (CBF) (2019) found that the reasons recorded for using physical restraint can be very vague, including preventing 'disruptive behaviour' without going into detail about what this includes. This evidence suggests that physical restraint may 'not' be used as a 'last resort' intervention, and its overuse may be going some way to normalise its usage rather than looking for alternative strategies (Dunlap et al., 2011).

Recording restraint incidents

In the UK, there is no legal obligation to record incidents of physical restraint in educational settings. A Freedom of Information request (Harte, 2017) found that there were around 13,000 incidents of physical restraint in the previous three years in educational settings in England, Scotland, and Wales. However, these were only the ones reported. A separate report in Scotland reported that at least 2,500 physical interventions were carried out with pupils in Scotland across three academic years (Macaskill & Allardyce, 2022). In the United States, it was found that around 122,000 pupils experienced restraint or seclusion at school during the 2015–16 academic year (Schifter, 2019).

Hodgkiss and Harding (2023) suggest that of those pupils who have had their incidents of physical restraint recorded, the majority have special educational needs and disabilities (SEND). Gage et al. (2020) found that pupils with disabilities were seven times more likely to be physically restrained in the United States, with the percentage of pupils being restrained in special needs schools at a significant 99%. Schifter (2019) also highlighted that whilst pupils with disabilities only make up around 12% of pupils enrolled on educational settings, they represent 71% of pupils who are physically restrained in those settings.

In the UK, the Challenging Behaviour Foundation (CBF) (2019) surveyed parents and carers of pupils who had been physically restrained at school and found that 88% of incidents reported in their survey were carried out with children or young people with a disability. These statistics suggest that the population receiving most physical restraints at school are highly vulnerable, and call into question whether these pupils are receiving their human right to freedom from 'inhuman or degrading treatment or punishment' upheld in comparison to pupils without disabilities, and their equitable access to education (Equality and Human Rights Commission (1998). It also suggests a lack of understanding of the causes of meltdowns and how school environments exacerbate dysregulation rather than demonstrate how the right support can reduce the frequency of meltdowns.

Harte (2017) for BBC News reported 731 injuries resulting from physical restraint over three years in the UK, with the actual number of injuries likely to

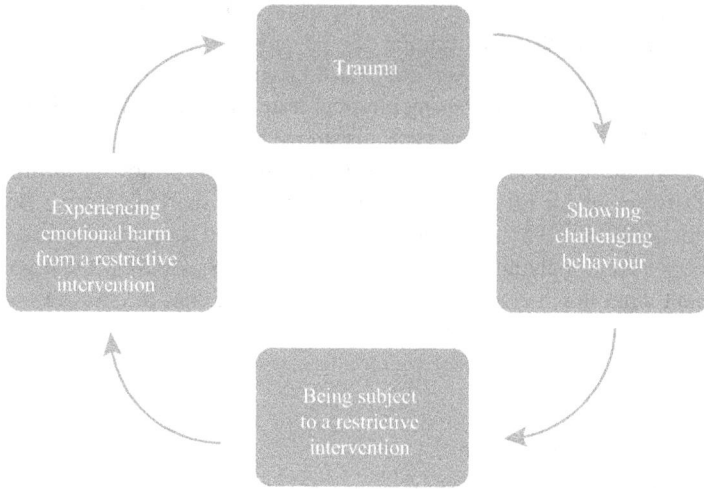

Figure 7.1 Trauma and restraint behaviours (Centre for Mental Health, 2020).

be even higher due to under-reporting. The article also summarises concerns from parents and carers around the physical impact of some forms of physical restraint, including positional asphyxia, choking, and bruising on the arms and chest.

The report from the CBF (2019) found that, of the incidents of restraint recorded in their survey, 58% led to the pupils being injured. However, 81% of these injuries were not reported by the school. Pupils also experienced significant negative emotional effects because of being restrained in schools. The report also found parents and carers reported some children were 'unable to communicate', had 'reduced trust in adults', 'low self-esteem' and 'anger towards staff', because of being physically restrained. In addition, special education staff members implementing physical restraint were found to experience physical and emotional harm regardless of the accuracy and success of the method of restraint used (Laymon, 2018). The use of restraint affects student–teacher relationships and trust, with pupils voicing a variation of positive, negative, and negligible effects of restraint on their relationship with staff members (Willis et al., 2021).

It was argued by the Centre for Mental Health (2020) that the psychological harm may manifest in further challenging behaviour, leading to a higher risk of being subject to restrictive interventions, so a cycle of trauma leading to restraint leading to trauma, see Figure 7.1.

What are the different types of restraint?

- 'Prone Restraint' means that the child is placed in the face-down position.
- 'Supine Restraint' means that the child is placed in the face-up position.
- 'Physical restraint' involves a person applying various holds using their arms, legs, or body weight to immobilise an individual or bring an individual to the floor.

- 'Mechanical restraint' includes straps, cuffs, tape, and other devices to prevent movement and/or sense perception, often by pinning an individual's limbs to a splint, wall, bed, chair, or floor.
- 'Chemical restraint' relies on medication to dull an individual's ability to move and/or think.

The Equality and Human Rights Commission (2021) defines these (see Figure 7.2):

- Physical interventions (active): a method of restrictive practice in which a pupil's actions or movements are controlled by the active use of force.
- Physical interventions (passive): a method of restrictive practice that involves direct physical contact, but not active force, to restrict or control a pupil's movement or actions.
- Seclusion: the withdrawal of a pupil from a classroom or other school situation against their will and involuntary confinement of a pupil, apart from others, in a place where the pupils must remain alone and separate from other pupils.
- Mechanical restraint: the use of materials or equipment by school staff to restrict a pupil's ability to move or act, such as arm splints, belts, or cuffs. This also includes the removal of an auxiliary aid such as a wheelchair or walking stick to prevent a pupil from being able to move independently.
- Chemical restraint: when assistance is sought from a medically trained member of staff to administer medication to control or subdue a pupil's behaviour.

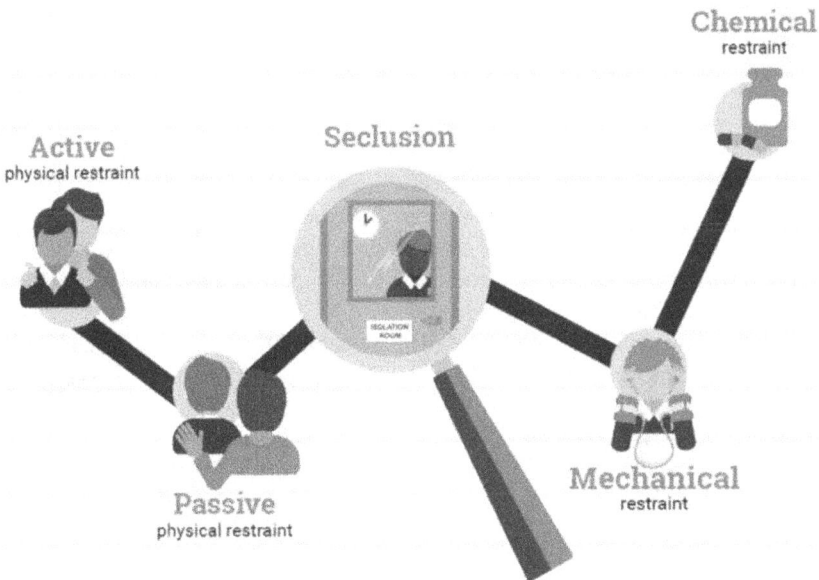

Figure 7.2 The different types of restraint (Equality and Human Rights Commission, 2021).

As there is no legal requirement for schools in England and Wales to monitor restraint, current (non-statutory) guidance for schools in England does not include mandatory requirements for recording or monitoring the 'use of force' (Department for Education, 2013). It advises that 'it is good practice for schools ... to consider how best to record such serious incidents'. If schools do choose to monitor restraint, the guidance provides them with little advice about the approach they should take. The Equality and Human Rights Commission (2021) argue that this is different from other areas of society where the use of restraint is legally required to be recorded and monitored: prisons, hospitals, and children's residential homes.

The Equality and Human Rights Commission's report (2021) found that when considered as a proportion of 'all' schools (including those that do not have a policy), 84% had a policy that requires all incidents of restraint to be recorded. 71% had a policy that also covered the analysis of those incidents. This dropped to 63% for mainstream secondary schools. Their survey found that most schools (93%) had a policy covering the use of restraint, and a small proportion (6%) did not have such a policy. One of the purposes of having a policy is transparency, so that staff and parents are clear about the approach schools must use to restrain. In the evidence we received, many parents whose children had been restrained in school expressed concerns about a lack of transparency.

However, on closer inspection, their sample of 641 primary, secondary and special schools surveyed in England and Wales (out of a possible 25,500 schools) suggests an unrepresentative sample. The lack of response would mean no restraint policy in place:

- 97% of all schools that use restraint said they record all incidences of active physical restraint.
- 25% of schools used passive physical intervention but did not always record this.
- 17% of schools said they did not always record their use of seclusion.
- 11% of schools said they used mechanical restraint, and 9% of schools used chemical restraint, but they did not record these incidents.
- While only a small number of schools said they used these forms of restraint, both have the potential to seriously affect a pupil's physical and/or mental health. Such incidents must be recorded.
- 23% of schools that did not record all incidents said they did not record all 'minor or passive' interventions. This rose to 44% in ten special schools surveyed.
- 25% of schools that did not record all incidents said they did not know why this was the case, and a further 12% said there was no reason.

What are the signs of restraint/seclusion?

While many children with autism are non-verbal or minimally verbal, there are some ways to tell whether restraint/seclusion techniques have been used. These can include:

- Bruising or abraded, reddened skin on arms, wrists, or ankles
- Unusual injuries

- Sudden regressions
- The emergence of new and unexplained behaviour problems at home such as sleeplessness, nightmares, increased anxiety levels, or emotional outbursts
- The appearance of new problem behaviour at school
- The appearance or intensification of self-injurious behaviours and/or increased aggression
- Fear of a particular teacher, aide, substitute, or staff member
- The emergence of a school phobia (especially when the child previously enjoyed attending school) or of a more generalised fear of leaving home
- Emergence of specific fears that may be related to aversive, restraint, or seclusion techniques (such as fear of spray bottles, seatbelts, or closets)
- Acting out of the traumatic experience(s) in play (e.g., a child who experiences physical abuse may begin to play roughly with dolls or peers)
- Not wanting to be alone
- Loss of interest in things he/she used to enjoy.

Vulnerable non-speaking autistic children are one of the largest groups to be subjected to restraint and seclusion, according to Tidd (2020). Restraint and seclusion are the inevitable outcomes of the failure to understand the causes of behaviour. Autism isn't a 'behavioural problem', it only becomes one when autistic people are denied appropriate accommodations and mistreated. The behaviours schools are trying to modify are distress, not wilful. Tidd argues that meltdowns are a non-volitional neurological event, not a volitional temper tantrum. The focus must be on preventing escalation by listening to the child and responding to their needs.

Maybe a new perspective is called for, seeing and talking about children not being 'challenging'. Children having meltdowns feel challenged, most often, by their caretakers/teachers/support workers. The simple truth is that most meltdowns are in response to the denial of reasonable accommodations and lack of awareness/ training.

Restraint and seclusion are crisis management strategies. Physical restraint is exactly what it sounds like; it is a personal restriction that immobilises or reduces the ability of a student, used in many schools worldwide. A personal restriction that immobilises or reduces a student's ability to move his or her torso, arms, legs, or head freely. Seclusion is the involuntary confinement of a student alone in a room or area from which the student is physically prevented from leaving. These interventions are dangerous and have led to serious injuries and even reported deaths.

Case study (Leighday, 2022)

Kent County Council, which ran Five Acre Wood Special School in Maidstone, admitted that the school breached its own Policy, and the Department for Education's guidance by using mechanical restraint Hardrock chairs against Samuel and Jacob Montague when they were aged between five and eight years old.

Now aged 17, the brothers were removed from the school by their parents Annie and Mark Montague in 2013 after the school continued to mechanically restrain the boys, strapping them into the chairs despite their parents' objections and protests. The brothers started at Five Acre Wood School in 2009, aged four, and the intention was that they would attend until age 19.

However, when Annie and Mark went to a school concert in 2010 when the boys were aged five, they were shocked to see them wheeled onto the stage strapped into wheelchairs. When they protested to the school, they were told that the use of the mechanical restraint, Hardrock chairs, was the only way the boys could participate in such a concert, and the incident was a one-off.

However, the parents became concerned that Samuel and Jacob were being routinely restrained while at the school. In June 2011, a clinical psychologist visited and witnessed one of the boys strapped into the Hardrock chairs in the classroom. The parents protested, but the chairs continued to be used. On one occasion, the boys' mother and their carer attended a school sports day where other children were outside and running around. Jacob was strapped into the chair and was visibly distressed. The boys' autism means they interpret the world through touch and movement, so the use of the chairs completely undermined their human rights, said their parents. After Annie and Mark took Samuel and Jacob out of the school, they home-schooled them, the boys have flourished. The couple brought a civil case under the Human Rights Act against Kent County Council, saying the restraints had been used unlawfully because the school failed to consider less restrictive options and failed to put in place a plan to reduce the use of restraint.

Kent County Council admitted multiple failings in the legal case and accepted its liability to pay the boys compensation following a court hearing.

His parents have personally asked this author to add 'despite repeated assurances by the school of the abandonment of restraint being used on the boys, an incident occurred to Samuel of such severity that involved hospital treatment and subsequent Child Protection Proceedings being instigated, thus involving the Police. As we all know, the Police failed the boys and indeed did not even enter the school, let alone speak to any teacher, despite overwhelming evidence. It was for this reason that they were removed from the education system for their safety. So, it would appear the Police are reluctant to get involved when an autistic individual needs their protection and help, yet are proactive in facilitating the pipeline, as this author has described, into the prison system.'

A joint research study carried out by the charities CBF (2019) and Positive Behaviour Support Scotland (PBSS) attempted to assess the use of restrictive practices on children with additional needs in schools across the UK, including Northern Ireland. The research included a survey conducted by CBF with 204 parents whose children have additional needs, as well as an analysis of 566 case studies of families being supported by PBSS gathered over 12 months. The survey revealed:

- 88% of parents reported that their child had been restrained in school, with 35% stating this happened regularly.
- 71% of families reported that their child had been secluded in school, with 21% stating this was happening daily.
- 50% of respondents' children had been prescribed medication specifically to manage challenging behaviour.
- Most of the restrictive interventions reported in the CBF survey took place in schools; for example, 68% of the physical interventions.
- Over half of the cases of physical intervention or seclusion reported were of children between the ages of five and ten.

Calum's Law

Adams and Jarvis (2023), along with Morrison (2023), and a report by Labour MSP (Member of the Scottish Parliament) Daniel Johnson, launched a consultation on a new member's bill after what happened to Calum Morrison, calling it 'Calum's Law'.

This consultation aims to establish legally enforceable physical restraint guidelines in UK schools and ensure compulsory training for all teachers on how to de-escalate difficult situations.

Morrison (2023), his mother, has been campaigning for more than a decade over what happened to her son Calum, who has learning disabilities, autism, and epilepsy. Calum was physically restrained on the floor for 40 minutes by four adults until he became unconscious whilst attending a special school in Dundee.

Calum was just 11 years old and was very small for his 11 years when riding an adapted disabled bike in the gym at his school. Having never ridden a bike before, one can imagine his excitement. This teacher was giving instructions, but Calum, who had the developmental age of a toddler, could not process her instructions. When (as she saw it) he did not do as he was told, so he was physically pulled off the bike and got such a fright that he was kicked out (had a meltdown). That resulted in four staff members tackling Calum to the floor, face down, with so much pressure that he couldn't breathe. He lost consciousness and wet himself. Whilst still in the process of coming round, still soaked in his urine, staff forced Calum into a chair. One of them stood over him with an egg timer to make sure he understood he was being punished (he did not). She said, "My husband and I were devastated. We had no idea that a school could do this to a vulnerable child with profound learning disabilities".

The bruises healed, but the trauma is still with Calum 13 years later. His mother said "Calum is still suffering the aftermath of that incident. It changed his life, and ours. We know of children with broken ribs, petechial haemorrhaging, severe bruising, cuts, broken collarbones and limbs, broken noses, bleeding lips and broken teeth". As there is no mandatory recording of incidents, parents say that they are often left in the dark.

Morrison said,

> *If a parent left a child bruised, there would be an immediate social work investigation. But this is happening every day in our schools, and it is virtually unheard of for any teacher or staff member to be investigated or questioned by the police. Schools are carrying on restraining our children and putting them into isolation rooms for hours.*

His mother explains,

> *Our children are the most vulnerable in Scotland. They use their behaviour to communicate because it is all they have. What are we doing, restraining children on the floor for discipline, for punishment, to make them comply? It is about control; it is not about care. That's got to change.*

Morrison (2023) wants the current guidelines on physical restraint to become legally enforceable, with mandatory recording and reporting of all incidents. She also wants compulsory training for all teachers and support staff on how to de-escalate difficult situations and understand children's needs so that physical restraint can and should be avoided. She told the BBC that since she started campaigning 12 years ago, more than 2,500 other families had contacted her because their children had been hurt while being physically restrained. She notes that hundreds of cases were reported to her each year, and almost all the children who had been injured were of primary school age, and all of them had additional support needs. "Some of the injuries being reported to me are horrific and, more often than not, restraint and isolation are being used as a punishment".

> *We are talking about the most vulnerable, disabled, non-verbal children from the age of three years old being tied to chairs or being physically pinned to the ground because they apparently did not follow orders. These children are not deliberately misbehaving. They are showing a distress reaction because they do not understand what is being expected of them. We are talking about severely disabled children who cannot speak or understand.*

The Labour MSP told the BBC, "We have now had over a number of years reports showing there is an alarming use of restraint and seclusion, sometimes literally putting them in cupboards".

A Scottish government spokesman said,

> *The reality is that ASN (additional learning support) provision has been under-resourced for many years, with serious implications for young people in our schools. There has been a significant decline in the number of specialist ASN staff employed in schools, while the number of young people with an identified additional support need has also increased substantially over the last few years.*

The United Nations Convention on the Rights of the Child-UNCRC (UNICEF, 2012) rules explicitly prohibit the use of restraint, isolation, and seclusion as disciplinary measures in schools and care settings. They state that it must only be used as a last resort and to prevent harm. The latest figures from 'Positive and Active Behaviour Support Scotland-PABSS' indicate that 6% of children being restrained are just three years old. By age eight, the figures rise to 33%. However, not one incident has been reported of a child older than ten years.

The Scottish Government has confirmed that "Restraint and seclusion in schools must only ever be used as a last resort to prevent the risk of harm, and existing guidance on physical intervention and seclusion", published in 2017, remains in place.

Scott (2024) reported on a case where a teacher restrained a five-year-old autistic pupil by pinning him down as he screamed for help. Joseph Morton's first days at Gilmerton Primary School in Edinburgh were so traumatising that the little boy has been terrified ever since of going to school. Edinburgh City Council upheld a complaint that the school breached their Relationships, Learning & Behaviour policy despite staff 'consistently' describing the practice as being "in the interests of enabling Joseph to engage with school". His father Alan, 37, said What we did not realise then was that those few moments would haunt Joseph and us, leaving him terrorised and afraid of going to school. Staff continued to grab him, restrain him and drag him into the classroom until our son became terrified that every adult would do that to him".

Restraint research

Salvatore et al. (2022) and Newcomb and Hagopian (2018) suggest that severe behaviour, such as aggression, self-injury, and property destruction, is more common in individuals with autism than their neurotypical peers. Most research on severe behaviour in individuals with autism is limited to children, and prevalence estimates vary widely. Hill et al. (2014) estimate that between 8% and 68% of children with autism engage in aggressive and destructive behaviour, while others suggest as many as 82% (Murphy et al., 2009) to 93.7% (McTiernan et al., 2011) exhibit challenging behaviour. This discrepancy in estimates has been attributed to differing operational definitions of severe behaviour, assessments used, and study participants (Hill et al., 2014), suggesting barriers to understanding this topic.

Salvatore et al. (2022) argue that applying restraint is a common strategy for managing severe behaviour, despite indications of increases in the individual's risk of depression, anxiety, and post-traumatic stress disorder following restraint implementation (Friedman & Crabb, 2018). Mechanical restraint entails using equipment such as arm splints or waist straps to restrict movement. Use of physical restraint, in which at least one person uses their body to restrict an individual's ability to move their torso, arms, legs, or head, is associated with distrust of medical professionals (Wong et al., 2019). Both physical restraint and chemical restraint, which entails using medication (e.g., benzodiazepines) to inhibit patient movement and manage emergent behaviours, can cause serious injury, functional decline, and even death (Friedman & Crabb, 2018).

Initiatives to reduce restrictive behaviour management for individuals with autism are associated with positive outcomes, such as improved safety, and decreased long-term costs such as staff training, reformed organisational policies, reduced staff sickness, and mindfulness-based interventions (Sturmey, 2018). Nonetheless, restraint is still commonly used in institutional, residential, day habitation, vocational, and school settings. Similarly, healthcare professionals have identified alternative approaches to restraint, for example, clearer communication and visual cues; with guidelines that physicians should only use restraint after all safer alternatives have been exhausted (Blumberg & Roppolo, 2021).

Although many educational and residential providers recognise that restraint should be a last resort, studies have reported an increased risk of inappropriate restraint use in children with autism and intellectual disability due to limited staff training and knowledge of autism (Gabriels et al., 2012). Recent research indicates that children with a diagnosis of autism and intellectual disability continue to experience higher rates of restraint compared to those without those diagnoses (O'Donoghue et al., 2020).

Professionals should ask why severe behaviour manifests, and rather than advocating restraint, to better try understand what the behaviour is communicating in the first place. For example, an individual with autism may engage in severe behaviour to escape the distress caused by bright lights in an examination room. For this person, dimming the lights could be a simpler, safer, more effective strategy than restraint. Kupzyk and Allen (2019) reviewed behavioural interventions to increase medical compliance, finding that graduated exposure and contingent reinforcement are most used, followed by modelling and prompting, distraction or relaxation, and behavioural momentum.

Restraint due to self-injury

The National Autistic Society (NAS) (2020) discusses the causes of self-injurious behaviour. There might be several factors causing someone with autism to self-injure (not self-harm, which is to injure oneself on purpose), which might include:

- They feel they are not listened to
- They have been told off
- They have little or no choice about things
- They have been bullied
- They are involved in arguments or hear other people arguing
- They are feeling unwell
- They have memories of a bereavement
- They have memories of abuse.

The NAS (2020) offers other reasons that may include:

- Communicating – The person might have no other way of telling you their needs, wants, and feelings; this may be more the case with a person with limited speech or being non-verbal. Head slapping, or banging the head on a hard surface, maybe a way of telling you they are frustrated, a way of getting an object or activity they like, or a way of getting you to stop asking them to do something. Hand biting might help them cope with anxiety or excitement. They might pick their skin because they are bored. Ear slapping or head banging might be their way of coping with discomfort or saying that something hurts.

- Mental health issues – Some self-injurious behaviour might indicate mental health issues such as depression or anxiety.
- Repetitive behaviour – Some forms of self-injury might be part of a repetitive behaviour, an obsession, or a routine.
- Developmental stages – The person might still do some things that most people stop doing as young children, such as hand mouthing – putting their fingers or hand into their mouth – causing injury.
- Learned behaviour – The person might learn that self-injurious behaviour can be a very powerful way of controlling the environment. A behaviour, for example, head-slapping, which they did at first because of physical pain, could eventually become a way of avoiding or ending a situation, they don't like, for example, turning the television off, or interrupting an argument taking place nearby.

The Dementia and Disabilities Unit (DDU) (2017) quotes the National Institute for Health and Care Excellence (2015) guidelines that children and young people with learning disabilities, autistic spectrum disorders/autism, and mental health issues may often respond with challenging behaviour (verbal or non-verbal) when they are confronted with situations they do not understand, which cause anxiety or fear, and for which they have not been prepared. The likelihood of such behaviour can often be anticipated by those who know the child best.

The BBC News team investigated 50 cases of restraint in UK schools (Clegg & Adnitt, 2024):

- Leah, who's 18 and from the north of Scotland, is autistic and has Attention-Deficit Hyperactivity Disorder (ADHD) and a learning disability. One of Leah's most painful memories of her former school is the time she was held down (restrained) for so long by members of staff that blood vessels burst in her face. She says restraint was used so often on her there that she once forced a screw into her toe as a plea for help. Her family had been told that an independent special school, which charges her local council £250,000 per year for a placement, would be able to meet her complex needs. However, although Leah initially settled at the school, she found herself being repeatedly restrained. The distress this caused, led to self-harm – she shaved her hair and eyebrows and pushed Blu Tack into her ears as she tried to get out of the school. "It was so scary", she says. "I never felt safe".
- Charlene says she felt she had won the golden ticket when she finally found a specialist school in the south-east of England that would meet her children's needs. After 40 schools had rejected her two autistic daughters, Isla, 13, and Skye, 11, she thought that, at last, this independent special school – costing the local authority £100,000 per child per year – would allow them to thrive. Charlene says

her daughters, Isla and Skye, were failed both academically and emotionally. But a couple of years later, she says the girls are still traumatised and out of education. At one stage, she says, her younger daughter was being restrained daily.

Clegg and Adnitt (2024) argue that due to a lack of provision in the state sector, and the growing number of children being identified as having special educational needs and disabilities (SEND), councils are increasingly turning to private provision. Last year, local authorities in England spent £1.6 billion on sending children to independent special schools – sometimes at more than £1 million a place. The majority are privately owned and run on a profit-making basis. Experts have told the BBC that the issues they raise are common across the sector. They include:

- An unnecessary and excessive use of restraint, and concerns that it is being used as a punishment
- A lack of qualifications – parents told us how some of those teaching their children had very little or no teaching experience
- Children making poor academic progress

The UK's Local Government Association – which represents councils in England and Wales – describes the SEND system as 'broken', and notes that the number of children being placed in independent special schools has more than doubled over the past decade. It is calling for 'urgent reform' and long-term funding so that children can be supported in the mainstream sector. There are more than 800 independent special schools across the UK, catering for about 21,000 children. They can offer a different learning environment for children who have struggled in mainstream education, and for many, they are the only establishments that can cater for such complex needs (Clegg & Adnitt, 2024).

Dr. Cath Lowther, the general secretary of the Association of Educational Psychologists (in Clegg & Adnitt, 2024) has concerns over the quality of the services some schools are offering. *"I worked in local authorities, and I saw independent special schools who are promising the earth and then charging the same, but then not delivering". Dr. Lowther argues that as soon as a school changes into independent ownership the culture changes, sometimes overnight. One parent said of the change, "It felt like the environment our children thrived in, vanished". "A huge turnover of staff followed, and Charlene says the ethos of the school completely changed...The escalation in the amount of restraint use was huge."* Many of the families told the BBC the complaints process is so complex, and often opaque, that they feel powerless when they do raise concerns to local authorities.

"Collectively as parents, we were all very alarmed about what we were seeing, because most of the children were in absolute crisis".

The Mental Health Act, autism, and assessment and treatment units (ATUs)

After much campaigning, the new UK Labour government of 2024 has agreed to limit the detention of those with learning disabilities and autism in hospitals, along with changing the entry requirement from needing to be sectioned under the UK's Mental Health Act. The National Autistic Society (NSA) (2024a) described the move as 'long overdue' adding that since 2015 there has been a 116% rise in autistic people without a learning disability being locked up in mental health hospitals, from 38% to 68% of all patients. The NSA said,

> *The inclusion of the Mental Health Act in the King's Speech is a vital opportunity to change the law so autism is no longer defined as a 'mental disorder' and autistic people cannot be detained in mental health hospitals just for being autistic.*

Previous reports (Kelso, 2019) have found more than 40 people had died while detained in these ATU units, since 2019 another 35 have reportedly died.

As of May 2024, the NSA (2024b) note that:

- In total, 2,025 autistic people and people with learning disabilities are in inpatient mental health hospitals in England.
- 1,380 (68%) of these people are autistic.
- There are 215 under 18 years old in inpatient units who are autistic or have a learning disability. Of these, 98% are autistic.

NSA (2024b) notes the average length of a time an autistic person staying at inpatient units is 4.9 years, and "we continue to hear alarming cases of overmedication, seclusion and unnecessary restraint", making them unsuitable for autistic young people to be in. ATUs are supposed to provide short-term assessment, treatment, and stabilisation of inpatients. However, many people are held miles away from their families for many years.

Joshi (2019) highlights the campaign of the father of Bethany, a young autistic girl who was detained in a single room for 24 hours a day. Bethany has autism and was sectioned under the Mental Health Act when she was 15 years old because she was deemed a risk to herself and others. She was locked up for almost three years. Her father notes. There is no furniture except a mattress on the floor that she sleeps on. There is no access to fresh air, not a window she can see out of. It's incredibly bright. Beth's sensory needs [include having] somewhere calm. It's noisy, you can hear people in the secure ward. People who are distressed.

She was moved there after her community placement broke down because she had not been given the proper support she needed, this was accepted after Jeremy fought a legal battle against NHS England, St Andrew's Healthcare, and his local authority. Her father argued successfully they were failing in their duty of care for Bethany. The case was settled out of court with all parties (NHS England, St Andrew's Healthcare, and his local authority) accepting that Bethany's care was inappropriate.

Sky News (2019) reported on Tony, a 41-year-old with autism, who has lived away from his family for more than 17 years. It all began to change when he was around 13 years old. His parents were advised by his school and the respite services that Tony needed to start medication, as he was difficult to manage, and the school couldn't help him. That was when his personality began to change. Tony never was aggressive but got aggravated. His parents reported he was hard to manage at home, and someone needed to be on call 24 hours a day, also he was going through puberty, so it was a difficult combination. No one knew back then about autism, his parents had no help or advice, so they were just told to start a support group. Roy, Tony's dad, said,

> *I knew how to deal with our son, and we still managed to care for him and enjoy a family life. However, as we got older, we realised that we aren't going to be around forever so we wanted to make sure Tony had his own home and wouldn't have to rely on us. But it completely backfired on us, and I now look back on it as the worst decision we ever made.*

Our local authority told his parents the best option was residential care. He went to two other secure units before ending up in a hospital unit. Originally, his parents were told it would only be for nine months until the council found somewhere more suitable that met his needs. Tony has now been in that unit for more than 17 years. His parents say it's destroyed their family, being over 120 miles away from their home. His parents have been told he doesn't belong to them; he is not their son anymore and belongs to the state because they pay the money. They feel they have no rights. His parents note that over the years, he has been restrained, sedated, and secluded. He has been held face down and injured, having black eyes, a broken arm, wrist burns, and bruises.

The Care Quality Commission (2022) report also reported that some people were admitted without proper assessment and did not have an assessment of their needs while in hospital. As a result, many of the people they met did not have a clear care and treatment plan in place. Often when people did have care plans, they were of poor quality, with no treatment plan to support them to leave the hospital (therefore suggesting they would never be released). Many of the plans they saw did not take account of individual needs. A common theme was that people felt they were seen as a collective of behaviours to be 'managed', rather than understanding the underlying causes of their distress.

Case study (Quinn, 2018)

Below is the story of Alexis, 34, an academic, international athlete and schoolteacher (Quinn, 2018). Alexis was restrained many times before she was able to leave the hospital system.

I was living with my family, but I felt overwhelmed. I sought help from my GP, and after a year and a half of misdiagnosis and mistreatment, I was lucky that an autism specialist witnessed one of my meltdowns and recognised my condition immediately. A specialist autism psychiatrist diagnosed me officially after a lengthy assessment while I was an inpatient. She explained that there was nothing wrong with me, but that my brain functioned differently and that I would need to learn to work with it.

I needed support, so I was told about an autism assessment and treatment unit – an ATU – in the south of England and decided to go there for a three-month assessment as a voluntary patient. I arrived in December 2014, and my nightmare began that very first day. When I admitted myself, everything was taken from me, including the phone I used to communicate with my daughter and parents who lived more than 200 miles away. I was searched, then left with only the clothes I was wearing, and one extra T-shirt and some underwear.

I entered the hospital for an initial 72 hour intervention. Due to a catastrophic clash between my autism and the environment when my brother died, I became overloaded and entered a damaging cycle.

It felt cruel, like I was set up to fail. I would never, ever be able to tolerate the lighting, the noise, the chaos and the sensory-charged box I was kept in. My different and sensitive autistic neurology was at the mercy of those who held the keys. I began to look as they described, 'violent and dangerous', because I couldn't control myself.

In total, I was restrained 97 times and secluded 17 times. I was forcibly drugged. The drugs took over every aspect of my very being. My body was battered and bruised, and my identity was fractured. They didn't like the autistic part of me. I tried to tell them that autism is all of me, it's who I am. I argued that my autism couldn't be treated. They said I lacked insight. Knowing I couldn't change, and being labelled as "treatment resistant", I grew to hate myself, and I lost hope. I'd never get out.

Alexis noted the irony of being in a unit dedicated to helping those with autism was that nothing about the way it operated was conducive to autistic people. The chaotic, noisy and often distressing environment made my meltdowns far more regular. Routines were constantly disrupted, making us all stressed and increasingly depressed.

After three and half years of restrictive practice in 12 different hospitals around the UK, I fled to Paris and then Africa whilst on a midweek at the unit and the weekends at home plan. There, I created a routine. I made my days predictable and my home autism friendly. Nothing in my house aggravated my sensory system. I weaned myself off the strong drugs, sought private psychology for the trauma I experienced (starting with the death of my brother). After six weeks, I started work as a teacher again. The key to success is creating the right environment and treating psychological differences with dignity and respect.

Case study (Nicholls, 2021)

Nicholls reports on Aaron, a young man with a diagnosis of autism and a learning disability. He was first admitted aged 18, in 2012, after attending a specialist autism school before a residential school placement. In 2012, Aaron's behaviour became increasingly challenging, so he was sectioned, and after 15 months in an ATU he was moved to a specialist autism hospital. His parents initially agreed to a short period of assessment in the ATU as they had become exhausted due to the lack of support and hoped that Aaron would get the professional support he needed. His mother told us that she was told "this would set him up for adult life". Unfortunately, Aaron had a traumatic experience in both the ATU and the specialist hospital. A serious case review later found that these placements had 'completely failed'. It further noted that "A very vulnerable young man suffered a sequence of traumatic experiences which may adversely affect him for many years". This included heavy reliance on restraint (including floor restraint), even though Aaron had never been restrained previously. It also involved over-medication, seclusion, and many safeguarding incidents and injuries.

At the specialist hospital, professionals removed Aaron's autism diagnosis without a proper assessment. As a result, he was arrested for assaulting staff – following 11 hours of floor restraint. Furthermore, he did not have access to an Independent Mental Health Advocate, and an independent social worker was excluded from meetings by the provider after raising concerns about the use of floor restraint. His anti-psychotic medication tripled in eight months. He had been restrained in an ambulance by seven people and had to wear a spit hood. Within three weeks of moving placement, his Haloperidol dosage had been reduced from 40 mg a day to 9 mg a day. A positive behaviour strategy was also put into action. The unit reassessed Aaron and reinstated his diagnosis of severe autism and a mild learning disability.

The report for the National Autism Society (Nicholls, 2021) was particularly concerned about the use of medication, in particular psychotropic medication. Research from Public Health England (2015) also indicates that people with a learning disability or on the autism spectrum are at greater risk of over-medication, with widespread inappropriate use of medication. Many of the families in the report spoke about the use of restraint as a significant issue, which should only be used as a last resort. A serious case review following Aaron's (case study noted above) discharge from an inpatient unit found that restraint (including prone restraint and a spit hood) had been relied upon, with damaging results. In one instance, he was arrested, handcuffed, and taken away in a police van. Although it appears that all the other parties have acknowledged that this was wrong, it is concerning that the provider has not apologised. The case study also notes a young person's autism diagnosis being removed, and later reinstated, suggesting a lack of training by some mental health professionals.

The Care Quality Commission (2022) report found that of the 43 assessment wards they inspected, they were not therapeutic and focused on

> *restraint and seclusion. Noting that young adults and adults with autism and learning difficulties need to be cared for in a person-centred way that meets their individual needs. They, therefore, recommended to the government, "They should be discharged as quickly as possible back home or to more suitable accommodation in the community where they live".*

Assessment ward staff told The Care Quality Commission that they did not always have the necessary training and skills to understand people's needs. People who care for people with a learning disability need to be able to properly understand them. Staff often lacked training on communication skills such as PECS (Picture Exchange Communication System and Makaton, and not being able to help people communicate caused patients further distress, which can lead to an increase in restrictive practices. Overall, hospital wards were not therapeutic environments. The noisy and chaotic nature of the wards could add to people's distress, particularly for autistic people (e.g., sensory overload). Often, autistic patients communicated this distress in ways that others found challenging, and this behaviour (likely to be autistic meltdowns) was then used as a rationale (vicious cycle) for using restraint, seclusion, and segregation.

The use of restraint varied across the services the Care Quality Commission visited. In some of the hospitals, they found that it was rarely used, but in others, it was a daily occurrence. In adult social care services, restraint was used more than seclusion or segregation. This is concerning, as currently there is no national oversight on the use of restraint and restrictive practices such as seclusion and long-term segregation. Seclusion was another option used to manage difficult situations safely. It is only meant to be used for the shortest time possible, but they found evidence that despite people being calm and settled, seclusion was not ended as it should have been. In some cases, people were living under these conditions for a long time. The environment and conditions of many of the seclusion rooms in hospitals that we saw were unacceptable and did not help people get better. For example, few seclusion rooms had access to natural light or fresh air, and only some had access to bathrooms or toilets. Most rooms were bare, without personal belongings or access to a TV or music. In addition, people in seclusion were not allowed to take personal possessions with them (even items that gave them comfort). While this was often for the safety of the individual, in some cases, we found that it was due to blanket restrictions.

References

Adams, L., & Jarvis, H. (2023). Calum's law plans to curb physical restraint in schools. *BBC Scotland*. 20 June 2023. Retrieved 23/07/2024. https://www.bbc.co.uk/news/uk-scotland-65930204

Blumberg, G.K., & Roppolo, L.P. (2021). Restraint and seclusion in the emergency department. In L.S. Zun, K. Nordstrom, & M.P. Wilson (Eds.), *Behavioural emergencies for healthcare providers* (pp. 249–256). Springer.

Cabinet Secretary for Education and Skills (2022). Physical intervention in schools: Draft guidance. *Scottish Government*. 21 June 2022. Retrieved 06/08/2024. https://www.gov.scot/publications/included-engaged-involved-part-3-relationship-rights-based-approach-physical-intervention-scottish-schools/pages/12/

Care Quality Commission (2022). Out of sight – Who cares? Restraint, segregation and seclusion review. 25 March 2022. Retrieved 22/07/2024. https://www.cqc.org.uk/publications/themed-work/rssreview

Centre for Mental Health (2020). 54: Trauma, challenging behaviour and restrictive interventions in schools. January 2020. Retrieved 09/07/2024. https://saphna.co/wp-content/uploads/2020/01/Briefing_54_traumainformed-schools.pdf

Challenging Behaviour Foundation. (2019). *Reducing restrictive intervention of children and young people*. Chatham, Kent: Challenging Behaviour Foundation.

Clegg, R., & Adnitt, J. (2024). Restrained and scared – The £100k schools failing vulnerable children. *BBC News*. 30 August 2024. Retrieved 04/09/2024. https://www.bbc.co.uk/news/articles/c4ge00wp9vgo

Committee on the Rights of the Child. (2016). *Concluding observations on the fifth periodic report of the United Kingdom of Great Britain and Northern Ireland*. Geneva: Committee on the Rights of the Child.

Dementia and Disabilities Unit – DDU. (2017). *Reducing the need for restraint and restrictive intervention children and young people with learning disabilities, autistic spectrum disorder and mental health difficulties*. Draft Guidance for Consultation. Prepared by the Department of Health and the Department for Education. Retrieved 08/07/2024. https://assets.publishing.service.gov.uk/media/5a81e9c3e5274a2e8ab56808/Reducing_the_Need_for_Restraint_and_Restrictive_Intervention.pdf

Department for Education – DFE (2013). *Use of reasonable force: Guidance*. London: HM Government.

Dunlap, G., Ostryn, C., & Fox, L. (2011). *Preventing the use of restraint and seclusion with young children: The role of effective, positive practices*. Tampa, FL: Technical Assistance Center on Social Emotional Intervention for Young Children (TACSEI).

Equality and Human Rights Commission (1998). Article 3. Freedom from torture and inhuman or degrading treatment. Retrieved 06/05/2025. www.equalityhumanrights.com/human-rights/human-rights-act/article-3-freedom-torture-and-inhuman-or-degrading-treatment

Equality and Human Rights Commission (2021). *Restraint in schools inquiry: Using meaningful data to protect children's rights*. Published June 2021. Retrieved 09/07/2024. https://www.equalityhumanrights.com/sites/default/files/2022/our-work-inquiry-restraint-in-schools-report.pdf

Friedman, C., & Crabb, C. (2018). Restraint, restrictive intervention, and seclusion of people with intellectual and developmental disabilities. *Intellectual and Developmental Disabilities, 56*(3), 171–187. https://doi.org/10.1352/1934-9556-56.3.171

Gabriels, R.L.; Agnew, J.A.; Beresford, C.; Morrow, M.A.; Mesibov, G.; and Wamboldt, M. (2012). Improving psychiatric hospital care for paediatric patients with autism spectrum disorders and intellectual disabilities. *Autism Research and Treatment, 2012*(7). https://doi.org/10.1155/2012/685053

Gage, N. A., Beahm, L., Kaplan, R., MacSuga-Gage, A. S., & Lee, A. (2020). Using positive behavioral interventions and supports to reduce school suspensions. *Beyond Behavior, 29*(3), 132–140. https://doi.org/10.1177/1074295620950611

Harte, A. (2017). Hundreds of 'restraint injuries' at special schools. *BBC News*. 9 April. Retrieved 10/06/2022. https://www.bbc.co.uk/news/uk-39530915

Hill, A.P., Zuckerman, K.E., Hagen, A.D., Kriz, D.J., Duvall, S.W., Van Santen, J., Nigg, J., Fair, D., & Fombonne, E. (2014). Aggressive behaviour problems in children with autism spectrum disorders: Prevalence and correlates in a large clinical sample. *Research in Autism Spectrum Disorders, 8*(9), 1121–1133. https://doi.org/10.1016/j.rasd.2014.05.006

Hodgkiss, B., & Harding, E. (2023). Reducing physical restraint in educational settings: A systematic literature review. 22 April 2023. Retrieved 23/07/2024. https://doi.org/10.1111/1471-3802.12598

Joshi, A. (2019). 'She's not an animal': Autistic teen girl locked up 24 hours a day. Thu 31 October 2019 21:37, UK. Retrieved 18/07/2024.

Kelso, P. (2019). 40 People died in 'barbaric' secure hospitals the government pledged would close. Thu 11 April 2019 16:43, UK. https://news.sky.com/story/40-people-died-in-barbaric-secure-hospitals-the-government-pledged-would-close-11540038

Kupzyk, S., & Allen, K.D. (2019). A review of strategies to increase comfort and compliance with medical/dental routines in persons with intellectual and developmental disabilities. *Journal of Developmental and Physical Disabilities, 31*(2), 231–249. https://doi.org/10.1007/s10882-018-09656-y

Laymon, S.R. (2018) Experiences of special education teachers performing physical restraints involving students with disabilities: A transcendental phenomenological study. Unpublished PhD dissertation, Department: School of Education, Liberty University.

Leighday (2022). Special school apologises for use of mechanical restraint against severely autistic twin boys. *Leighday website.* 25 March 2022. Retrieved 09/07/2024. https://www.leighday.co.uk/news/news/2022-news/special-school-apologises-for-use-of-mechanical-restraint-against-severely-autistic-twin-boys/

Macaskill, M., & Allardyce, J. (2022). I've been kicked and slapped by pupils, says teacher as level of violence in schools is revealed. *The Times.* 16 July. Retrieved 18/06/2024. https://www.thetimes.co.uk/article/ive-been-kicked-and-slapped-by-pupils-says-teacher-as-level-of-violence-in-schools-is-revealed-w9sbswnms

Marques, A. R., & Barnard-Brak, L. (2023). Restraint and seclusion procedures with children with autism spectrum disorder. *Intervention in School and Clinic, 59*(1), 70–74. https://doi.org/10.1177/10534512221130071

McGill, P., Murphy, G., & Kelly-Pike, A. (2009). Frequency of use and characteristics of people with intellectual disabilities subject to physical interventions. *Journal of Applied Research in Intellectual Disabilities, 22*, 152–158. https://doi.org/10.1111/j.1468-3148.2008.00483.x

McIlwain, L. (2015). Restraint & seclusion. A guide for autism parents. 21 January 2015. Retrieved 30/07/2024. https://nationalautismassociation.org/restraint-seclusion-a-guide-for-autism-parents/

McTiernan, A., Leader, G., Healy, O., & Mannion, A. (2011). Analysis of risk factors and early predictors of challenging behaviour for children with autism spectrum disorder. *Research in Autism Spectrum Disorders, 5*(3), 1215–1222. https://doi.org/10.1016/j.rasd.2011.01.009

Morrison, B. (2023). Calum's Law and why it's time to talk about restraint in schools. *The Herald Newspaper.* 27 September 2023. Retrieved 23/07/2024. https://www.heraldscotland.com/business_hq/23816024.calums-law-time-talk-restraint-schools/

Murphy, O., Healy, O., & Leader, G. (2009). Risk factors for challenging behaviours among 157 children with autism spectrum disorder in Ireland. *Research in Autism Spectrum Disorders, 3*(2), 474–482. https://doi.org/10.1016/j.rasd.2008.09.008

National Autistic Society (2020). Self-injurious behaviour – A guide for all audiences. 14 August 2020. Retrieved 24/07/2024. https://www.autism.org.uk/advice-and-guidance/topics/behaviour/self-injurious-behaviour/all-audiences

National Autistic Society (2024a). Our response to the King's speech. 17 July 2024. Retrieved 24/07/2024. https://www.autism.org.uk/what-we-do/news/our-response-to-the-kings-speech

National Autistic Society (2024b). Number of autistic people in mental health hospitals: Latest data. 21 June 2024. Retrieved 24/07/2024. https://www.autism.org.uk/what-we-do/news/number-of-autistic-people-in-mental-health-ho-20

National Institute for Health and Care Excellence – NICE (2015). Challenging behaviour and learning disabilities: Prevention and interventions for people with learning disabilities whose behaviour challenges. *National Institute for Health and Care Excellence*. Retrieved 08/07/2024. https://www.nice.org.uk/guidance/cg142

Newcomb, E.T., & Hagopian, L.P. (2018). Treatment of severe problem behaviour in children with autism spectrum disorder and intellectual disabilities. *International Review of Psychiatry*, *30*(1), 96–109. https://doi.org/10.1080/09540261.2018.1435513

Nicholls, T. (2021). Transforming care: Our stories. *National Autism Society.* Retrieved 22/07/2024. https://www.challengingbehaviour.org.uk/wp-content/uploads/2021/03/trans formingcareourstories.pdf

O'Donoghue, E.M., Pogge, D.L., & Harvey, P.D. (2020). The impact of intellectual disability and autism spectrum disorder on restraint and seclusion in pre-adolescent psychiatric inpatients. *Journal of Mental Health Research in Intellectual Disabilities*, *13*(2), 86–109. https://doi.org/10.1080/19315864.2020.1750742

Public Health England (2015). Prescribing of psychotropic drugs to people with learning disabilities and/or autism by general practitioners in England. Retrieved 14/05/25. clok.uclan.ac.uk/17970/

Quinn, A. (2018). 'I went from being a teacher with a first-class degree to losing my power of speech': New mother reveals how she was drugged and locked up in solitary confinement until she became suicidal after she was diagnosed with autism. Mail on Sunday. 3 November 2018. Retrieved 19/07/2024.

Robison, J.E. (2018). Restraint of people with autism and developmental disability: Some institutions can restrain people against their will. Should it be allowed? *Psychology Today.* 12 December 2018. Retrieved 08/07/2024. https://www.psychologytoday.com/gb/blog/my-life-aspergers/201812/restraint-people-autism-and-developmental-disability

Salvatore, G.L., Simmons, C.A., & Tremoulet, P.D. (2022). Physician perspectives on severe behaviour and restraint use in a hospital setting for patients with autism spectrum disorder. *Journal of Autism Developmental Disorders*. 2022 October, *52*(10), 4412–4425. https://doi.org/10.1007/s10803-021-05327-8. Epub 2021 Oct 16. PMID: 34657221; PMCID: PMC8520455.

Schifter, L.A. (2019). The need for federal legislation on seclusion and restraint. *The Century Foundation.* 28 February. Retrieved 18/06/2024. https://tcf.org/content/commentary/need-federal-legislation-seclusion-restraint/?agreed=1

Scott, M. (2024). Fears child will die as report on restraint of disabled pupils reveals more than 200 cases. *Scottish News in The Sunday Post*. 30 June 2024, 2:05 pm. Retrieved 08/07/2024. https://www.sundaypost.com/fp/restraint-of-disabled-pupils/

Sky News (2019). Line 18: 'My autistic son deserves a life, but he's locked up'. Fri 12 April 2019, 14:31, UK. Retrieved 19/07/2024. https://news.sky.com/story/line-18-my-autistic-son-deserves-a-life-but-hes-locked-up-11539937

Sturmey, P. (2018). Reducing restraint in individuals with intellectual disabilities and autism spectrum disorders: A systematic review group interventions. *Advances in Neurodevelopmental Disorders*, *2*(4), 375–390. https://doi.org/10.1007/s41252-018-0088-y.

Tidd, J.L. (2020). Autism isn't a crime. *Alliance Against Seclusion and Restraint, Inc.* 19 June 2020. Retrieved 08/07/2024. https://endseclusion.org/2020/06/19/autism-isnt-a-crime/

UNICEF (2012). A summary of the UN Convention on the Rights of the Child. 12 July 2022. Retrieved 24/07/2024. https://www.unicef.org.uk/wp-content/uploads/2019/10/UNCRC_summary-1_1.pdf

Webber, L.J., Richardson, B., White, K.L., Fitzpatrick, P., McVilly, K., & Forster, S. (2019). Factors associated with the use of mechanical restraint in disability services. *Journal of Intellectual and Developmental Disability*, *44*(1), 116–120. https://doi.org/10.3109/1366 8250.2017.1310814

Webber, L.S., McVilly, K.R., & Chan, J. (2011). Restrictive interventions for people with a disability exhibiting challenging behaviours: Analysis of a population database. *Journal of Applied Research in Intellectual Disabilities*, *24*, 495–507.

Willis, J., Harrison, A., & Allen, J.L. (2021). Pupils with social, emotional and mental health special needs: Perceptions of how restrictive physical interventions impact their relationships with teaching staff. *Teaching and Teacher Education*, *97*, 103219.

Wong, A.H., Ray, J.M., Rosenberg, A., Crispino, L., Parker, J., McVaney, C., Iennaco, J.D., Bernstein, S.L., & Pavlo, A.J. (2019). Experiences of individuals who were physically restrained in the emergency department. *Journal of the American Medical Association Network Open*, *3*(1), e1919381–e1919381. https://doi.org/10.1001/jamanet workopen.2019.19381

8 Exclusions

Ambitious about Autism (2018a) argues that secondary education is a time of vulnerability for autistic young people due to challenges associated with mainstream schools' environments, timetabling, and social pressures, along with relationships (Makin et al., 2017). Whilst it is expected that educators support the learning needs of autistic children (Makin et al., 2017), difficulties can be regularly experienced in providing such support (Trussler & Robinson, 2015).

The lack of autism training and the time to implement strategies proposed to help the diagnosed/undiagnosed autistic child can mean teachers react in ways that can trigger adverse reactions from these vulnerable students, for example, meltdowns.

Research indicates that 25% of children diagnosed with autism have been excluded from school at some point during their education (Ambitious about Autism, 2014). It is argued that compared to other groups of children with Special Educational Needs and Disability (SEND), autistic children are being excluded from mainstream secondary in disproportionate numbers. As a result, many end up in a pupil referral unit (PRU) – an Alternative Provision (AP) option for children who are unable to cope with mainstream education. See Figures 8.1 and 8.2.

Ambitious about Autism (2018) notes that exclusions for children with autism rose sharply, between 2011/12 and 2015/16 being up by almost 60% across

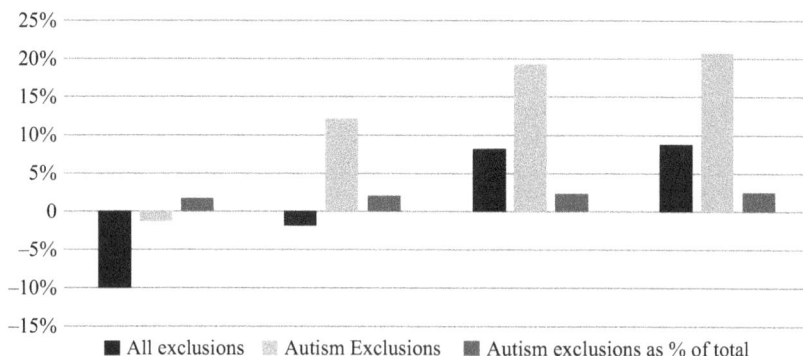

Figure 8.1 Year-on-year percentage changes in exclusions, 2011/12 to 2015/16 (Ambitious about Autism, 2018).

DOI: 10.4324/9781003614432-8

England, in five years. In every English region, exclusions of children with autism increased by at least 44%; in contrast, overall exclusions have risen by only 4% in the same period. Autism seems to be unfairly targeted by school leaders, forcing out higher needs students from schools.

Case study (Ambitious about Autism, 2018b)

My son Josh is 13. In secondary school last year Josh was unlawfully excluded for seven mornings and a further six half days prior to his Education Health and Care Plan (EHCP) application.

Josh is a great kid; he enjoys playing sports though this can cause a few problems as his oppositional defiance disorder and other mannerisms can lead to unwanted outbursts. But generally, he's polite, he loves maths and is very good at it. Before the exclusions began, he used to say he wanted to be a Maths teacher. The half-day morning exclusions were when the school was giving Josh 'Intensive Day punishments' which meant he had to go in at 2 p.m. till 5 p.m. on those days. The school recorded him as present in the morning sessions on the legal registers, even though he wasn't allowed to go to school until 2 p.m. This is unlawful – he had been excluded – and they need to report every time they exclude pupils.

This didn't just happen for Josh, 'intensive days' are part of this school's policy for dealing with pupils with challenging behaviour. They are habitually, illegally excluding children, across the school. At first, we didn't know it was unlawful to call parents to pick up during school time without recording it and telling us our rights. On one occasion, I was called in to take him home as he was upset and wandering the school and not listening to them. I asked how they were recording this when they called us to pick him up as they couldn't cope. I wanted to be sure they had evidence that Josh needed extra support. The school decided that they would mark these occasions in the registers as 'C' (collected by parents) with a notation next to it. We agreed to this, as we believed this would help us collect the evidence that Josh needed extra support, and because we didn't know that technically this was an exclusion. Beforehand, they were marking the times we were called in to collect, as Josh was present in school for the whole day. I now know both of these actions were unlawful – and worse, our complying with the school in the hope it would build evidence that Josh needed more support achieved the opposite. He wasn't recorded as excluded – so no one thought to assess if his needs were being met. He was being failed twice.

Despite the fact I had confirmation in writing that the school had acted unlawfully in the way they had excluded my son, and that they'd refused to record it correctly even when directed to by the local education authority, no one could help. I knew my child's rights – but it didn't make any difference. In desperation, I called the police. His school were acting unlawfully and had knowingly supplied incorrect records to their funding body – surely someone could act. But no – the police told me my only option was to make a civil case – and like most parents, I simply can't afford to.

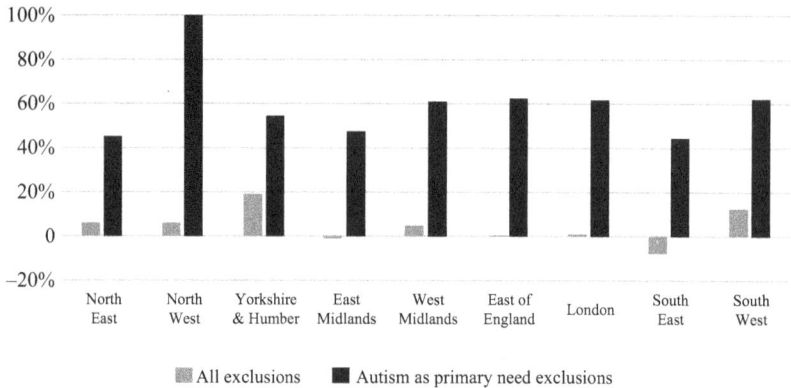

Figure 8.2 Regional percentage changes in all exclusions, and exclusions for children with autism, 2011/12 to 2015/16 (Ambitious about Autism, 2018).

Case study (Ambitious about Autism, 2018)

Billy is seven years old. He was diagnosed with autism at the age of 2. He's a bright boy but can become overwhelmed by too much noise and can find it hard to focus for long periods. His school was made aware of his needs right from the start and he was given varying levels of support from teaching assistants throughout nursery – who would change frequently. This resulted in Billy falling behind academically. When he reached Year 1 he was supported by a teaching assistant who specialised in special educational needs and his progress improved considerably – to the point where he caught up with the rest of the class. However, in September 2017, Billy's school was taken over by a new head and many staff, including Billy's teaching assistant, left the school. Billy was placed with a new teaching assistant which he found difficult, and this resulted in an outburst of behaviour that led the school to formally exclude Billy for 4 days. Following his first exclusions, his mum Stacey and the school agreed that he wasn't coping in a mainstream school and needed to be in a special provision. However, the school later changed its mind – following intervention by the local authority – and said Billy could cope in another mainstream school. This has resulted in the local authority refusing to sort an emergency placement for Billy in a special school or unit. Billy was subsequently excluded 17 times and then in December the school decided to permanently exclude him from school. Following this decision Billy was left with no education for two months – which had a massive impact on him. During this time, he didn't want to go outside and felt very anxious. He was bored and didn't have any structure in his life. Also at this time, Stacey was told she couldn't take Billy out of their house between 9 a.m. and 3 p.m. or else she would get fined by the local authority.

Exclusion explained

There is increasing awareness of data on the exclusion of children in England from education being hidden (Gazeley et al., 2015) and that there are several ways schools exclude a pupil using unofficial or illegal measures. Parsons (2018) identifies nine ways in which a pupil can be excluded:

• Permanent exclusion
• Fixed-term or temporary exclusions
• PRUs or alternative provisions
• Managed moves
• Elective home education
• Reduced timetables
• Extended study leave
• Attendance Code B – approved off-site educational activity
• Children missing education

Department for Education (DfE) (2020) data for 2018–19 from state-funded primary, secondary, and special schools indicate that 155 pupils with autism as their primary need were permanently excluded and 5,607 received a fixed-term exclusion. Autistic young people were found to be approximately twice as likely to be excluded from school as pupils who do not have special needs. Despite the rates of permanent and fixed-term exclusions for autistic pupils being above the national average, the scale of the problem is likely to be much higher. For example, official data does not include the number of undiagnosed or misdiagnosed autistic pupils in schools. In addition, government data only records 'official' exclusions (see section above on unofficial and illegal exclusions).

Ambitious About Autism (2018b) reported that 56% of parents of autistic children who responded to their survey said that their children had been unlawfully sent home from school or denied an education. They also saw a rise in the number of exclusions as a new and distinct trend; however, there has also been an increase in the number of children with autism as their primary SEND need at school.

Reasons for exclusions

There are 11 'official' UK school reasons for exclusion that head teachers refer to when deciding to exclude a pupil, being:

• Physical assault against pupil
• Physical assault against adult
• Verbal abuse/threatening behaviour against pupil
• Verbal abuse/threatening behaviour against adult
• Bullying
• Racist abuse
• Sexual misconduct
• Drug and alcohol related

- Damage
- Theft
- Persistent disruptive behaviour
- Other (includes incidents which are not covered by the categories above, but this category should be used sparingly).

The 2018–19 DfE dataset in Guldberg et al. (2021) indicates the most common reason for permanent and fixed-term exclusions in the general school population was persistent and disruptive behaviour. For autistic pupils, the most common reasons given for permanent exclusions were 'physical assault against an adult' (32%) and 'persistent disruptive behaviour' (21%). For fixed team exclusions 21% of schools reported 'physical assault against an adult' as the reason, with 'persistent disruptive behaviour' given as a reason in 22% of cases. In the DfE categories of reasons for excluding, there is an option for the school to select 'other'. It is unclear what fits in this category, and a deeper understanding of the 17% of permanent and 14% of fixed-term exclusions categorised as 'other' would provide insights into the reasoning behind and purpose of some exclusions made of autistic pupils that are not covered by the standard list of exclusions.

In Guldberg et al. (2021), 15% of teachers reported making unofficial exclusions, mainly because they felt the child could not have dealt with school 'events'. These findings resonated with the experiences of most parents, manifesting as part-time timetables, and informal exclusions associated with 'events' such as school trips and Ofsted inspections. Parents frequently regard the reasons schools give them for excluding their child to not be the true reasons. Almost two-thirds of parents surveyed thought that there was an alternative reason, mostly highlighting the failings of the school and a lack of teacher knowledge. It is worth noting, however, that official guidance requires schools to make reasonable adjustments to accommodate a pupil's autism and to consider whether the behaviour resulting in a possible exclusion was a consequence of the pupil's autism.

Exclusion is the end of a chain of events

Graham et al. (2019) indicate that there is commonly a 'chain reaction' to an event which leads to a young person ultimately being excluded. The path to exclusion may begin with distress, disengagement, or boredom, then behaviour that challenges, disciplinary action, and finally exclusion (Briggs, 2010). Looking at this from the perspective of autistic children and young people, a child or young person might get stuck in a cycle of lack of support, exclusion, distrust, and limited opportunities, and that cycle is then in the hands of adults and the child or young person does not have any control of that cycle.

> ...the evidence suggests that this guidance is simply being ignored and that children on the autism spectrum are regularly unlawfully excluded, with consequences for their academic progress, self-esteem and mental health. Of the parents who completed our survey, one in four told us that their child had

been 'informally' excluded at least once in the last year. Four in ten of the teachers who responded to the survey said that their school had excluded an autistic child, either lawfully or unlawfully, in the last year.
(APPGA: Autism and Education in England, 2017).

The UK's 2017 APPGA [National Autistic Society (NAS) 2019] report recognised that a lack of assessment or slow assessment processes meant many autistic learners' needs were not being met within schools. 70% of parents surveyed for the report agreed that support was not put in place quickly enough for their child. Nearly 70% waited more than six months for support and 50% waited more than a year. This lack of early assessment and intervention meant reasonable adjustments were not being made within schools to enable autistic pupils to access learning effectively. The Timpson Review (2019) reported that autistic children with an EHCP (with individual statutory SEND funding) are less likely to be excluded than those without an EHCP, suggesting that EHCPs are protective in some ways for the autistic child not being excluded. Indeed, the statutory guidance for headteachers on exclusion states that the head teacher should make every effort to avoid permanently excluding a pupil with an EHCP. However, this does not mean they are supported adequately in schools.

Around 70% of children and young people on the autism spectrum meet the criteria for a mental health condition, most often anxiety (Simonoff et al., 2008). The existence of co-occurring psychiatric conditions both leading up to exclusion (Sproston et al., 2017) and because of exclusion happening (Contact a Family, 2013). The question that needs to be asked is: Are these secondary or co-occurring conditions caused by the lack of correct support (or any support in some cases) for the person's primary autism diagnosis?

To illustrate, a boy with autism is then also diagnosed with anxiety and depression following bullying. He is treated for anxiety and depression, but the cause was from bullying which was likely due to the lack of support for his autism. The same could be said for obsessive compulsive disorder (OCD) tendencies, being a means to control their environment which is not autistic-friendly. Medical professionals seem more willing to treat OCD, anxiety, and depression with medication than support primary needs such as autism which require much more time, training, environmental, and institutional changes to the way schools or society act.

The increased risk of bullying and social isolation that many autistic students experience means they are at higher risk of exclusion, given that both bullying and being the victim of bullying emerged as a potential trigger for exclusion in the Timpson literature review (Graham et al., 2019). However, in the DfE statutory guidance for teachers on exclusion, the head teacher 'should' be considering bullying as a contributing factor in explaining an exclusion event. The DfE (2020) reports that children with SEND have much higher levels of unhappiness regarding school (Barnes & Harrison, 2017) and have more frequent conduct problems, hyperactivity, and poor peer relationships. Many of these factors may explain why autistic pupils are at risk of exclusion reoccurring and why some autistic individuals may display persistent and disruptive behaviour as a way of escaping school.

"Being excluded taught me that if I lashed out, I could go home to get peace and quiet" Autistic Adult (Guldberg et al., 2021). This suggests a coping strategy, albeit a negative one.

"Exclusions aren't a sanction for a child who is stressed and in need. It reinforces the behaviour to get them out of a difficult situation. It re-enforces their belief that school is a stressful and unsafe place". Parents of an autistic child are excluded at age 6 from a primary mainstream (Guldberg et al., 2021).

Mazurek et al. (2013) argue that given the increased rates of behaviours found in pupils with autism, such occurrences could be avoided by making environmental adjustments. Therefore, it is important to look beyond the tip of the iceberg to identify why these behaviours might be taking place, and by better understanding them and factors that may lead to meltdowns, autistic young people can be better supported in likely stressful environments.

The House of Commons Education Committee (2018) suggests firstly the rise in so-called 'zero-tolerance' behaviour policies in schools creates environments where pupils are punished and ultimately excluded for incidents that could and should be better managed within the mainstream school environment. Secondly, Brede et al. (2017) highlight that the social, institutional and environmental complexity of mainstream school settings means that autistic pupils can come under significant pressure which is an underlying reason for their increased rates of stress and behavioural issues. Thirdly, children and young people may be more likely to exhibit behaviours that challenge when moving to secondary school, where there may be less willingness to adjust teaching/lessons for their specific needs by teachers. Some reports have suggested that the rigid, pressurised, and uncaring environment in mainstream secondary, compared to primary schools is a cause for behaviours that challenge and exclusion (Levinson, 2016; Farouk, 2017).

Brede et al. (2017) researched the experiences of children and young people on the autism spectrum who had previously been excluded from education. Interviews with their parents identified that they felt schools and teaching staff failed to understand and accommodate their children's often complex needs. School staff used inappropriate methods to deal with resulting behaviours that challenged them. This led to the children becoming unable to engage in and access education. In most cases, they were permanently excluded from school. Brede et al. reported that autistic children in their study were aware that their difficulties (peer relations and communication problems), as well as the school's reluctance to adapt (lack of teacher training), were key factors in the decline in school performance and behaviour issues.

The House of Commons Education Committee (2018) also cited the unidentified and unmet special educational needs of many pupils as being a key reason for their school exclusion. Evidence was also presented that some schools may be deliberately failing to identify a pupil as having SEND as it is more difficult to permanently exclude them. That schools were justifying permanent exclusions of pupils with SEND, by claiming that they will get the support that they need in alternative provision, and exclusion will speed up the assessment process.

This author has been involved with cases where schools proposed that suspended students with undiagnosed SEND needs should be sent to a pupil referral unit (PRU), even though the school did not understand their needs, and therefore the PRU did not know whether they could meet their needs. Most were on a long waiting list with CAMHS for an autism and/or attention-deficit/hyperactivity disorder (ADHD) assessment. Speaking with a Deputy Head of a local PRU, they confirmed that most of the students coming to them had undiagnosed SEND needs, and even they could not gain faster assessments for these vulnerable students.

Brede et al. (2017) studied excluded autistic students, finding that 64% did not have their diagnosis at the time of exclusion, but had a broad range of additional difficulties around the time of exclusion, argued to be secondary manifestations of unmet SEND needs. This included anxiety, depression, sleep, and attention problems. Common feelings before exclusion occurred were stress, confusion, worry, and anger. 81% of autistic adults reported being bullied before exclusion occurred. Comments from respondents included

- "Because I did not fit in"
- "Because I was being bullied"
- "Because I was too slow"
- "Because I was too different"

UK school suspension/exclusion data supports the view that persistent and disruptive behaviour is commonly given as a reason for suspensions and exclusions. The difficulty is when the secondary manifestations of unmet SEND needs are used as the reason for the exclusion, and the primary unmet SEND needs are not addressed, then students feel rejected, unsupported, and misunderstood by teachers/schools. It also suggests that mainstream schools are not suitable for students with SEND needs, and if you have severe needs, then school can be a harsh environment.

All respondents in Brede et al. (2017) felt that they were unsupported by the teachers, and a large proportion (80%) reported that things worsened or stayed the same when they re-joined education after suspension/exclusion. Furthermore, many highlighted that exclusion led to school refusal, as they no longer felt safe or welcome in school, leading to a lack of trust and a breakdown in relationships.

As stated by several different respondents (Smith, 2024)

- "I was glad to be excluded because I felt better at home."
- "I was too scared to say much to staff after that in fear of things getting worse."
- "Teachers labelled me and didn't give me a chance!"
- "If I had been diagnosed with autism perhaps, they would have had more idea of how to help me."

In two studies that drew on the perspective of parents, they were asked about what factors led to school exclusion (Sproston et al., 2017; Brede et al., 2017). Parents highlighted:

- A lack of adaptation in sensory environments
- Conflict between staff and pupils
- Damaging peer relationships (including bullying)
- Limited understanding of the needs of autistic pupils and a lack of transition planning when moving from their previous school.

Parents spoke of promises of support not being upheld by staff, a lack of empathy and care shown by teachers, and a limited understanding of how autistic individuals manage stress. Parents in the study said that the relationships with teaching staff were often poor and they only ever got in touch when there was something negative to say (Sproston et al., 2017).

Smith (2024) found that:

- 84% of parents felt their child's autism was not considered when decisions on exclusion were made. As stated by one parent: "They couldn't deal with her extra needs - which weren't many. However, in other areas they shone and couldn't be faulted".
- 85% of parents felt unsupported.
- 93% thought the exclusion could have been avoided.
- 63% were unaware of their school's behaviour policy before exclusion occurred, and parents commented on a lack of communication about the process, with one stating: "School called me and said my son cannot come back to school. [However,] there was no official letter of exclusion".

As found in Smith (2024), interviews with the specialist support service teams highlighted that commonly there were unmet needs, including a lack of understanding of autism, and behaviour being misunderstood by school leaders and teachers. Precursors to permanent exclusion included missed opportunities to prevent exclusions, and school leaders seeing misbehaviour as a 'problem' rather than a signal for specialist support needs. Parents in Smith (2024) commented that it felt like schools would rather send a child somewhere else rather than try to make themselves an appropriate place, providing the reasonable adjustments they were required to legally provide.

Anxiety was a key underlying feature of behaviours that challenged autistic pupils, but these were not recognised in the behavioural approaches of schools (Smith, 2024). Schools predominantly drew on behaviour policies, which tended to not specifically reference autism/ADHD, or their unique needs, therefore indicating a lack of understanding around why behaviour happens, and the reason why a child or young person might behave in a certain way.

Impact of exclusion

Qualitative interview data suggests that exclusion can lead to social isolation from peers and future risk of bullying. Smith (2024) indicated that most of those who moved into AP seemed to have a more positive experience there compared to the mainstream school they came from and had better relationships with staff. In the medium term, half of respondents felt that the exclusion process had been negative, stigmatising and affected prospects, whereas almost a fifth regarded being excluded as a positive experience.

Parent data on the impact of exclusion highlighted that exclusion led to:

- Negative impact on self-esteem (83%)
- Isolation from friends (58%)
- Feeling let down by education system (54%)
- Impact on academic performance (50%)
- The child feeling stigmatised (48%)

Staff training on autism

The 2017 APPGA Report (NAS, 2019) found that 60% of young autistic people said that having a teacher who understood autism was the main thing that would improve their experience of school.

In contrast, the same report indicated that only 50% of teachers surveyed felt confident about supporting a child on the autism spectrum. It is argued that a lack of autism knowledge in teaching staff can negatively impact the school experiences of autistic children and reduce pupils' opportunities to succeed (Humphrey & Symes, 2011; Wittemeyer et al., 2011). Therefore, staff development is critical in terms of enhancing practice and outcomes for autistic children and young people, and in reducing exclusion rates (Parsons et al., 2011). Ambitious About Autism (2018) highlighted that this is needed not just in initial teacher training but for all school staff, including school governors.

No autistic child or young person should be at greater risk of getting into trouble with the criminal justice system just because they're autistic and schools have failed them. However, NAS (2020) found that this is too often the case, and the impact can be devastating. The damage this has caused can't be underestimated or undone. Their stories and experiences, alongside those of families and professionals, show clearly the areas where change needs to happen.

NAS (2020) heard from 203 autistic people, 167 family members, 40 criminal justice professionals, and 115 professionals working with autistic people outside the criminal justice system. The autistic people we spoke to who had previous involvement with the criminal justice system under the age of 25 had at least one experience with the police, - experience with solicitors and courts, experience within the prison system and experience on probation.

Committing a crime to gain an autism diagnosis

Current NHS statistics show that despite the National Institute for Health and Care Excellence (NICE) recommending 13 weeks between referral and first assessment, many wait much longer, with around 100,000 people currently on the waiting list for an autism assessment National Autistic Society (2021, 2022). This risks people developing secondary needs and autistic people falling into crisis unnecessarily.

The most common co-occurring conditions in the NAS (2021) study were anxiety (59%) and depression (53%), and for children, they were anxiety (58%) and ADHD (41%). Furthermore, throughout the study results, there was a clear demand for more mental health services and crisis support. Autism is not a mental health condition; however, incredibly high numbers of autistic people experience poor mental health. 70% of autistic children have a mental health problem (such as anxiety or depression), and 40% have more than one. In addition to this, between 7% and over 40% have self-harmed and/or attempted suicide. These stark figures show an urgent need to support autistic young people better, and long waiting lists for assessment make already vulnerable young people even more vulnerable.

> *For 18 months, I'd been suffering from severe suicidal ideation... The GP still did nothing... so I tried other ways of getting help and therapy, but that had led to nowhere because waiting lists were so phenomenally long, so I committed the index offence in the context of trying to draw attention to my plight and need.*
>
> *Autistic adult* (National Autistic Society, 2022)

NAS (2021, 2022) argues that autistic pupils are being denied their basic right to education, as figures reveal the number persistently off school has increased by 166% in four years.

Research by Gray et al. (2023) indicated that more than a quarter of autistic children in England – 51,000 out of about 200,000 children – are persistently absent, meaning they have missed 10% or more of the school term. And of the nearly 20,000 autistic children persistently absent from state secondary schools, four out of five experienced mental health issues, according to government data.

NAS (2021) argues that autistic pupils are more than twice as likely to be excluded from school than their peers. 25% of autistic children wait more than three years to receive the support they need at school, and almost 60% wait more than a year. In 74% of cases, parents said their child's school place did not fully meet their needs, with more than half of autistic pupils not having a quiet place to go to at school or someone to turn to if they need support.

Jolanta Lasota, Ambitious About Autism's Chief Executive Officer, remarked that the perception that children were being excluded because they were violent or aggressive was wrong. "Many are excluded from school simply because they can't conform to the high behaviour expectations of [mainstream] schools who don't have sufficient funding or staff to provide autistic children with the policy adjustments required from them by law," she added (Hill, 2024).

"There is strong existing evidence that autistic children are commonly failed by the education system...The fact that autistic children and young people commonly underachieve in school is an area of extreme concern." Prof Simon Baron-Cohen, the director of the charity Autism Centre of Excellence (Hill, 2024)

Gray et al. (2023) recruited 12 autistic pupils, who had previously experienced school avoidance and/or exclusion, from one local authority in England, UK. Through semi-structured interviews with the young people themselves, ten of their parents, eight of their current teachers, and nine local authority professionals, including six educational psychologists and three specialist autism teachers, the following was learnt:

- **Sensory overload:** how mainstream classrooms were "very big" [PU10], "the lights were too bright" [PU1], which made it difficult to "filter out background noise and deal with distractions... so I basically just mentally logged out" [PU5].
- **Social overload:** how the sheer "number of people was just intimidating" [PU6]—in part because they didn't "get on with a lot of the people" [PU11] and were "bullied" [PU10], and in part because "I didn't know what they were going on about" [PU7].
- **Academic overload:** especially with homework, which "was extremely stressful", and which often led "to lots of sanctions" leading to "lots of distress" [EP4]. Many young people attributed their "hate" for homework to "a straight separation between school and home" [PU6]: "In Year 7, I tried to do homework, but I was having like breakdowns and crying every other day; it was not a happy time" [PU5].
- **More support and help needed:** commonly reported that staff were "unknowing of either my condition or needs" [PU6] and, as a result, felt unfairly treated "like, they were just always telling me off, they'd always assume I was up to something" [PU3]. "The teachers shouted a lot, and they were like really aggressive... they would start shouting at me because I tend to zone out a lot as well, and I always ask the person next to me what's going on, so then I got told off for that, and I got sent out a lot" [PU7].
- **Prolonged experiences of anxiety:** resulted in their children "being desperately unhappy" [PA5] and eventually "shutting down" [PA6] "I had to take him to casualty I was so worried about him" [PA4]. They reported self-harm and suicide attempts, as well as "mental health breakdown... you just couldn't reach him, he was catatonic, non-communicative" [PA10].
- **Reasons for self-exclusion:** or "decided to leave... it's effectively the same thing [as being excluded]" [AT1]. For those who instead decided to leave school, it was often because young people had severe mental health difficulties, which reached the point at which there was "pure unwillingness to go, I just couldn't go in there" [PU6], were "on the verge of suicide, because I felt like that's not where I am supposed to be" [PU8], or "had slid into a deep depression and wouldn't even get out of bed" [PA10].
- **Mental illness causing long-term absence:** Parents also reported their children being "signed off [school] through anxiety... since he started secondary school, he didn't have much schooling" [PA9]. These avoidance and informal exclusion experiences meant that young people were "actually out of education for a long time" [PA5], usually between 1 and 3 years, oftentimes not accessing any education at all "he's missed a good two years of education" [PA8].

- **Schools lacking the expertise:** Teachers lacked the resources to support children. "I've seen more pupils this year permanently excluded or at risk of permanent exclusion, managed move than I've ever seen... schools are just saying 'we've not got the funding to put in the extra support you're all talking about'" [EP4]. School "had had enough of him and they wanted him out" [PA2]. "it's the ones that have the angry outbursts that tend to get permanently excluded or managed moved. And it's those who have anxiety and really struggle that then refuse to go back to school" [EP3].
- **Behavioural reasons for exclusion:** for "setting off fire alarms, stuff like that" [PU2], getting "involved with the police because they were saying I punched someone in the face, and I didn't" [PU8], being "caught vaping—but just general naughtiness, they were already on the edge there, just waiting for any excuse to kick me out" [PU3] and "hitting a boy on the head with the tennis racket—he was 4 at the time" [PA7].
- **Strategies before excluded:** Some young people reported that, prior to exclusion, school "put me on a reduced timetable" [PU7] or "a different timetable to normal" [PU3] "I was in school but only for about two hours" [PU4].
- **Advantages of alternative education:** In sharp contrast to their previous school experiences, parents and young people were overwhelmingly positive about their placement "it's all pretty good at the moment" [PU3]. One key factor in its apparent success was that "it's relaxed but structured". The "smaller school space" [PU3] with "less people" [PU1] meant that there "were less distractions, and less opportunity for [student] to make wrong choices" [T2] and staff "can actually cater more for what the child's needs" [PA9].
- **Parent support in alternative education:** Parents agreed that their children's new placements were more flexible "they don't mind too much if he has a day off... it's like, 'oh, that's a wobble, move on'" [PA6]. Another parent also appreciated how the teachers "are very good at not saying, 'right, these are the rules'; they gradually over time get the kids to modify their behaviour" [PA5]. This flexibility made young people feel that they were "able to learn" [PU5]. Only one pupil felt that mainstream school "challenged me [him] a lot more" [PU1].
- **More caring in alternative education:** Critically, young people emphasized the importance of strong, trusting relationships with their teachers at their alternative provision: "it's just like everyone cares" (subtheme 3.3). They spoke of how they valued "caring and fun teachers" [PU6], who "I can get along with" [PU5] and "don't shout—at my old school, all of my other teachers used to shout a lot because they didn't get it" [PU7]. Parents "could see a change in [child]" [PA2] in multiple ways. Young people were "better at dealing with anxiety" [PU5] and "much more open to understanding his emotions" [PA4], which had positive effects on their behaviour, including fewer "big meltdowns" [PA3] and being "not so aggressive—[school] have managed to bring out the child I knew was there" [PA6]. These positive changes extended to their academic work, in which many had "just flourished" [T6].

Totsika et al. (2020) described school non-attendance in students with autism by surveying 486 parents (student mean age: 11 years):

- 43% school refusal was the most frequent reason
- 9% of absences was due to school exclusion
- 9% of absences was due to school withdrawal
- Truancy was almost non-existent
- 32% of absences describe non-problematic absence that is mostly due to medical appointments and illness

What are the top reasons for permanent exclusions from UK schools?

Recent UK suspension and exclusion data from the Department of Education (2024) indicates that firstly the overall numbers have grown substantially between 2021–22 and 2022–23 (see Figure 8.3), with the most common reasons being (see Table 8.1):

- Suspension – Damage
- Suspension – Drug and alcohol-related
- Suspension – Persistent disruptive behaviour
- Suspension – Physical assault against a pupil
- Suspension – Physical assault against an adult
- Suspension – Verbal abuse or threatening behaviour against a pupil
- Suspension – Verbal abuse or threatening behaviour against an adult
- Permanent – Persistent disruptive behaviour
- Permanent – Physical assault against a pupil
- Permanent – Verbal abuse or threatening behaviour against an adult

Headline facts and figures - 2022/23

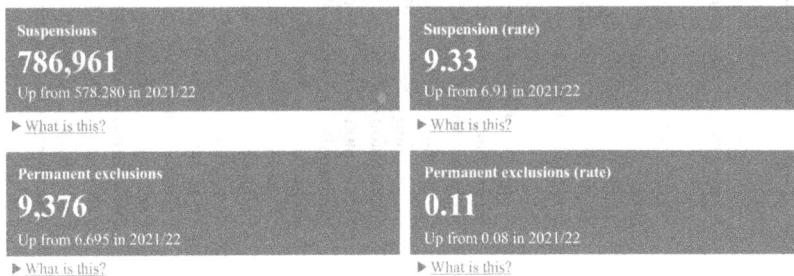

Suspensions	Suspension (rate)
786,961	**9.33**
Up from 578,280 in 2021/22	Up from 6.91 in 2021/22
▶ What is this?	▶ What is this?
Permanent exclusions	Permanent exclusions (rate)
9,376	**0.11**
Up from 6,695 in 2021/22	Up from 0.08 in 2021/22
▶ What is this?	▶ What is this?

Figure 8.3 Indicating 2021 to 2022/23 rises in UK school suspensions and exclusions. (Department For Education, 2024).

Table 8.1 'Suspensions and permanent exclusions – by multiple reasons (2020/21 onwards)' for state-funded secondary in England between 2021/22 and 2022/23 (Department For Education, 2024)

		2021/22	2022/23
State-funded secondary	**Suspension – All exclusions**	**558,804**	**774,246**
	Suspension – Abuse against sexual orientation and gender identity	2,377	2,633
	Suspension – Abuse relating to disability	216	299
	Suspension – Bullying	6,198	7,668
	Suspension – Damage	**13,112**	**15,562**
	Suspension – Drug and alcohol related	**21,803**	**22,941**
	Suspension – Inappropriate use of social media or online technology	9,807	10,810
	Suspension – Persistent disruptive behaviour	**256,556**	**402,019**
	Suspension – Physical assault against a pupil	**81,796**	**97,693**
	Suspension – Physical assault against an adult	10,431	14,105
	Suspension – Racist abuse	8,189	9,785
	Suspension – Sexual misconduct	5,650	5,137
	Suspension – Theft	5,168	6,432
	Suspension – Use or threat of use of an offensive weapon or prohibited item	11,708	12,566
	Suspension – Verbal abuse or threatening behaviour against a pupil	**25,387**	**32,751**
	Suspension – Verbal abuse or threatening behaviour against an adult	**98,460**	**131,122**
	Suspension – Wilful and repeated transgression of protective measures in place to protect public health	1,946	2,723
	Permanent – All exclusions	**7,155**	**10,411**
	Permanent – Damage	163	209
	Permanent – Drug and alcohol related	449	583
	Permanent – Inappropriate use of social media or online technology	105	78
	Permanent – Persistent disruptive behaviour	**2,633**	**4,279**
	Permanent – Physical assault against a pupil	**1,250**	**1,667**
	Permanent – Physical assault against an adult	571	836
	Permanent – Sexual misconduct	123	118
	Permanent – Use or threat of use of an offensive weapon or prohibited item	498	600
	Permanent – Verbal abuse or threatening behaviour against a pupil	346	537
	Permanent – Verbal abuse or threatening behaviour against an adult	**816**	**1,256**
	Permanent – Wilful and repeated transgression of protective measures in place to protect public health	16	54

Table 8.2 'Year group, by type of SEN provision and type of need – 2016 to 2024' for autistic spectrum disorder, non-maintained special school, social, emotional, and mental health, state-funded AP school in England between 2022/23 and 2023/24 (Department For Education, 2024)

		Autistic spectrum disorder		Social, emotional, and mental health	
		2022/23	2023/24	2022/23	2023/24
State-funded secondary	**Year group 7**	14,386	16,712	25,110	2.7,514
	Year group 8	13,790	16,232	24,151	27,403
	Year group 9	13,180	15,169	24,077	26,605
	Year group 10	12,754	14,412	23,085	25,737
	Year group 11	11,554	14,073	21,522	24,616
	Year group 12	3,042	3,453	3,326	3,568
	Year group 13	2,633	2,913	2,658	3,035
State-funded alternative provision (PRUs) school	**Year group 7**	30	36	192	231
	Year group 8	68	65	793	884
	Year group 9	96	122	1,292	1,735
	Year group 10	113	154	1,965	2,373
	Year group 11	177	195	3,003	3,426
	Year group 12	33	21	110	89
	Year group 13	24	16	39	42
State-funded special school	**Year group 7**	5,423	5,881	2,444	2,518
	Year group 8	5,186	5,714	2,532	2,708
	Year group 9	4,743	5,372	2,664	2,851
	Year group 10	4,407	4,920	2,747	2,781
	Year group 11	3,897	4,486	2,567	2,837
	Year group 12	2,280	2,564	390	412
	Year group 13	1,784	2,023	244	285
Non-maintained special school	**Year group 7**	156	115	57	49
	Year group 8	154	132	53	57
	Year group 9	156	163	73	55
	Year group 10	139	159	55	64
	Year group 11	154	121	43	51
	Year group 12	107	101	25	19
	Year group 13	85	89	22	19

Where have all the autistic students gone?

Table 8.2 looks at the UK data for mainstream secondary schools, secondary alternative provision, and state special schools, for two types of SEND needs. 'Autism' and 'Social Emotional and Mental Health' (SEMH) are census terms used to describe those with autism and ADHD. Whilst the data suggests a large drop of students from years 7 to 11 with autism in mainstream schools, there is no increase in alternative or special school provisions, so where have they all gone? The same is not true for those with SEMH, commonly how ADHD is categorised, where they do seem to move from mainstream secondary school to alternative provision.

Interestingly, the data also suggests a staggered drop of autistic students in special schools between years 7 and 11, and these are provisions with specialist teachers and resources. Could it be that even with such provision these students are unsuited to traditional school settings? Again, SEMH student data seems constant between these age groups.

References

Ambitious about Autism (2014). Excluded from school. Retrieved 06/05/2025. https://www.ambitiousaboutautism.org.uk/sites/default/files/resources-and-downloads/files/we-need-an-education-exclusions-report.pdf

Ambitious about Autism (2018a). We need an education: Excluded from school. Retrieved 25/07/2024. https://www.ambitiousaboutautism.org.uk/sites/default/files/resources-and-downloads/files/we-need-an-education-exclusions-report.pdf

Ambitious about Autism (2018b). The exclusions review leaves a 'big question mark' over support for autistic pupils in school. Retrieved 15/08/2024. https://www.ambitiousaboutautism.org.uk/about-us/media-centre/news/exclusions-review-leaves-big-question-mark-over-support-autistic-pupils

APPGA (2017). Autism and Education in England 2017. Available at: https://www.autism.org.uk/getinvolved/campaign/appga/highlights.aspx

Barnes, M., & Harrison, E. K. (2017). The wellbeing of secondary school pupils with special educational needs. UK: Department for Education. Retrieved 15/08/2024. https://openaccess.city.ac.uk/id/eprint/17866/1/Barnes%202017_Wellbeing%20and%20SEN.pdf

Brede, J., Remington, A., Kenny, L., Warren, K., & Pellicano, E. (2017). Excluded from school: Autistic students' experiences of school exclusion and subsequent re-integration into school. *Autism & Developmental Language Impairments, 2,* 2396941517737511.

Briggs, D. (2010). The world is out to get me, bruv: Life after school exclusion. *Safer Communities, 9*(2), 9–19.

Contact a Family (2013). Falling through the net. Illegal exclusions, the experiences of families with disabled children in England and Wales. Retrieved 06/05/2025. https://contact.org.uk/wp-content/uploads/2021/03/falling_through_the_net_-_illegal_exclusions_report_2013_web.pdf

Department for Education (2020). Permanent and fixed term exclusions in England: 2018 to 2019. Retrieved 16/07/2024. https://www.gov.uk/government/statistics/permanent-and-fixed-period-exclusions-in-england-2018to-2019

Department for Education (2024). Special educational needs in England. *Data grid'.* Retrieved 16/07/2024. https://explore-education-statistics.service.gov.uk/data-tables/special-educational-needs-in-england/2023-24?subjectId=a9e2821b-c468-4050-7f05-08dc74d49ccd

Farouk, S. (2017). My life as a pupil: The autobiographical memories of adolescents excluded from school. *Journal of Adolescence, 55,* 16–23.

Gazeley, L., Marrable, T., Brown, C. & Boddy, J. (2015) 'Contextualising inequalities in rates of school exclusion in English schools: beneath the 'tip of the ice-berg'.' *British Journal of Educational Studies, 63*(4), 1–18.

Graham, B., White, C., Edwards, A., Potter, S., & Street, C. (2019). *School exclusion: A literature review on the continued disproportionate exclusion of certain children.* c-ertain.

Gray, L., Hill, V., & Pellicano, E. (2023). "He's shouting so loud but nobody's hearing him": A multi-informant study of autistic pupils' experiences of school non-attendance and exclusion. *Autism & Developmental Language Impairments.* 2023 October 18, *8,* 23969415231207816. https://doi.org/10.1177/23969415231207816. PMID: 37860824; PMCID: PMC10583514.

Guldberg, K., Bradley, R., Perepa, P., & Macleod, A. (2021). Investigation of the causes and implications of exclusion for autistic children and young people in England. Retrieved 14/07/2024. https://www.autismeducationtrust.org.uk/sites/default/files/2022-01/ exclusion-research-report_final.pdf

Hill, A. (2024). Autistic pupils in England denied right to education as absenteeism surges, says charity. Retrieved 14/07/2024. https://www.theguardian.com/society/2024/ mar/05/autistic-pupils-in-england-denied-right-to-education-as-absenteeism-surges- says-charity

House of Commons Education Committee. (2018). *Forgotten children: Alternative provision and the scandal of ever increasing exclusions.* London: House of Commons. https://publications.parliament.uk/pa/cm201719/cmselect/cmeduc/342/342.pdf

Humphrey, N., & Symes, W. (2011). Inclusive education for pupils with autistic spectrum disorders in secondary mainstream schools: Teacher attitudes, experience and knowledge. *International Journal of Inclusive Education, 17*(1), 32–46. https://doi.org/10.1080/ 13603116.2011.580462

Levinson, M. (2016). 'I don't need pink hair here': Should we be seeking to 'reintegrate' youngsters without challenging mainstream school cultures? *International Journal on School Disaffection, 12*(1), 23–43.

Makin, C., Hill, V., & Pellicano, E. (2017). The primary-to-secondary school transition for children on the autism spectrum: A multi -informant mixed-methods study. *Autism & Developmental Language Impairments, 2*, 2396941516684834.

Mazurek, M.O., Kanne, S.M., & Wodka, E.L. (2013). Physical aggression in children and adolescents with autism spectrum disorders. *Research in Autism Spectrum Disorders, 7*(3), 455–465.

National Autistic Society (2019). The Autism Act, 10 years on: A report from the All Party Parliamentary Group on Autism on understanding, services and support for autistic people and their families in England. Retrieved 09/07/2024. https://pearsfoundation.org. uk/wp-content/uploads/2019/09/APPGA-Autism-Act-Inquiry-Report.pdf

National Autism Society (2020). *Youth justice report.* Retrieved 26/07/2024. https://nas.chorus. thirdlight.com/link/n4bhhjjwhbxk-as0nu1/@/preview/1?o

National Autistic Society (2021). School Report 2021. Retrieved 23/05/25. https://www. autism.org.uk/what-we-do/news/school-report-2021

National Autistic Society (2022). "My Life could be so different" Experiences of autistic young people in the youth justice system. Retrieved 23/05/25. nas.chorus.thirdlight.com/ link/n4bhhjjwhbxk-as0nu1/@/preview/1?o

Parsons, S., Guldberg, K., MacLeod, A., Jones, G., Prunty, A., & Balfe, T. (2011). International review of the evidence on best practice in educational provision for children on the autism spectrum. *European Journal of Special Needs Education, 26*(1), 47–63. https://doi.org/10.1080/08856257.2011.543532

Parsons, C. (2018). *The Continuing School Exclusion Scandal in England. In FORUM: for Promoting 3–19 Comprehensive Education* (Vol. 60, No. 2, pp. 245–254). Symposium Books Ltd.

Simonoff, E., Pickles, A., Charman, T., Chandler, S., Loucas, T., & Baird, G. (2008). Psychiatric disorders in children with autism spectrum disorders: Prevalence, comorbidity, and associated factors in a population-derived sample. *Journal of the American Academy of Child & Adolescent Psychiatry, 47*(8), 921–929.

Smith, A.E. (2024). Educators' perspectives on supporting autistic children at Pupil Referral Units following their exclusion from mainstream secondary school. *British Psychological*

Society. Retrieved 14/07/2024. https://www.bps.org.uk/educators-perspectives-supporting-autistic-children-pupil-referral-units-following-their-exclusion

Sproston, K., Sedgewick, F., & Crane, L. (2017). Autistic girls and school exclusion: Perspectives of students and their parents. *Autism & Developmental Language Impairments, 2,* 2396941517706172.

Timpson Review (2019). London: Department for Education. Retrieved 15/08/1968. https://assets.publishing.service.gov.uk/government/uploads/system/uploads/attachment_data/file/807862/Timpson_review.pdf

Totsika, V., Hastings, R.P., Dutton, Y., Worsley, A., Melvin, G., Gray, K., Tonge, B., & Heyne, D. (2020). Types and correlates of school non-attendance in students with autism spectrum disorders. *Autism*. 2020 October, *24*(7), 1639–1649. https://doi.org/10.1177/1362 361320916967. Epub 2020 May 18. PMID: 32419486; PMCID: PMC7545649.

Trussler, S., & Robinson, D. (2015). Inclusive *practice in the primary school*. SAGE Publications, Inc. https://doi.org/10.4135/9781473916975

Wittemeyer, K., Charman, T., Cusack, J., Guldberg, K., Hastings, R., Howlin, P., McNab, N., Parsons, S., Pellicano, L., & Slonims, V. (2011). Educational provision and outcomes for people on the autism spectrum. *Autism Education Trust*. Retrieved 10/01/2025. http://www.autismeducationtrust.org.uk/

9   Autism and Criminal Behaviours

It should be noted early on that evidence regarding the prevalence of offending in autism is equivocal; however, it is generally agreed that people with autism are more likely to be victims of crimes rather than perpetrators (Lindsay et al., 2019; Fitzgerald, 2013). Nevertheless, people on the autism spectrum do offend, and it is therefore helpful for treatment and management purposes to consider whether there are any particular risk factors for offending behaviour in this population.

Weinman (2023), an autism advocate in the United States, discusses the chances that a young person with autism could be arrested. She notes that most defendants she works with tell her they did not intend to commit a crime or harm another person. Instead, any criminal acts are a reaction to a given situation. They acted in the only way they knew to protect themselves from a perceived threat.

She offers several scenarios:

- You receive an alarming call from your son's school. The police are there to arrest your son for striking a teacher. You later discover that your son was reacting to something the teacher said.
- You and your son are at the supermarket. You proceed down an aisle with your son close behind. Suddenly, you hear a scream. You quickly turn to see a stranger face down on the floor, and your son nearby. A store employee calls the police, who arrest your son for assault. Later, you learn your child believed the stranger was staring at him.
- Your 20-year-old son is attracted to a girl he sees walking down the street. Being naïve and possessing the emotional maturity of a much younger child, he approaches her and inappropriately touches her buttocks.
- A 21-year-old male was arrested for stalking. It all started when he was sitting behind the wheel of his parked car for hours outside the victim's home, binoculars in hand and food in the passenger's seat. A concerned neighbour called the police. The police arrived, ordered the driver out of the car, and proceeded to arrest him. When I asked my client whether he understood why what he did was wrong or illegal, appearing puzzled, he answered, "No." As the trial date got closer, I approached the prosecutor to plead the uniqueness of my case. After all, my client's future hung in the balance. I told her, "It is not what it looks like." In disbelief, she responded, "Are you kidding? There were binoculars and

DOI: 10.4324/9781003614432-9

food in the car." I passionately persisted in my attempt to make her understand. She resisted at first, but I could bring her to my way of thinking. The case never saw the inside of a courtroom, and my client avoided a criminal conviction. Not all criminal defendants with autism are so fortunate.

The following are a few relevant case studies, which will help the reader understand the fascination and fixations symptomatic of autism:

Case study (Haskins & Silva, 2006)

Case of Mr B., a middle-aged substitute teacher accused of touching several adolescent female students. Mr B was unable to develop friendships or relationships. He failed to recognise how the students and others might perceive his actions. The compulsive nature of his touching behaviour is consistent with repetitive and stereotyped behavioural patterns.

Vulnerabilities to crime, Risk factors

Howlin (2006) states that autistic individuals might be particularly vulnerable to crime for the following reasons:

- A fascination or 'special interest' could be fatal, for example, fire or poison. She cites the example of a young man interested in washing machines who would break into shops and people's houses to examine them!
- A strong dislike, such as a baby crying or a dog barking, might lead to an aggressive outburst.
- A lack of knowledge of appropriate and inappropriate touching could lead to accusations of sexual harassment. Individuals may love the feel of a particular texture or material, such as velvet, and think nothing of stroking the back of the lady if she is wearing a velvet jacket.
- Unexpected violence and outbursts are provoked by specific, random, and unexpected environmental triggers, for example, a fire alarm, a fire, roads being shut, or a train or bus breaking down.
- A preoccupation/adoration for an individual could lead to stalking.
- Activities appropriate in childhood can be perceived as inappropriate in adulthood, for example, picking up or tickling toddlers who belong to strangers.

Davis and Schunick (2002, pp. 45–46) argue that individuals with autism might encounter the police for the following autistic symptomatic reasons:

- Self-stimulatory and self-injurious behaviour such as hand flapping, pinching oneself, self-biting, repetitive actions, and thrashing.

- Wandering alone, for example, children dressed inappropriately for the weather, wandering alone or darting into traffic.
- Some children with autism are attracted to water and may be especially at risk near pools, ponds, and lakes.
- Peering into windows.
- Turning water faucets on and off.
- Behaviour may mimic drug abuse or mental illness.
- Bizarre or disruptive behaviour such as lining up objects, eating inappropriate objects, toe walking, and robotic-like speech.
- Hitting or biting people.
- Involvement in altercations, for example, they may commit a crime without realising what they have done wrong.
- Suspected child abuse, parents may be restraining the child with what may appear questionable force.

For example, in a situation that involved interaction with a police officer, they could:

- Behave in an extremely socially inappropriate way.
- Offend without being aware they are doing so.
- Appear aloof, rude, egocentric, or insensitive.
- Not knowing how to react to certain unknown situations and other people's feelings.
- Have difficulty understanding and using non-verbal communication.
- Not like being touched.
- Have extreme intolerance to certain sounds, smells, or other sensory stimuli.
- Take things literally.
- Not understand the implied meaning or follow a long set of instructions.

A criminal intent study by the Welsh Assembly (2010) interviewed autism specialists, police officers, and autistic youngsters about their experiences with the police and their parents. Some of the autistic youths said they had found themselves in situations where their social communication had led to misunderstandings.

For example, one young man said, "I have been in trouble and they (the police) thought I was being cheeky, but I was just being honest." When asked by a police officer, "Do you promise never to do this again?". One young man had answered, "No, I do not know if I will ever do it again". In his mind, he did not want to make a promise that he genuinely did not know if he would be able to keep. Another, when asked if he had been involved in a shoplifting incident, answered "Yes". He had not committed the crime, but he had been in the shop at the time when the incident occurred. His interpretation of the word 'involved' was very different from that of the police officer, which may lead him to be arrested. Therefore, individuals with autism may appear to be behaving uncooperatively when they are trying to be as open and honest as they can be.

Autistic individuals sometimes comply with requests to please and make friends. They can be easily manipulated, which makes them vulnerable. For example, they may get involved with drug dealing because they see it as a way of having friends without thinking about or realising the consequences of their actions. Professionals need to assess whether the person with autism understands that they have committed a crime. Sometimes, a person with autism will not realise that their behaviour is illegal. Conversely, an individual with autism may not understand that a crime against them such as robbery or rape has been committed.

Symptoms of autism, such as a tendency to misread the behaviour of others, constitute a risk factor for offending behaviour. Studies indicate that a diagnosis of autism is more prevalent amongst those who have committed some categories of offence, for example, some sex offences, than for other psychiatric diagnoses, whereas autism is less prevalent amongst offenders convicted of other categories of offence, such as property crimes.

A qualitative analysis of predisposing and precipitating factors for offending in autism (Allen et al., 2008) suggested that predisposing factors included a lack of concern for, or awareness about the outcome of certain behaviours, social naïveté, impulsivity, and misinterpretation of rules and obsessions. Factors that appeared to precipitate offending behaviour included social rejection, bullying, sexual rejection, family conflict, deterioration in mental health, change of living arrangements, or professional support and bereavement.

The following examines various risk factors/vulnerabilities and how they may lead an autistic person to criminal activity.

Lack of empathy

Specific aspects of autism may predispose individuals to offend. A lack of empathy is an important factor in offending with a 'history of rather bizarre antisocial acts' (Wing, 1981). The associated phenomena of poor theory of mind (ToM) (Baron-Cohen, 1995) and misinterpretation of social cues may make a person with autism likely to act in an offensive way towards others. It is argued that ToM refers to the capacity to understand other people by ascribing mental states to them. A ToM includes the knowledge that others' beliefs, desires, intentions, emotions, and thoughts may be different from one's own.

Social behaviours

Those with autism may be vulnerable to committing or suffering from antisocial, offending behaviour, or stalking behaviour; for example, they may misunderstand social signals (Stokes et al., 2007). Woodbury-Smith et al. (2005a and b) compared individuals with high-functioning autism (HFA) who had and had not committed criminal offences compared to typically developing (neurotypical) controls. They examined ToM, executive function, and emotion recognition. Those with autism who had offended were less able to recognise fear in others than non-autistic adults. A lack of ability to recognise fear responses may cause individuals with autism to carry on with behaviours that can be distressing to others, as they fail to register their impact, and may not understand non-verbal responses regarding consent.

Social naivete and 'joint enterprise'

Being socially naïve may result in those with autism being easily led into criminal behaviour by others (Howlin & Moore, 1997). People with Asperger's syndrome (AS) may seek out friendships with others to gain status without realising the risks associated with a particular group's community identity (e.g., criminal gangs, terrorist groups) and their vulnerability to exploitation (Shine & Cooper-Evans, 2016).

"He was being taken advantage of and being influenced by the wrong individuals." Parent of an autistic young person (National Autistic Society, 2022)

"They could be and still are influenced by others to fit in with a crowd; he didn't understand he was being used." Parent/carer of an autistic young person (National Autistic Society, 2022)

They may also accompany others who are committing crimes, simply to please them. However, if caught, they would be judged equally guilty under 'joint enterprise' legislation (where persons who assist or encourage another to commit a crime. Such persons are legally known as accessories or secondary parties in the crime committed). There have been recent cases of this with autistic individuals, but it has been very hard to argue their innocence, Alex is one such young man convicted for joint enterprise with undiagnosed autism, guilty for murder, even though he did not kill anyone because he was 'in the wrong place at the wrong time' (Henry, 2018; O'Brien, 2014).

Robins (2022), a special adviser to the UK's All Party Parliamentary Group on Miscarriages of Justice, notes, "The justice system cruelly stacks the odds against the neurodivergent". He says that it is striking how many cases in the sorry history of miscarriages of justice feature the wrongful conviction of people with significant cognitive impairment – for example, Stefan Kiszko, the shy Inland Revenue clerk with the mental age of a 12-year-old who served 16 years after being wrongly convicted of the murder of Lesley Molseed; or Stephen Miller of the Cardiff Three, mental age of 11, who confessed to killing Lynette White (after more than 300 denials); or any number of 'joint enterprise' cases in which autistic people (e.g., Alex Henry) have been convicted of murder under the controversial common law doctrine.

Barry Sheerman MP, chair of the all-party parliamentary group on miscarriages of justice, challenged Justice Secretary Dominic Raab on the iniquity of joint enterprise, which is often characterised as a 'dragnet'. As Sheerman pointed out, "Many of the young people charged and convicted of joint enterprise are later found to be on the autistic spectrum".

Case study (Godfrey, 2022)

The BBC News website reported that an autistic 23-year-old young man was arrested and jailed for being around a group of youths, known as a 'joint enterprise'. It is argued that he was not fully aware of the crimes being

> *committed, and therefore, due to his autism, he was incapable of committing the offence and was not given a fair process in court, when arrested, and whilst he is serving a prison sentence. His mother is working with lawyers, who allege institutional discrimination, to overturn a 'miscarriage of justice'. His lawyers said that the joint enterprise principle – in which guilt may be deemed by an individual's presence within a criminal group – was an option available to the jury at Mr Brown's trial, although the extent to which the jury applied it when making convictions was unclear.*

Joint enterprise: where persons who assist or encourage another to commit a crime. Such persons are legally known as accessories or secondary parties in the crime committed.

Robins (2022), Henry (2018), and O'Brien (2014) have studied 'joint enterprise' and note that it is very hard to argue an autistic individual's innocence, as it seems so unlikely a person would be so naïve, even with very eminent supporting expert witnesses like Professor Baron-Cohen. However, there are many cases of miscarriage of justice regarding those with autism. Barry Sheerman MP points out, "Many of the young people charged and convicted of joint enterprise are later found to be on the autistic spectrum".

Case study (Robins, 2020)

On August 6th, 2013, Alex Henry had been shopping with friends. Two of the friends were on their way home when confronted by the brothers Bourhane and Taqui Khezihi, and two of their friends. On Henry's account, he saw a friend in trouble. As he approached, he claimed to have picked up a dropped mobile, thrown it at one of the attackers and attempted to punch another. That, he claimed, was the extent of his involvement. The facts are disputed. Bourhane claimed Henry had 'a shiny object' in his hand, and another told the police it was a knife, but he was not confident at trial.

On of Henry's group, Cameron Ferguson, joined in the fray. He had a knife hidden in a bag and stabbed Taqui and Bourhane. Taqui's injury proved fatal. Alex Henry claimed that it was only hours later, when they regrouped in a park, that they realised that Ferguson had 'poked' the brothers.

Alex Henry, together with his friend, Janhelle Grant-Murray, was found guilty at the Old Bailey for the murder of Taqui Khezihi and wounding his brother Bourhane. Midway through a six-week trial, Ferguson changed his plea to guilty, admitting to the stabbing.

Alex Henry is currently serving a sentence of life imprisonment with a non-parole period of 19 years. According to his legal team, a conditional exercise of the royal prerogative would swap a lesser sentence with the original and would 'not expunge his conviction' but allow Her Majesty to correct a significant injustice.

A mercy petition has been sent to the UK's Lord Chancellor this week, arguing that Alex has been the subject of 'a catalogue of events that have led to grave injustice'. The petition states that Henry has been the subject of 'a catalogue of events that have led to grave injustice'. It cites the 2016 Supreme Court ruling, which held that the law on joint enterprise had taken 'a wrong turn' in 1984. 'The effect of unprincipled and harsh mandatory sentencing laws... caused injustice to Alex and were applied without knowledge of Alex's autism,' it argues. It also criticises 'the morally and medically insensible decision' by the Court of Appeal to reject the expert evidence of Professor Baron Cohen.

Prof Baron-Cohen is Britain's leading expert on autism. In June and December 2014, he met Alex twice at his category A prison. He recorded the interview. 'I didn't start the fight, and I didn't stab anyone,' Henry told him. He told the doctor of his past antics – how, when he was young, he was 'proper naughty'.

Henry told the doctor that he had always been conscious of being 'different'. "I talk to people in the prison a bit randomly. I play snooker, but I don't get involved in conversation".

On Prof Baron-Cohen's autism spectrum quotient questionnaire, which aims to test whether adults have the condition, Henry scored 'a very high' 35 out of 50. The majority of males tend to score 17, and the average score for females is 15. If someone scores over 32, then this suggests that they may have Asperger's syndrome (high-functioning autism).

Focus on detail

A focus on the details of an event rather than the whole picture, or 'weak central coherence' according to Happé and Frith (2006), can also be a characteristic of individuals with autism, which may make it harder for them to see the consequences of their actions. Interestingly, Murrie et al. (2002) described a man with autism who was trying to get custody of his child. He attempted to murder the psychologist who was carrying out the custody evaluation because he feared the evaluation would be unfavourable. He believed that by shooting the psychologist carrying out the evaluation, he would improve his chances of retaining custody of his child, as it would mean the court would not receive the unfavourable evaluation.

Narrow focus

Some offenders with autism have engaged in criminal behaviour on account of their narrow focus and preoccupation with a special interest (Barry-Walsh & Mullen, 2004; Haskins & Silva, 2006). For example, in one case, a man obsessed with city transport systems was arrested for driving underground trains and buses without authorisation and directing traffic around construction sites.

Obsessions

As will be discussed, the relatively high proportion of computer offences noted amongst offenders with autism (e.g., Freckelton, 2011a and b) may reflect computing being a common special interest in those with autism, and a skill strength for many autistic individuals. Obsessions with individuals, sometimes including celebrities, can also be a mechanism that leads to stalking offences.

Property damage

An excessive preoccupation with routines associated with cognitive rigidity and inflexible thinking patterns may be common in autistic individuals. If routines are disrupted, or fixed attitudes and assumptions are challenged, then this may lead to extreme anxiety, fear or anger manifesting in aggression towards others or property damage. Many parents who have experienced their child, mainly boys with autism, have noted how their home looks, broken doors, holes in walls, broken televisions and computers. All resulting from autistic meltdowns. In the case of one of my students, his meltdown anger was so intense and controlled, he broke a bottle and badly cut his hand, as a result requiring stitches. I needed to check carefully with his mother that it was not intended self-harm or attempted suicide.

Sensory fascination

Hyper- or hyposensitivity to or fascination with sensory aspects of the environment (lights, smells, textures, sounds) may play a role in the antisocial or offending behaviours exhibited by some people with autism (Bjørkly, 2009). For example, in one case, a young man with autism was fascinated with the colour and texture of long blonde hair, and this led to his detention after he followed and assaulted a young woman to touch her hair. Those with autism may have disproportionate reactions, including violence and other forms of offending behaviour, to sensory stimuli, such as loud noises or bright lights.

Stimming, repetitive behaviours

Repetitive behaviours often increase when an autistic person is feeling anxious or stressed (Howlin et al., 2004). Other examples of stimming may include pacing, spinning, tapping, or hitting an object, such as hitting/tapping one's head or hitting one's head on something. See Appendix 4 for a long list of different stimming strategies.

For example, a young autistic man in his 'day-setting' wanted to shake everybody's hand whenever he saw them. This was potentially an issue, but generally manageable. The problem stemmed from the fact that he would constantly have his hand down his trousers as well! Combine the two, and suddenly, numerous issues arise. How he reacts to others not shaking his hands and running away or having strange reactions to him forcing his dirty hands in their direction, may lead to a meltdown.

The type and intensity of the repetitive behaviour can make the difference between acceptable and unacceptable. This is undoubtedly true, but other issues such as age (Howlin et al., 2004), gender, the person's size, and even the autistic person's visible level of disability are also important – if a person looks the same as other people, then there is an expectation they will act the same.

In another example, a young child in public wishing to smell a person's hair or touch a particular type of clothing someone is wearing because they like the material may be seen as 'odd' or 'strange', but within the realms of acceptability. However, a 6-ft adult male behaving in the same way is going to be interpreted very differently, maybe threatening. It might lead to police involvement and even criminal proceedings.

It could be argued that all stimming behaviours that can be easily misinterpreted as unsocial or threatening should be discouraged by families, carers, or professionals in childhood. However, this is not always realistic or desirable for the autistic person. Attwood (2002) makes the point that autistic people often have very few enjoyable activities, so rather than stop all (unsocial/threatening) repetitive behaviours, a level of compromise is needed. For example, boundaries are set such as, this is a home or a bedroom activity, not one for outside.

Whilst this seems a sensible approach, as with most things there is a level of risk involved. If an autistic adult finds themselves in a new and unexpected situation, for example, their normal travel route is blocked, or a train is cancelled, then this may lead to enormous anxiety and a need for comfort from a certain repetitive activity, the fact that they are not at home can become irrelevant due to their immediate situation. The use of stimming is used by many autistic people to avoid meltdowns; however, when prevented from being able to stim, this may lead to autistic meltdowns and possible explosive manifestations.

Sims (2016) in Aspis (2023) for a submission to the UK Parliament for the draft Mental Health bill noted how those with autism are criminalised by their behaviour:

- "A young autistic man in his 'day-setting' wanted to shake everybody's hand whenever he saw them. This was potentially a slight issue, but generally manageable. The problem stemmed from the fact that he would constantly have his hand down his trousers too! Combine the two and suddenly numerous issues arise."
- "A child in a public place smelling a person's hair or touching a particular type of clothing because they like the material may be seen as 'odd' or 'strange', but a 6-ft adult male behaving in the same way is going to be interpreted very differently. It might lead to outsider intervention, possibly to police involvement and even criminal proceedings."
- "An autistic gentleman who would seek out sensory stimulation in terms of smell found himself attracted to women's public toilets. Lots of complaints were received, the police became involved, and he was detained in a special hospital."

Many autistic people appear to be anxious of the police (Mclelland, 2016) and therefore being confronted by them in an already volatile environment can lead to an escalation. If the behaviour is seen as serious enough and the autistic adult is taken into custody, then the anxiety levels are almost certain to increase further. Therefore, the stimming increases too and there is a huge risk of a meltdown, and if the police believe they are a danger to themselves and others, they may section the person so that they can be moved to a hospital for psychiatric observation, as per the case studies highlighted in this book.

Types of crime committed by people with autism

Research seems to separate between those with 'autism' and those with 'HFA', formerly called 'Asperger's syndrome'. The two are split here; however, a crossover in the studies using the term autism or autism spectrum disorder (ASD) should be recognised, as of 2013, the American Psychiatric Association grouped all autism-related disorders as ASD (autism spectrum disorder, the medical term for autism). So older research may use either term, but newer research combines them.

According to Rutten et al. (2017), symptoms of autism, such as the overactive sense of right and wrong and the unwillingness to break the law, tend to protect people with autism from committing criminal behaviour. However, other symptoms could be argued to be risk factors.

Crimes committed by individuals with autism vary, a review of court decisions in Freckelton (2011) found that offenders with autism tended to disproportionately commit arson, computer offences, stalking offences, sexual offences, violence and neglect offences, and dishonesty offences.

Common crimes manifested in those with autism are believed to be:

- Stalking
- Knife use and collection
- Computer crimes, stalking, and getting into hard systems
- Intensive anger during a meltdown hurting people
- Intensive anger to kill people
- Carrying drugs after being befriended and exploited
- Sexual offences.

In a study comparing 45 autistic people with 43 non-autistic patients admitted to low secure services in England, Haw et al. (2013) found that those with autism had less extensive offending histories (including violence, sexual, fire-setting, property damage, acquisitive, and other forms of offending) and significantly fewer previous convictions than the non-autism group. Esan et al. (2015) also compared 42 autistic patients with 96 non-autistic patients admitted to an intellectual disabilities service in England and found that the autism group had lower rates of previous convictions for violent, sexual and arson offences than the non-autism group.

It has been suggested that autistic offenders may be more likely to engage in certain types of crime than others (King & Murphy, 2014); specifically that they are more likely to engage in crimes against the person such as sexual offences, assault, and robbery (Cheely et al., 2012; Kumagami & Matsuura, 2009) and less likely to engage in property crimes such as burglary, arson, trespass, driving offences, and drug offences (Cheely et al., 2012; Kumagami & Matsuura, 2009).

In terms of offences, the most common crime category found in a study by Hofvander et al. (2023) was violent crime, present in three-quarters (75.5%) of the prosecutions. Sexual crimes were the second most common crime (16.1%). This is in line with previous studies where different interpersonal crimes are dominant among offenders with ASD. Due to experiences of victimisation and social isolation (Collins et al., 2022), compared to individuals with ASD in general, these individuals commit various offences, but there appears to be a high proportion of violent offences, particularly arson and sexual offences (Hofvander, 2018).

High-functioning autism, formerly called Asperger's syndrome

Studies have suggested that those with HFA are more likely to commit arson (Hare et al., 1999; Siponmaa et al., 2001) or criminal damage (Woodbury-Smith et al., 2006) than other crimes.

Allely (2019a,b and c) suggests that the most common crimes are more commonly committed by persons with HFA:

- Threats to kill
- Arson
- Sexual offending
- Criminal damage
- Stalking

Kawakami et al.'s (2012) study of the characteristics of individuals with HFA suggests those who exhibit criminal behaviours. In this study, the most common criminal behaviour was theft (55.6%), followed by sexual misconduct (25.0%), violence (25.0%), and running away (19.4%). In the present study, 94.4% of participants in the criminal group exhibited 'multiple recurrent incidents with a current episode of criminal behaviour' or 'multiple recurrent incidents without a current episode', 5.6% of participants reported only once and no recurrences of illicit behaviours at the time of the assessment. This result corresponds with many previous case studies reporting that individuals with HFA repeat criminal behaviours (e.g., Baron-Cohen, 1988; Chen et al., 2003; Mawson et al., 1985).

Risk factors for offending behaviour by people with autism

Risk factors are proposed by Allely (2019) to better understand how those with autism can be drawn into criminal offences:

- Their increased social naivety may leave people with autism open to manipulation by others.
- Obsessive pursuit or engagement in circumscribed interest.

- Convictions for arson were preceded by an interest in fires (e.g., Barry-Walsh & Mullen, 2004).
- Tantam (1981) describes an individual with a fascination with National Socialism, who dressed in Nazi uniform before assaulting a soldier.
- Attempts to discourage certain repetitive behaviours could trigger reactive aggression from individuals with autism, accounting for the association between repetitive behaviours and aggression.
- According to Bjorkly's (2009) literature review of risk factors for violence in AS (HFA), 35% of violence towards others was reportedly attributed to social misinterpretations of the victims' intentions.
- Burdon and Dickens (2009) highlighted that impairment in understanding social cues may influence criminal behaviour in individuals with AS (HFA).
- Can have difficulties with developing and maintaining friends.
- The Internet provides a safe environment (degree of control).
- Internet/social media 'Friends' who validate skills and promise 'justice' and 'moral certainty' can influence an individual very quickly (Al-Attar, 2018, 2020).
- Technical skills coupled with social impairments can make an individual with autism target for exploitation (Al-Attar, 2018, 2020).

Hammond et al. (2021) note remarks by Professor Simon Baron-Cohen that

Autistic people are vulnerable to being misunderstood and to ending up in the criminal justice system, accused of crimes when they have had no criminal intent. It is vital that they have well-informed advocates and legal advice and that the police and the courts are well-trained to make reasonable adjustments for an Autistic defendant. Autistic people deserve proper support, especially when they make mistakes, given their disability.

National Autism Society (2020) 'Youth Justice Report' (2020) investigated 203 autistic people, 167 family members, 40 criminal justice professionals, and 115 professionals working with autistic people outside the criminal justice system. The samples were made up of autistic people and their families who had been involved in the criminal justice system (aged 25 years and below).

Professionals and criminal justice professionals in the study noted that the main risk factors in school-aged autistic young people are, in the highest frequency order: difficulties with socialisation (98%), being easily led (85%), violence/aggression (68%), school exclusions (58%), inappropriate sexual behaviour (55%), special interests (45%), property damage/fire-setting (33%), and taking/dealing drugs (33%).

Lack of training by arresting police officers

Fallon (2024) reported on a school-based police officer in a UK school who assaulted an autistic child having a meltdown at school. In this case, a police officer is seen threatening to kick a ten-year-old boy lying on the ground. The officer then grabs him and drags him along the floor into a room. The police officer who resigned after losing a disciplinary hearing regarding this incident highlights the need for more autism training.

The following case studies suggest that autistic people are adversely affected by a lack of autism training in police officers, leading to arrest, where understanding would be more likely to result in a more positive resolution to situations.

Powell (2021) in a national newspaper reported on a 12-year-old boy diagnosed with autism, on his first day at a school, being challenged for his trainer shoes, which was an agreed allowance for his autism. He was challenged, started to be dysregulated and pushed out, resulting in a dinner lady being pushed. Classed as an assault by the school, he was then physically restrained by a police officer. This mum arrived to see her son restrained by a police officer, pinned down in handcuffs on a table, being treated like a 'criminal'. She filmed the incident, which has been watched more than 900,000 times on Facebook. Whilst not arrested, the school suspended Rayan and then removed him from their school roll.

A 14-year-old with autism had an altercation with a police officer that left him with multiple cuts and bruises (CBS News, 2017). The 21-minute encounter at a park in Buckeye, outside Phoenix, was caught on the officer's body camera. The police officer tackled the boy after mistaking his mannerisms for signs of drug use, not knowing he was autistic, leaving him with multiple cuts and bruises as well as an ankle injury. "He pushed me down on the grass and he just hit me on the tree, and he tackled me and then he didn't stop," Connor said. The Buckeye Police Department's internal investigation cleared the officer of wrongdoing, finding there was no excessive use of force, and because of his training as a drug recognition expert, they determined it was a reasonable stop.

A UK court reported a case of an autistic man, Parr, 21 years old, resisting arrest and biting a police officer on the arm after being confronted outside McDonald's, who had suffered a sensory meltdown at the time (Cooke, 2019). Connor was part of a group of people whom police found outside the restaurant following reports of a fight that had been going on at the premises. When the police approached him to talk to him, he panicked and began shouting and swearing and was eventually pava sprayed (an incapacitant spray like pepper spray) multiple times to the face.

When he was told he would be detained, he told the policeman he had autism, attention-deficit/hyperactivity disorder, and post-traumatic stress disorder and started to lose his temper, calling them a bunch of "f***ing w*****s," he said. Shortly afterwards, Parr ran away and was chased and detained, and during the struggle, pava-pepper spray was used again, and the officer then felt a sharp sensation in his arm and noticed he was being bitten when restraining Parr.

After calming down, his anxiety levels then rose and then suffered 'a complete and utter meltdown'. Parr argues he was fighting for his safety and had no filter about what he was saying or doing. Parr, 21, pleaded guilty to assaulting a police constable acting in the exercise of his functions as an emergency worker on April 16 when he appeared before Somerset Magistrates. He also admitted using threatening or abusive words or behaviour or disorderly behaviour likely to cause somebody harassment, alarm, or distress. In court, the judge said, "It is accepted the defendant has mental health issues, but this does not give him a blank cheque to do what he wants." Parr's father addressed the court and acknowledged his son's autism was no excuse for his behaviour, but was a reason for it. He said, "For Connor, it was like being an animal trapped in a corner, and that is how he reacted. It was fight or flight". His condition is never going to go away, and he cannot change that, but when he does things, it is on impulse, and he has no control. He had ordered him to pay the officer £500 compensation for the assault as punishment for the offence.

Case study (Pring, 2016)

A young autistic man was arrested and held in a police cell for nine hours without medical treatment after he was the victim of a vicious disability hate crime in a local park. Smith was charged with two counts of assault by beating but was only cleared by Corby magistrates of the offences last week after they accepted that he had been acting in self-defence.

His family have now launched complaints against both Northamptonshire police and the Crown Prosecution Service (CPS). Smith was enjoying a weekend visit to his family in Rushden, Northamptonshire, from his assisted living placement in Devon when he was set upon by a stranger and punched in the face and body. The attack last October appears to have been the result of some innocent remarks he made to a couple of teenage girls, one of whom had been taking pictures of him. One of the teenagers called her father, who arrived at the park because he wanted, he admitted to police later, to "sort him out for being weird" after being told – wrongly – that Smith was taking pictures of children in the park.

Smith, who is 26, was left bloodied and bruised, and as he was making his way to report the assault to police, he was picked up by officers and arrested just yards from the station. He twice told Northamptonshire police that he was autistic, once when he was arrested and later after he had been placed in custody, but his family say it was "completely ignored" by officers, spending nine hours in a police cell, without medical treatment for his injuries, even though he told officers he had just been defending himself against "the bullies", while they did not attempt to contact his family to tell them where he was.

The Police also ignored the photographs he had taken of the two local men who were responsible for the attack and failed to notice that there were no photographs of children on his phone, say his family. Daniel's father, Owen, described the police's behaviour as "archaic, bullying, cruel, unintelligent and inept".

He said his son had required help from his family every day since the attack and had experienced "meltdowns, illnesses, screaming and vomiting". He said, "Our main concern is that this was either missed by multiple officers through incompetence or laziness, or it was simply ignored because they didn't like the look of my disabled son, judging him on face value."

Stephen Brookes, a coordinator of the Disability Hate Crime Network, said: "While we haven't got the full detailed report of the case, the fact is that once again a police force has shown itself to have fallen well short of acceptable standards in dealing with disabled people". "The fact that a few police officers appear to have ignored Smith telling them he was autistic is nothing less than scandalous, particularly when we have seen far too many cases in which disabled people have been unjustly accused of being the criminal before being subjected to vicious beatings".

Autism and offending behaviour: understanding their criminal act

For each case of offending, the relationship between autism and the act has the potential for complexity. The facts of the case, the nature of the behaviour itself, and the burden of impairment are crucial considerations. Typically, offending behaviour in autistic people can be explained concerning ToM (knowledge that others' beliefs, desires, intentions, emotions, and thoughts may be different from one's own), executive functioning, central cohesion deficits, social naivety, overload of environmental stimuli poor emotional regulation, and problems with moral reasoning in those with autism may raise the risk of an offence (Lerner et al., 2012).

The capacity for empathy is normally regarded as protective against the victimisation of others (Farrington, 2007); however, in those with autism, this can be impaired, and these empathic deficits have been implicated as factors in offending behaviour (Wing, 1981; Woodbury-Smith et al., 2005). The interplay of emotional regulation difficulties, interpersonal anxiety and hypersensitivity, maladaptive cognitive coping skills, and a sense of alienation from others is cited as a prominent feature of interpersonal violence in autism (Murphy, 2010). In terms of re-offending, poor appreciation of the consequences of criminal behaviour and limited scope for the consideration of the impact of these actions on others further raise the risk in the context of transfer to less-secure therapeutic settings, or onward into the community (Wing and Gould, 1979; Hare et al., 1999).

For parole/release, a prisoner needs to recognise their crime and work towards not reoffending; however, where the person has autism and does not recognise and acknowledge their crime, then this will delay any release or parole. This has the potential to hold many autistic prisoners in prison without release, and speaking with a UK expert in this matter, it's a frequent occurrence.

Involvement in crime

National Autism Society (2020) studied 203 autistic people, 167 family members, 40 criminal justice professionals, and 115 professionals working with autistic people outside the criminal justice system. The samples were made up of autistic people and their families who had been involved in the criminal justice system (aged 25 years and below). Participants indicated early concerns about their children with autism. This data suggests that this starts with being easily influenced by others and aggression towards others/property damage (likely through meltdowns) and being excluded from school, leading to being stopped, cautioned, or arrested by the police, and the police visiting the family home.

Early concerns regarding criminal activities by families included: being easily influenced by others/easily led (66%), violence/aggression towards others (52%), being excluded from school (38%), damaging property/fire setting (38%), threats to harm others (23%), and taking/dealing drugs (20%).

Autism and violent-physical crimes

In relation to physical violence, the clinical picture is not of a reservoir of simmering rage, or of an acute persecutory oversensitivity to imagined slights; however, research does talk about the culmination of events during the day and the event that leads to violence or property damage is the 'tip of the iceberg', as they are pushed 'over the edge'.

The final event may occur in the face of a sudden, distressing invasion of personal space (Freckelton & List, 2009). The reaction of a person with an autism spectrum disorder can be instant and intense, reflecting a primitive fight-or-flight response to a threat. It is not connected with dislike, or with emotional interpersonal rage; it is, rather, an impulsive and unconscious response arising from highly attuned personal radar to what is experienced as a repugnant, intolerable intrusion. In that context, what is to the perpetrator a reflexive self-protective stance is, to the object (the other person or property), an experience of physical, even violent, assault. The person with an autism spectrum disorder may well be perplexed by the intensity of the reaction by others and personally distressed that he or she had caused such an unexpected, confusing, and severe response in others.

Mawson et al. (1985) were the first to report in detail the co-occurrence of AS/HFA and violent crime. They described a 44-year-old man who had a long history of violent behaviour that led to frequent admissions to psychiatric hospitals and long-term detention in Broadmoor Hospital, a UK high-security special psychiatric hospital. Subsequently, Baron-Cohen (1988) described the assessment of violence in another case, a 21-year-old man with AS/HFA with a history of recurrent violence towards his girlfriend and others. Within the context of a social-cognitive model of autism, Baron-Cohen hypothesised the underlying cause of the offender's violence as an inability to appreciate the mental states of his victims. Baron-Cohen conducted a psychometric assessment and a series of semi-structured interviews with the offender. The interview data gathered added some credence to the hypothesis and revealed that feelings/behaviours associated with the clinical features of AS/HFA were important factors in the offender's violence. In line with Mawson et al. (1985), Baron-Cohen considered it possible that a co-occurrence between AS/HFA and violent behaviour is perhaps more common within the secure prison estate than has been previously recognised.

Looking at research by Mawson et al. (1985) and Baron-Cohen et al. (1985), one can ask whether the violence noted is due to dysregulation and, therefore, a meltdown rather than a person who chooses to be violent due to a provocation. Was the use of violence a means to unconsciously control their environment due to their helplessness or to extinguish built-up extreme danger?

Our daughter becomes extremely violent when she suffers acute anxiety. We couldn't access any help despite contacting various agencies, including GPs and CAMHS. She would smash our house up, hit us, and hit others. I was very concerned as she became older, about how we would be able to help her control her temper and protect herself and others.

Parent/carer of an autistic young person
(National Autistic Society, 2022)

When in periods of high anxiety and overwhelm/meltdown, my daughter's behaviour escalates to using violence against others. Now we have an assessment/diagnosis of pathological demand avoidance autistic profile, we can attempt to provide a low/no-demand environment and have had no incidents for almost two years; however, before this, we were having weekly incidents.

Parent/carer of an autistic young person
(National Autistic Society, 2022)

Case study (this author)

An 11-year-old student diagnosed with autism and obsessive-compulsive disorder (OCD) suffered from emotionally-based school avoidance and had huge emotional and physical eruptions at home but never at school. His eruptions were due to dysregulation caused by his autism, with his OCD likely to be a manifestation of control over his environment. Frequent eruptions would lead to property damage and loud shouting, so much so that their neighbours would call the police for fear of domestic violence or serious harm. Several police officers would attend and physically hold him down as he was highly dysregulated and could cause harm to others. The offer of an ambulance to take him to the hospital was rejected by his parents for fear of his being sectioned for his safety. In a rage, he broke a bottle and severely cut his hand as a result, requiring stitches. He refused to attend CAMHS mental health clinics and so was unable to be prescribed suitable anxiety medication by psychiatric teams. This family felt trapped by the inability to access suitable professional help.

His uncontrolled anger caused several home moves due to neighbour/ police complaints. The student was intelligent but could not cope with mainstream school, and tutor services would not support him at home due to tutor safety concerns.

The local authority was now offering a holistic autism specialist school, a 30-minute drive away from the family home, as a more suitable option to return him to education, which he had been off for the last 6 months.

Fixations

Intense interests and repetitive behaviour can be a source of enjoyment for autistic people and a way of coping with everyday life. But they may also become obsessions and limit involvement in other activities, causing distress or anxiety. Many autistic people have intense and highly focused interests, often from a young age. These can change over time or be lifelong. It can be art, music, gardening, animals, science, space travel, postcodes, or numbers. For many younger children, it's Thomas the Tank Engine, dinosaurs, or cartoon characters (National Autism Society, 2020).

Autistic people might also become attached to objects (or parts of objects), such as toys, figurines, or model cars, or more unusual objects like milk bottle tops, stones, or shoes. An interest in collecting is also quite common. Autistic people often report that the pursuit of such interests is fundamental to their well-being and happiness, and many channel their interests into studying, paid work, volunteering, or other meaningful occupations. This interest can

- Provide structure, order, and predictability, and help people manage the uncertainties of daily life
- Give someone a way to start conversations and feel more self-assured in social situations
- Help someone relax and feel happy.

It is the intensity and duration of a person's interest in a particular topic, object, or collection that marks it out as an obsession:

- Is the person unable to stop the activity/interest independently?
- Is the interest impacting the person's learning?
- Is the interest limiting the person's social opportunities?
- Is the interest causing significant disruption to other people, for example, parents, carers, and family?

If your answer to any of the questions above is 'yes', then their interest may have become an obsession which is affecting them, you, and/or other people in their life.

> *My mind was constantly whirring with thoughts, worries, and concerns. The time spent with my intense interest was the only time in which I had a clear mind—it gave me that much-sought-after relaxation.*
> Autistic young person
> (National Autism Society, 2020).

When does a fixation become an obsession that can lead to potential criminal activity? As those with autism have delayed empathy and the ability to read non-verbal communication, there is a chance that the obsession turns into stalking. Also, where the fixations are related to sexually related stimming activities (e.g., masturbation), the chances of moving into criminal activity increase.

Interestingly, there are case studies in this book regarding fixations on smells, which led them into ladies' toilets and other sex-based crimes. A fixation regarding ladies' underwear and the lengths/hyper-focus the autistic individual went to gain such personal property are symptomatic of autism.

In the case of a young schoolboy with autism (National Autistic Society, 2022), he expressed an interest in military history, firearms, and explosives at school, as part of an English lesson studying Private Peaceful. He researched weapons, vehicles, and uniforms that would have been in the First World War. Without thinking, he brought in expended shell casings that would have been from the First World War. The school thought that it was live and called the police. Someone reported that he had access to firearms, which he didn't, but was still put in segregation for six weeks whilst they investigated the allegations.

Autism and sexual crimes

The most frequent sexual offences committed by autistic people are child exploitation material possession (Allely et al., 2019), public masturbation acts (Creaby-Attwood & Allely, 2017), and child molesting (Hart-Kerkhoffs et al., 2009a and b). However, it is important to emphasise here that there are no studies which have found that individuals with autism are more likely to engage in violent sexual offences such as rape and sexual assault (Sevlever et al., 2013).

In evaluating why those with autism are involved in sexual crimes, it is important to have regard to the social deficits inherent in autism spectrum disorders, and the consequential limitations of socialisation associated with those deficits. For example, concerning sexual assault, there is evidence that sexually assaultive behaviour occurs in the context of the inability of an autistic person to interpret another person's, the victim's, negative response to sexual overtures.

It is questionable whether sexual offences were the intention, or how it has been categorised by others, namely the police. This is not condoning any crime that has taken place, but in court settings, the intention is an important part of any criminal prosecution.

An example of this is an autistic person who experiences normal sexual impulses (the initiator), as well as a desire to interact socially with the object of such impulses, and then their attempts to engage the target of their affection by physical touching or direct sexual contact. They are unable to interpret the other person's facial expression, tearfulness, or verbal response as being threatened or repelled by such a direct, possibly sudden, advance. In that context, the object of affection feels intimidated and frightened, even terrified, by what to the initiator is a harmless, even affectionate, overture. The initiator is puzzled, even distressed, by the realisation that 'something is seriously wrong', struggling to interpret the meaning of the other person moving away, along with their verbal or non-verbal cues. The autistic person understands that they have committed a social offence but is unable to construct a coherent meaning from the signals they have received from the other person (Freckelton & List, 2009).

Payne et al. (2020a and b) interviewed nine autistic sexual offenders in prisons and probation services across England and Wales. Analysis revealed five main themes (social difficulties, misunderstanding, sex and relationship deficits, inadequate control, and disequilibrium). Analyses indicated that social skills difficulties, lack of perspective/weak central coherence, misunderstanding the seriousness of their behaviours, and a lack of appropriate relationships were the main reasons for offending reported by this group of autistic sexual offenders. Findings highlight a need to develop sex and relationship education interventions which are tailored to the needs of autistic individuals, to address both their reported reasons for offending and their reported lack of sexual knowledge and awareness.

Inappropriate behaviours can include:

- Giving a stranger a kiss
- Intruding on the personal space of an individual that they are infatuated with
- To inappropriate acts of masturbating (e.g., masturbating in a public place)
- Individuals with autism becoming sexually violent (however, this is seen as rare).

When judging and responding to sexualised behaviour and crime by autistic people, it is important to understand that, whilst having social impairments and difficulties with relating to the world around them, they also have a desire for attachment or sexual relations, as all people do. This mismatch of desire and poor understanding of social relations may subsequently lead to sexual offending behaviour (Murrie et al., 2002).

Murrie et al. (2002) described six cases of individuals with AS/HFA who had committed a wide variety of offences (arson, burglary, physical assault, sexual assault, sexual abuse, and attempted murder). Four of the six cases involved sexual offending and all four exhibited a lack of victim empathy, as they did not appreciate the harm their offence had on their victims. Murrie et al. consider this to be 'symptomatic of the core characteristics' of autism.

Although the lack of victim empathy is also found in neurotypicals who commit sexual offences, which is why many treatment programmes for such individuals include an empathy training component, this might be problematic for autistic offenders. 'Interpersonal naiveté' is another factor identified by Murrie et al. that may have contributed to the offence committed by the individuals in the case studies they describe. Murrie et al. discuss several other factors that may be contributing to sexual offending in individuals with autism, namely, sexual frustration, immediate confession (which may be associated with impaired deception and ToM ability), and sexual preoccupation.

Studies suggest that the majority of deviant or sexual offending amongst those with autism is often driven by symptoms inherent to autism rather than being the expression of malice or reflecting actual sexual deviance. Such symptoms include restricted, repetitive patterns of interests relating to sexuality, people, or objects (Allely, 2019; Søndenaa et al., 2014) as well as lack of social understanding

(Allely, 2019; Creaby-Attwood & Allely, 2017), impulse control, or empathy (Hart-Kerkhoffs et al., 2009).

These suggest that core features of autism, such as difficulties in social interactions and the presence of restricted and repetitive sexual interests, could substantially contribute to the manifestation of inappropriate sexual behaviours. Furthermore, the lack of communicative abilities and social understanding often observed in individuals with autism can lead to misinterpretations of interpersonal dynamics and social boundaries, and, ultimately, to inadequate sexual behaviours. Kohn et al. (1998) and Peixoto et al. (2019) highlight how difficulties in recognising nuances of intimate language could lead to misunderstandings and unintended sexual behaviours.

There is also evidence that other forms of sexual offences, including possession of child exploitation material, child molesting, solo peer offending, indecent exposure, and acts of public masturbation, may also be influenced by autism characteristics such as restricted and repetitive sexual interests, lack of impulse control, and difficulties in understanding others' emotions. Notably, deficits in social communication and interaction skills and sexuality-related restricted, repetitive interest patterns could be considered inherent traits, and stable over time. Margari et al. (2024) suggest that sexual offences committed by individuals with autism were predominantly non-violent, with no underlying motivation aimed at harming others.

Studies suggest that autistic adults describe less sexual and privacy knowledge (e.g., seeking privacy for sexual behaviours and awareness of rules) and demonstrate more public sexualised behaviour than neurotypical individuals (Mehzabin & Stokes, 2011). Research also reports that autistic adults describe less access to peers as a learning source, which may increase the risk of offending in relation to inappropriate sexual behaviours (Stokes et al., 2007). Therefore, the lack of appropriate sexual and relationship education at school should be considered a major contributing factor.

Social immaturity and a lack of sexual education

Individuals with autism tend to have delayed social maturity than their neurotypical peers. Peterson et al. (2007) compared social maturity levels among 16 neurotypicals and 27 autistic children aged 4–12 years, indicating that those with autism had lower social maturity levels than their neurotypical peers, even among the four-year-olds, who are just learning peer interactions. Social immaturity may have a negative effect on social and emotional well-being when individuals enter puberty and begin to learn about sex and relationships. Decreased well-being may result in social rejection and isolation that reduce opportunities to obtain sexual knowledge from peers (Brown-Lavoie et al., 2014). Interestingly, Mehzabin and Stokes (2011) compared the sexual knowledge among those with autism and neurotypicals and revealed that those with autism had less sexual knowledge and received less sexual education from social sources (parents, teachers), and more from non-social sources (television, internet), according to Brown-Lavoie et al.

(2014). This can result in inappropriate behaviour about courtship and dating since they do not have peers to teach them or share their experiences with.

This book looks at what sex and relationship education should look like, being different to those offered to neurotypicals, for example, more explicit and a more intense course. Such a course should be provided by specialist autism teachers, as their content may be too graphic and uncomfortable for mainstream teachers to deliver.

Fixations and obsessions

Chesterman and Rutter (1993) described an adult male with AS/HFA in London who was fixated on washing machines and would masturbate as he watched them in use. Police later arrested him for burglary as he attempted to break into a neighbour's residence to access their washing machine. Offences arise when such behaviour creates fear and psychological harm to victims; however, the behaviours were characteristics of the perpetrator's symptomology with no malicious intent. Autism training is needed for police officers, so they understand the motive of such behaviour.

Case study (Kellaher, 2015)

A young man with autism whose interest in wolves as a child transformed into a preferential canine zoophilia as an adolescent. This young man admitted that he was sexually excited at seeing and touching the fur and scrotum of a large wolf-like dog.

This is an example of an interest in the sensory parts of 'the whole' for sexual excitement. Kellaher argues that this partialism or body part fetishism (which is 'part' oriented as opposed to 'whole' other person-oriented) is relatively commonly identified in individuals with autism. So, for instance, "just as an autistic individual may be interested in the wheels of a car, he may also be drawn sexually to the feet or hair of another person".

"This is consistent with numerous case studies involving individuals with autism who have a paraphilia or sexual interest in a particular body part, such as feet."

"Having highly restricted interests and having sensory peculiarities in autism may set the stage for developing fetishism and other paraphilias in individuals with certain sensory profiles, among other factors"

Brendel et al. (2002) report on a 49-year-old male (never married), a computer programmer with a history of depression and a possible diagnosis of AS, but with obsessive-compulsive and attention-deficit disorders. Mr C revealed his 'obsession with pornography' was the main reason for his inability to get to sleep at night. Into the early hours, he would spend time viewing pornographic internet sites, with a pornography collection comprised of 'thousands' of videos, along with a significantly large collection of 'paper dolls' which were created from mainstream and pornographic magazines.

Milton et al. (2002) highlight the case of an autistic male in his early thirties. His convictions are categorised into three main groups (acquisitive offences, direct sexual assaults, and indirect sexual assaults). A history of recurrent sexual offences includes sexual touching of young females' private regions, watching women in public toilets, and pretending to be a gynaecologist and interviewing women about their experiences over the phone.

His focus of this fascination was the image of a woman being gynecologically examined by a doctor, and he would pose as a medical researcher and go on telephone 'chatlines' to ask the women he spoke to for details of their gynaecological examinations while he frequently masturbated. Milton et al. explored the combined impact of the individual's diagnosis of autism, his paraphilic behaviour, and the offending behaviour. Based on their formulation, they put forward the concept that the individual, in this case, may have not only obtained immediate sexual gratification from his behaviour but also received pleasure from the perceived power and a sense of mastery that he had over women.

The need for intimate contact

Many autistic individuals are rejected by those of their age, and their inability to understand that sexual contact with those younger than themselves, if they could recognise an underage person, is a reason why many with autism find themselves befriending underage young people, which would be a criminal offence. An unintentional danger many find themselves facing. Allely and Creaby-Attwood (2016) conclude that there is support for the notion that an individual with autism impaired ability to appropriately interpret the victim's negative reactions (such as facial expression, tearfulness, etc.) to their sexual advances (attempts to engage the target of their affection) is one of the factors which underlie their sexual offending behaviour (Freckelton & List, 2009).

Individuals with autism may have difficulty expressing their sexuality within the context of an appropriate relationship due to limited or no experience of being in any prior intimate relationship, which may contribute to offending behaviour due to sexual frustration (Murrie et al., 2002). Biologically, they may be adults, but emotionally, they may still be children. This conflict makes them vulnerable, along with peer pressure to have boyfriend/girlfriend relationships, which creates potentially dangerous situations.

Linked to this topic and the ability to form suitable and consenting adult relationships are those who have an impaired ability to recognise the expression of fear, which results in committed offences, for example, consent-based (Woodbury-Smith et al., 2005).

Case study (Griffin-Shelley, 2010)

This case reviews the five years of treatment for an adolescent sex offender and sex addict, who was adjudicated at 14 and was given a diagnosis of Asperger's syndrome/high-functioning autism.

He was caught engaging in inappropriate sexual contact with an 11-year-old nephew and a 9-year-old male family friend. The difference in age between him and his victims was only two and four years, respectively. This raises important issues surrounding whether this case involved sexual offending or normal sex play. There were also other inappropriate behaviours with two younger female siblings and two incidents of problematic internet sexual activity (viewing pornography). An evaluation carried out by an independent psychologist provided some detailed insight into the offending behaviour. The psychologist (Eichel) found that the individual in this case longed for interpersonal connectedness but was frustrated by not knowing how to successfully obtain such connectedness with someone, and also could not understand why he was odd and the responses he sometimes received from others. The psychologist suggested that it would be more clinically appropriate to consider these alleged sexually offending behaviours as manifestations of a "deeper, more autistic compulsivity combined with a deep but primitive longing for intimate physical contact". A combination of sexual offending and sexual addiction treatments is potentially the most effective.

Will, a 16-year-old male, was diagnosed at 7 years old with AS/HFA (Ray et al., 2004). Will had been involved in numerous incidents of both sexually coercive and aggressive behaviour towards both male and female children. Common behaviour was massaging or tickling the victims' feet. He reports being attracted to females who are of a similar age to himself, but his victims are grade-school-aged children, and he indicated that his 'social disability' is his rationale for targeting the younger age victims, as he is much less awkward socially with this age group. This is potentially problematic due to links between his deviant behaviours with young 'compliant' children and his sexual gratification.

In another case, Max, a small, 14-year-old male with autism, had an extensive history of sexually inappropriate behaviours that were becoming increasingly more offensive (Ray et al., 2004). Sexualised and/or violent behaviours were frequently and compulsively made. Recently, Max had developed a sexualised view of the world (made worse by his impaired social abilities). This manifests in his play, interpersonal interactions, and daydreaming about sex and violence. Physically and behaviourally, Max presents as someone much younger than his chronological age.

Sexual naivete

Murrie et al. (2002) examined six individuals with autism in forensic settings in Australia and described an adult male's preoccupation with intercourse who stated his courtship strategy was "hanging around a woman until sex happened".

The above examples of deviant behaviour imply social and sexual development delays and naiveté about forming relationships.

Deviant sexual behaviours may be the result of naiveté of courtship, inability to handle rejection, and/or inability to grasp social rules regarding socially appropriate behaviours. Wing (1981) described individuals with AS/HFA with sexual desires that led them to touch or kiss strangers. A common sexual behaviour described in the research on adolescent and adult males with autism was touching female strangers on the breasts and genitals (Stokes et al., 2007; Kohn et al., 1998). The example Kohn et al. (1998) provided was a 14-year-old male with AS/HFA who claimed he touched a female to "make her his girlfriend". Barry-Walsh and Mullen (2004) described a 16-year-old male with autism who approached a seven-year-old girl and her five-year-old brother, put his arms around them, and said he "wanted to take them to his place to do a naughty thing".

In the case of CD, a 27-year-old male diagnosed with AS/HFA is reported to have committed a sexual offence involving a teenage male (Murrie et al., 2002). CD felt he was making genuine attempts at sexual contact with someone and had a history of compulsive masturbation (since the age of ten he would masturbate five times a day) and had a collection of 'artificial vaginas' (both commercial and homemade). Murrie et al. propose that CD's sexual naiveté and his impaired understanding of social situations increased his likelihood of engaging in sexual offending behaviours.

In another case, a 27-year-old male, diagnosed with AS/HFA, was charged with a sexual offence involving a teenage male (Søndenaa et al., 2014). Allowing a homeless teenage boy to stay with him in exchange for sex, but after a while, the teenager left, stealing his stereo. Being unhappy about the theft, he went to the police to report the crime, but in doing so, he described the preceding events, which resulted in him being arrested for the sexual assault of a minor. Murrie et al. (2002) argued that the man's lack of understanding of social situations and sexual naiveté likely made him engage in sexual crime.

Private sexual behaviours in public

Allely and Creaby-Attwood (2016) suggest that a contributing factor in sexual offending with autistic individuals is the tendency to engage in private sexual behaviours in public places (e.g., masturbating or revealing private body areas), also found by Ruble and Dalrymple (1993), Van Bourgondien et al. (1997), and Kalyva (2010). This may also result in the sexual exploitation of individuals with autism (e.g., would-be friends convince an individual with autism to expose their genitals as a joke in a public place).

Another cringeworthy memory is how effortlessly I could be manipulated and, consequently, how my peers would wind me up for their own comedic purposes. It wasn't exactly difficult to get me to humiliate myself, because I was provoked by the most trivial of things.

Nita Jackson (2002).

Sevlever et al. (2013) suggest that this kind of sexual offending behaviour comprises the majority of sexual offences related to individuals with autism, which again brings about a discussion on the intention of any criminal act and mate crime, doing an act to attempt to remain friends with others without thinking through the consequences of the request actions.

Studies point to the more common deviant behaviours reported by parents and caregivers of autistic individuals, such as public masturbation (Mehzabin & Stokes, 2011; Ruble & Dalrymple, 1993; Stokes et al., 2007; Van Bourgondien et al., 1997), and undressing or exposing private parts in public (Hellemans et al., 2007; Nichols & Blakeley-Smith, 2010; Ruble & Dalrymple, 1993).

Fantasies

The cases in Murrie et al. (2002) give some support to the concept that the existence of paraphilias (defined as persistent and recurrent sexual interests, urges, fantasies, or behaviours of marked intensity involving objects, activities, or even situations that are atypical in nature) are relevant factors when carrying out risk assessments of individuals with autism. Individuals are reported to conduct particularly serious, violent crimes against women, fantasies of 'taking apart the body of a woman' and engaging in cutting female dolls (Allely & Creaby-Attwood, 2016). Murrie et al. (2002) crucially highlight that similar perverse fantasies in persons who are law-abiding do occur and do not escalate into a criminal offence. A court should take the presence of autism in a charged person when deciding on any criminal offence being committed.

Murrie et al. (2002) reported that a male (KL) was arrested following an assault on two women in the female toilets at the local zoo where he was a weekend volunteer and was subsequently referred for forensic evaluation. He was open and exhibited no embarrassment or hesitation when revealing intimate details about his life and his significantly active and aggressive sexual fantasies. KL reported feelings of isolation and loneliness. He had a crush on numerous women at work and would follow them when they moved around the building. He reported that his masturbatory fantasies involved following strange women, binding them using rope and climaxing while he used a knife to cut into their breasts.

Acting without thinking, or understanding the consequences of their actions

Other explanations put forward as factors contributing to sexual offending in individuals with autism are difficulties with impulse control and empathy, which result in the individual failing to appreciate the consequences of their behaviour and acting 'without thinking' (Haskins & Silva, 2006). It has also been suggested that the 'obsessional' interest often found in individuals with autism can lead to offending behaviour if the obsessional interest has a sexual component or is perceived by the individuals as being sexually related (Murrie et al., 2002; Haskins & Silva, 2006). Autistic individuals caught up in 'Mate Crime' may believe what is being asked of them is okay to do and would cement their friendship with others. Acting without thinking and acting without thinking through the consequences of requested actions are likely to get them into trouble, which may or may not be the intended outcome of the request.

Poorly influenced by others

Similarly, social misperception was highlighted by Sutton et al. (2013) in a report about a 12-year-old boy diagnosed with autism who committed a sexual offence influenced by a peer-group relationship. The peer group's sexual assault of another peer did not elicit any recognition of acting harmlessly until he was arrested, and he was likely guilty of 'joint venture'. This is another area of 'Mate Crime' where autistic individuals are too trusting of others and therefore influenced to do several actions (requests) which may or may not be legal. Autistic symptomology is to be too trusting and naïve to consequences, for example, an autistic person being asked to deliver a package for a friend sounds innocent, but not when the package contains drugs, and the autistic young person is then arrested for supplying drugs. It is unlikely that the police, when questioning them, would believe they were so naïve as not to know what was in the package and the possible dangers of such a request.

Stalking

For the autistic person who engages in stalking, whether in person or by the internet, the intention is often to learn more about the person or to communicate with them, rather than to cause distress or to harass. Related to this, compared to individuals without autism, individuals with autism may be more likely to engage in stalking behaviour (e.g., monitoring the movements of the target of their affection). Some researchers have found that individuals with autism engage more often in attempts to interact with a romantic interest, despite there being no evidence of reciprocation from the target to their affections/interests (Stokes et al., 2007); therefore, it is one-way. Such behaviours are increasing the chances of autistic individuals being questioned about criminal activity. Again, social naiveté appears to underlie the stalking behaviour in some individuals with autism (Sevlever et al., 2013).

McEwan et al. (2020) argue three general commonalities which help identify stalking as opposed to other offence types, which are as follows:

- The pattern and nature of the unwanted behaviour (conduct element)
- The intent of the perpetrator (mental element)
- Some requirements for a negative impact on the target of the stalking (impact, or harm, element)

Mullen et al. (1999) reviewed 145 individuals who stalked; they classified individuals based on their motivations, victimology, and stalking behaviours. They identified five overarching stalking types:

- Intimacy seeker
- Incompetent suitor
- Rejected

- Resentful
- Predatory

Of note, the 'incompetent suitor type' describes individuals who pursue people to whom they are attracted in a manner that causes distress and often fear. Victims are usually strangers or casual contacts. Incompetent suitors are typically motivated by the desire to make contact, usually seeking a date; however, social skill deficits often result in approaches that are clumsy, intrusive, and unsuccessful in achieving their aims. This seems to relate to the autistic profile.

The human desire for connection to others, which requires social skills and understanding, is universal. Romantic relationship experience among autistic individuals is a relevant yet understudied area of research (Strunz et al., 2017). As social skills and the ability to take the perspective of others are important for initiating and maintaining intimate relationships (Byers et al., 2013), autistic individuals, who may have deficits in these abilities, often experience difficulties in understanding and developing romantic relationships.

Although desiring a relationship, more than half of the participants without a romantic partner in the Strunz et al.'s (2017) study of individuals with HFA and romantic relationships shared that they were afraid of not fulfilling a partner's demands, did not know how to find a partner, and/or did not know how a relationship works. They also noted that finding contact with others was extremely exhausting. This suggests that a romantic relationship, even if desired, might overextend what autistic individuals can cope with.

Stokes et al. (2007) concluded that autistic individuals, compared to controls, were more likely to engage in inappropriate courting behaviours (e.g., touching the person of interest inappropriately; believing that the target must reciprocate their feelings; showing obsessional interest; making inappropriate comments; monitoring the person's activities; following them, making threats against the person). Stokes et al. also found that autistic individuals found it difficult to understand why the individuals they pursued were unresponsive in the way that they wanted, and could not understand why what they were doing was wrong. In addition, Stokes et al. found that autistic individuals focused their attention upon celebrities, strangers, colleagues, and ex-partners, and pursued their target longer than controls.

Rawdon et al. (2024) suggest that there are certain features of autism that can provide the context of vulnerability to engaging in stalking behaviours:

- Issues with empathy and awareness of social norms
- Restrictive preoccupations and interests
- An inability to understand the viewpoint of others (impaired ToM)
- An inability to attend to or recognise others' social cues (e.g., being impaired in their ability to pick up social cues from the individual who shows their discomfort/ distress in response to their unwanted pursuits)
- Lack of appropriate skills and knowledge and developmental lag (see Allely, 2022).

Regarding issues with empathy and awareness of social norms, Rawdon et al. (2024) found that some autistic individuals experience difficulties understanding that the strategies they used to pursue relationships were inappropriate and might even be distressing to the person of interest. Some of the features of autism which may contribute to this are their lack of awareness and understanding of social norms. These factors may explain why some autistic individuals are unable to accept rejection by the person in whom they are interested. These may also explain why they persist in their pursuits for much longer periods compared to their neurotypical peers (Stokes et al., 2007). Also being impaired in their ability to appreciate or understand that most people in society would consider their obsessive focus or fixations on others as intrusive.

With regards to a lack of appropriate skills and knowledge, some autistic individuals may lack the appropriate skills and knowledge which would enable them to successfully initiate such romantic relationships (Stokes & Kaur, 2005), as these were not taught or observed at school. Therefore, in their attempts to initiate interpersonal relationships, some autistic individuals may present naively in their courtship behaviours, which may be considered inappropriate and intrusive, and could be defined as stalking behaviours (Stokes & Newton, 2004). This issue of a lack of appropriate skills and knowledge may be further exacerbated by any present developmental lag.

Case study (Ventura et al., 2022)

A 40-year-old high-functioning autistic male patient was accused of stalking behaviour. Ventura and colleagues described that the male, in an inadequate attempt and desire for attachment and social relations, repeatedly called people he randomly selected from the telephone directory, which he had memorised from public phones, for several months. When he called people and engaged in these random phone conversations, he considered there to be reciprocity ('over-evaluating platonic interactions') and mutual interests between him and his victim. He failed to understand that his behaviour was illegal and that he was causing his victim's psychological harm. The authors described him as having no apparent remorse for his actions. Critically, the male in this case study believed that his actions were 'a straightforward path to making friends' and thought there would be mutual interest when approaching others by stalking them.

Case study (Rawdon et al., 2024)

Andrew, a 27-year-old, white, British male, was diagnosed with Asperger's syndrome/high-functioning autism in childhood and reported having periodic difficulties with managing depression throughout his adult life.

At the time of the study, Andrew was in prison awaiting sentencing after being convicted of stalking. Andrew's victim, Claire, was a fellow secondary school student and barely a casual acquaintance, whom he began to stalk during his time at school. He persisted with this behaviour for approximately ten years, since it began in secondary school, until his subsequent conviction and imprisonment.

Three superordinate themes and sub-themes were identified:

What she means to me ("She's special". "Unindulged obsession". "If I don't exist to her, my life has no validity").

2. Problematic, but unstoppable ("Stalking is a big problem for me". Community interventions are a chocolate fireguard).

3. Life after prison (The difficulty of letting her go. The inevitability of reoffending).

(1) What she means to me – This theme was interpreted as the richest theme and explored Andrew's sense-making of his stalking behaviours concerning the mean ing he attributed to Claire, as his victim. Andrew expressed a longstand ing admiration for Claire, which had predated his stalking behaviours. However, Andrew identified an incident during his time at school that had served as the trigger for his stalking. In brief, Andrew described how Claire had made a friendly approach towards him at a school event, to which he gave a 'rude' response, which he attributed to the difficulties his autism created for him in social situations. Andrew felt that this was a lost opportunity for both social acceptance amongst his peers and a potential relationship with a popular girl he admired. He described experiencing crippling disappointment and rumination at the event. This experience served to intensify his admiration for Claire and his fantasy of a relationship, which he believed contributed to his later stalking behaviours.

(2) Problematic, but unstoppable – This theme provided insight into Andrew's understanding of his stalking behaviours and how, or whether, he could desist from stalking. Andrew described his stalking behaviours as an 'ongoing problem', and this theme encapsulates how Andrew makes sense of why his stalking behaviours became problematic by directly connecting this to his mental health. Andrew experienced that 'depression intensifies [his] obsession', describing that although taking prescribed medication for his depression, there were times when they were less effective, and when he felt there was 'no logic to keep thoughts from turning into behaviour'. There was a sense that he was 'overcome' with the urge to contact Claire, believing that having her in his life would 'fix' him. He describes this as 'self-torment'.

(3) Life after prison – Ultimately, accepting that Claire should not be part of his life was at no point considered a viable option for Andrew. This suggests that Andrew's pursuit of his relational goal has persisted, even into prison, where he has not been exposed to external stimuli such as being able to access her social media accounts and has been unable to

physically pursue Claire. The reinforcement of this goal may be maintained at a lesser intensity by him continuing to think about Claire.

Andrew's stalking motivation appeared to mostly fit the incompetent suitor typology as described by Mullen et al. (1999) and Stokes and Newton (2004).

Stokes et al. (2007) investigated stalking and social and romantic functioning among adolescents and adults with autism spectrum disorder. Parental reports were obtained for 25 autistic adolescents and adults (13–36 years), compared to 38 neurotypical adolescent and adult controls (13–30 years). Not surprisingly, autistic individuals reported less access to their peers and friends as sources of learning to acquire social and romantic skills and knowledge. This is likely a reflection of the core deficits characteristic of autism itself, as impairments in communication and social reciprocity can lead to greater difficulties in socialisation and the development of meaningful social relationships. Although not surprising, social learning from peers and friends is a significant predictor of overall social functioning. This can be a 'vicious circle' in which individuals with autism have long suffered, leaving their desire for social relationships generally unfulfilled. Consequently, autistic young people are prevented from the typical development of overall social competence.

Levels of social competence are normally expected to increase with age, which would in turn increase the individuals' ability for meaningful interpersonal relationships; however, this was not found in this autistic group. Autistic adolescents and adults were found to be more likely to touch the person of interest inappropriately, believing that the target should reciprocate their feelings and show obsessional interest; however, this was not so, leading the autistic individual to make inappropriate comments, monitor the person's activities, follow them, pursue them in a threatening manner, make threats against the person, and threaten self-harm.

Autistic individuals were found to display behaviours indiscriminately across all types of targets. The study concluded that autistic adolescents and adults do not know how to discriminate between appropriate and inappropriate behaviours, or to be discerning in their choice of target. The complexity of addressing both exacerbates this situation. It appeared that individuals with autism tend not to engage in behaviours that require interpersonal contact (e.g., asking on a date, telephoning, attempting social contact); this may be due to a lack of awareness that such strategies to how people initiate relationships, or a lack of confidence in their reduced social competence.

Orsmond et al. (2004) investigated peer relationships and participation in social and recreational activities among 235 autistic adolescents and adults. Overall, 46.4% of the participants were reported to have no peer relationships. Of those individuals who were reported to have one or more peer relationships and friendships, the frequency of such relationships was inversely related to the strength of social impairment. While some traits associated with autism may improve or lessen with age, social dysfunction appears to persist.

Sexual functioning is commonly developed more slowly in autistic individuals, supporting a concept of developmentally delayed social development. Ruble and Dalrymple (1993) found autistic individuals (with a broad age sample of 9–39 years old) displayed more inappropriate sexual behaviours and reduced sexual functioning, even though many had been involved in normal social and formal sex education programmes. Both Stokes et al. (2007) and Ruble and Dalrymple (1993) report that parents of autistic individuals expressed concerns about how others may misconstrue their child's sexualised behaviours. Traditional sex and relationship educational programmes in schools are targeted at neurotypical young people and may not be long enough or explicit enough for those with autism.

As discussed earlier, in society, there is a blurry distinction between what constitutes acceptable and inappropriate relationship behaviours. To initiate a relationship, it is not unusual for a person to ask the target of their interest out on a date, telephone them, send them texts and emails, wait for them outside work, or make other attempts to initiate social contact. There is a subtle distinction between these appropriate and inappropriate forms of these behaviours. Persistent unwanted attention via any of these behaviours is typically utilised to distinguish between harassment and appropriate courting (Ravensberg & Miller, 2003), placing the intended subject at harm and the perpetrator in a potentially legally dangerous position. Stalking involves repeated or persistent unwanted attempts to communicate with or associate with another (Mullen et al., 1999).

The fine line between these two is not often clear. Most particularly, it may be unclear to a person who has experienced considerable social rejection and exclusion over their whole life, learning that associations with others are only available with persistence. Confusion, or lack of awareness, of what is and is not regarded as appropriate courtship behaviour, together with the desire for intimate relationships, limited socialisation, and inadequate overall social and sexual functioning, may likely lead to what is considered as stalking (Stokes & Newton, 2004).

Although autistic individuals lack social competence and have deficits in romantic functioning, many still possess a desire for social and romantic relationships and actively seek out such relationships. It is natural for many individuals with autism to desire a romantic partner, and this is often heightened by the belief that it is 'normal' to have a boyfriend or girlfriend, as 'everyone else has one'. The perception of 'normal' may be part of the challenge for those with autism. Social media is also to blame for setting what is 'normal', which may not be realistic or appropriate to where a person lives. What might be normal activity or dress in California, New York, or Rome may not be in Birmingham or London. Social media influencers may be more personally motivated by financial gain than by setting realistic expectations.

Stokes et al. (2007) argue that typical adolescents and adults appeared to be aware that their interest was not reciprocated and ceased their attempts. Due to autistic individuals' lack of empathy and awareness of social norms, they have difficulty understanding that the strategies they employ to pursue relationships are inappropriate and might be distressing to the person of interest. These factors may be important in explaining why autistic individuals do not accept rejection by the person of interest and persist in their pursuits for much longer periods than would be socially acceptable.

BBC News (2024) highlighted the case of a 17-year-old boy who was found guilty of murdering Holly Newton, 15, who was stabbed to death in January 2023. Holly had complained about the boy 'stalking' her hours before she was repeatedly knifed in an alleyway. The boy, who was diagnosed with autism, initially told the court his mind was 'blank' at the time of the attack, and he was trying to kill himself. He then admitted he attacked her out of anger, before backtracking and claiming he never intended to hurt her. Holly suffered 36 knife injuries, and the blade snapped during the minute-long assault, which only came to an end when two passers-by pulled the boy away. The Crown Prosecution Service said that they faced a 'significant challenge' in the early stages of the case to establish the defendant's fitness to plead, which had been raised as an issue by the defence. However, independent psychologists persuaded the court that the boy did have the capacity to enter pleas and to stand trial. It was also reported that he had a history of harming himself without really knowing what he was doing. Judge Mr Justice Hilliard told the boy that stalking meant 'following' or 'being obsessed' with a person and asked him: "Were you doing that, do you think?" The boy replied he didn't think so.

The case of Holly Newton suggests stalking, and a fixation by the autistic boy, that he would follow for a long time, and his mind was 'blank' at the point of stabbing, because he was not conscious of the act of stabbing. His motive for following/stalking is unknown, but he felt that Holly was going to be talking to him, suggesting a misreading of social signals. He admits harm but not murder, suggesting acknowledging the act but not the outcome, so the 'intention' to harm and kill. The intense anger is common amongst autistic individuals who become dysregulated and rejected (BBC News, 2024).

Sex and relationship education

Corona et al. (2016) found that whilst parents of adolescents with autism believe that their children are interested in sexual and romantic relationships, they are unaware of how best to effectively and appropriately instigate conversations with their child with autism regarding such topics.

Interviews with 18 parents of children with autism (6–13 years) in Ballan (2012) found that some parents believed that broad-ranging discussions about sexuality and relationships would not be relevant. Parents reported that their sexuality-related discussions with their children did not include topics relating to future social and sexual behaviours. Lehan Mackin et al. (2016) found that few parents of children with autism could quickly imagine the likelihood of their child ever experiencing a romantic relationship.

In a survey of individuals with autism and typically developing individuals, Mehzabin and Stokes (2011) found that individuals with autism have less adaptive sexual knowledge and behaviours, reported less social behaviour, less education about sex and sexuality, and less sexual experience.

Harris (2017), in a study of sex education for autistic young people, concluded that one of the major issues related to the successful teaching of sexual health education to autistic adolescents is that there is a deficit related to social skills and social cues within this population. This aspect of development hinders understanding of the social features of sexual and romantic relationships. For these reasons, researchers have suggested that sexual and relationship education programmes aimed at autistic adolescents should incorporate not only the typical information from the curriculum, but also characteristics to develop greater social skills, social understanding and social interactions. The following are suggested:

- Use of social stories – A Social Story is a short story with specific characteristics that describes a social situation, concept, or social skill using a format that is meaningful for persons with autism spectrum disorders. Social Stories have been associated with increased socially appropriate behaviours and decreased problem behaviours. Although there is little information regarding the use of Social Stories in sexuality education, it seems likely that they can be a useful tool to help individuals with autism navigate this natural developmental transition (Ballan & Freyer, 2017).
- Technology – Autistic young people have shown positive responses to the lack of social demand from a computer, the ability to have immediate and predictable responses, and a controlled environment in which they can learn and develop.
- Parent/caregiver support – Parents and caregivers in our society are assumed to take the role of instructor for their children when it comes to sexual health education. Whether the school environment plays a small or a large role in sex education, parents are supposed to fill in the gaps and be available for questions if needed. Even in the best situations, this private education between parent and child can be marred by an unwillingness to be open and honest with one another, awkwardness, or a general lack of age-appropriate, sexually positive and accurate information. Another component that would be to help parents and caregivers teach sexual education to their adolescents is if they receive support from healthcare providers and other staff who work with their youth's development.
- Nursing implications – Parents expect that providers have some skill in the areas of disability and sexual health, and when they do not, it can lead to miscommunication and a lack of perceived or actual support. One of the most important things that nurses can do for families looking for resources on teaching sexual health to their autistic adolescent is to form relationships with local community agencies that provide services specifically targeted to this population.

McCann (2016) suggests that a sex and relationship educational programme for those with autism should be individual and more explicit. Images (see Figure 9.1), role-play, social stories, videos, and mirrors help inform discussions.

Case study (McCann, 2016)

Peter, in Year 10, was following a girl he found attractive everywhere at school. He was put on report, but he continued. He was excluded for three days when he punched his fist through a window because a teacher had stopped him from going into a room where the girl was. One night, he followed her home and stood outside for an hour until her parents called the police. He said she had smiled at him, and that meant she liked him.

Peter had listened carefully in the Sex and Relationship Education lessons, but had taken it literally when the discussion explored how looking at someone and smiling was a way of expressing an interest in them. He'd also been watching television soaps for tips on getting a girlfriend, and one particular story about someone stalking a woman he liked had stuck in his mind. The school organised some sessions on anger management and brought in a monthly session with an external autism specialist, where he talked about his feelings about girls and his dreams of entering into a relationship, and received some positive advice and support using autism-friendly resources and social stories. The school also spoke to the girl and her parents. They dropped the police action, and Peter was able to apologise to the girl. The school worked with both students to agree not to pursue the matter, especially on social media.

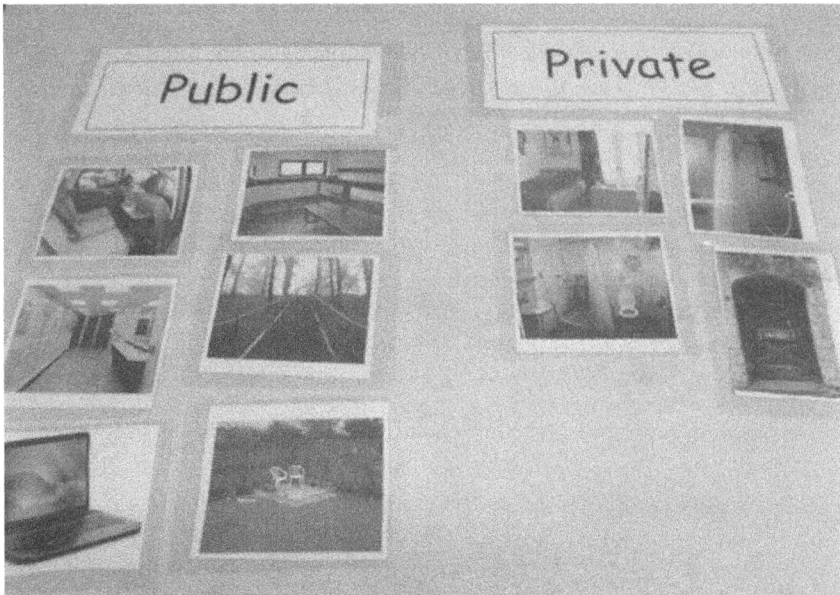

Figure 9.1   Photos of public and private places support a conversation about what constitutes appropriate behaviour in different contexts (McCann, 2016).

Relationship topics should include (McCann, 2016):

- Consent is a concept that needs to be taught in terms of respecting others and of agreeing to have sex.
- Knowing how to join in with others and how to leave a situation they are not comfortable with safely.
- Recognising teasing and bullying and knowing what to do about it.
- Finding out what is safe and enjoyable in relationships, who they can trust, and where they can get help when they need it.
- Understanding how relationships evolve as people move from childhood through adolescence into adulthood, and the different types of relationships they might have. Include parenthood if appropriate.
- Reading social signals, including flirting, touch, facial expression and body language. This could be turned into a guessing game, where students apply their 'social detective' skills to a series of photos or video clips.
- Conversation skills. How to give compliments, arrange meetings, and ask good questions to find out about others (including someone they are interested in).
- Developing their moral framework. Explore sexual relationships in the context of religious, secular and legal frameworks and support the young person to say what they think is important to them.

Case study (McCann, 2016)

Jamie, in Year 5, became very angry when anyone mentioned birthdays. It had always been an issue, and people had learned not to talk about his birthday, but this year it had got much worse, so much so that he would attack any child who mentioned that a birthday was coming up. He had started targeting pupils by looking at the birthday list on the wall. He also spoke in a very high-pitched voice. Jamie had a deep fear of growing up. He had heard about puberty in a lesson, and he had teenage brothers. He had been frightened when their voices changed, and was a child who already found change very difficult.

Jamie was given some extra lessons in a small group of boys who were his friends. They started by looking at how we can tell how old someone is and what stage of life they are at (discrimination), and arranged lots of magazine pictures of people into categories of baby, toddler, child, teenager, adult and elderly. As he listened to the other boys talking about what they were looking forward to when they were older, staff supported Jamie to understand that growing up is a natural process and that it happens gradually, not on a specific day (a birthday). He then made a book charting his own growth from babyhood, noting what was the same as well as what had changed. A social story was written reiterating the messages that had come out of this work, with lots of positive and affirmative.

Child pornography, pornography, especially on the internet

This is a complex topic with many layers. Autistic individuals may explore the internet for sexual education or to satisfy sexual needs due to a lack of sexual outlets with peers/friends. However, according to Allely (2019), many autistic individuals have average or above-average intelligence, while their social maturity is that of someone much younger. This frequently results in them being more interested in befriending people who are much younger than themselves, but who are socially and emotionally at the same level, so developmental age rather than chronological age.

Regarding viewing child pornography, issues occur when autistic individuals are unaware that what they have done is a criminal offence. One explanation for the lack of awareness, according to Allely (2019), is that they have committed a crime due to their inability to recognise the facial expressions in the images of the children. Such an inability to recognise facial expressions (such as fear) is supported by many studies (e.g., Woodbury-Smith et al., 2005; Uljarevic & Hamilton, 2013).

Therefore, many autistic individuals may inadvertently view child pornography because of their inability to correctly guess the age of the individuals in the images, and sometimes the boundaries/distinction between an adult and a child is blurry (Allely, 2019), made worse by both being readily available on the internet. This is important to understand given that the legality and severity of the offence are determined by the age of the victims in the images being viewed by the defendant (Mahoney, 2009).

For individuals with autism, exploring sexuality on the internet through child pornography is one way for them to try to understand relationships and sexuality, in a safe and controlled environment, as opposed to being a precursor to any sexual offending towards a minor. As with many things that interest them, and are commonly found as an autistic trait, the desire for this material can end up being particularly excessive and compulsive in individuals with autism. The perception that everything on the internet is safe and suitable for parents and their autistic children leads many with autism to potentially illegal collections of images.

Numerous cases have been reported where autistic individuals have been found to have large collections of pornographic material (e.g., involving children), as part of the ritualistic nature of autism, with thousands of files not even opened. Unaware of the broader issues like where and how they got those files, who else might be able to access them and what the consequences (and impact) are for the minors in the images they are viewing (Mesibov & Sreckovic, 2017).

Due to their literal view of the world, they are unlikely to consider that illegal images can be so freely available on the internet. Our media is fraught with marketing materials with risky images of teenage models or images where they have made the older models look 'barely legal'. Such images can be confusing for individuals with autism, making it more difficult to determine what is illegal pornography (Mesibov & Sreckovic, 2017).

Also, a lack of sexual outlets with age-appropriate peers may lead individuals to explore the internet for sexual education to satisfy sexual needs (Attwood et al.,

2014). Lastly, looking at extreme sexual material is not always a reflection of the presence of deviant sexuality. Instead, it can be what is referred to as 'counterfeit deviance' (e.g., naïve curiosity) in offenders with autism (Mahoney, 2009).

Mahoney (2009) highlights the many factors that can contribute to an autistic individual engaging in the viewing of IIOC (Indecent Images of Children):

- Unbridled curiosity of individuals with ASD (autism spectrum disorder)
- Autistic individuals' interest is not necessarily deviant – 'counterfeit deviance'
- IIOC's mere existence on the internet sends the message of legality to the autistic teen or young adult
- Autistic individuals' inability to intuit social mores and legal rules
- Empathic deficits (but note that individuals with autism do have empathy when told that the children in the images are victims and are in distress, etc.)
- Unless explicitly explained, autistic individuals fail to see the harm in merely viewing or receiving IIOC
- Distinction between of-age and underage females is intentionally blurred by the media and pop culture and legal 'adult' porn (Mahoney, 2009).

In a case study, Allely (2020) investigated PJ, highlighting the association between autism and the viewing of IIOC is poorly recognised and understood both by the public and clinical and legal professionals. The ownership and sharing are seen as one and the same offence; however, in the case of PJ it was just collecting and ownership.

Case study (Allely, 2020)

PJ was 30 years old when he was charged and 31 years old when he was convicted. He was sentenced to 13 months in prison.

PJ was first exposed to IIOC when he was 12 years of age by a friend (who was 11 years old) at school. It was clear to PJ that he had been sharing this material for some time. PJ states, "[...] my offending was based on habits created when I was exposed to such material at the age of 12, when I was of similar age to those in the images I accessed and the actual searching for and downloading of the images was what gave me comfort rather than the content". Taken within the psychological context of someone with autism, the images will have become fixated at this stage and this type of material, as PJ himself says "gave him comfort". This became his preoccupation or obsessive interest in the same way that an individual exposed to trains at that age might develop a fixation or preoccupation with trains. Ceasing or interrupting the pursuit of these interests can cause individuals with autism significant distress and anxiety. His diagnosis of autism came after 72 days in prison when he was released on bail. His parents paid privately for the assessment.

> However, PJ reports that there was a lack of certainty as to whether his diagnosis of autism would make any difference at his appeal hearing. He states, "My lawyers were so unconvinced that the submission of a diagnostic report would make any difference, that they did not present it to the High Court, until we insisted that they do so on the day of the Hearing. This was due to their lack of experience with the significance of an autism diagnosis". However, the diagnostic report was pivotal during the appeal. The High Court Judges quashed his sentence and reduced it to a community payback order (with 200 hours of unpaid labour) without hearing any testimony from PJ's advocate.

Autism, arson, and property damage crimes

Fire setting

In the context of the arsonist with an autism spectrum disorder, Freckelton (2011) argues there is often an obsessive preoccupation with flames, cinders, colours, and heat, rather than an intention to damage property or put lives at risk.

Allely (2019) investigated cases regarding autistic individuals who engaged in fire-setting or were convicted of arson and argued it was clear that autism traits contributed in various degrees to the behaviour, including

- An impaired ability to understand and appreciate the possible consequences or harm of setting fires (such as damage to property, possible injury or death)
- Fire-setting is being viewed as the only way to solve problems
- Impaired victim empathy and having a preoccupation and special interest in fire and fire-setting (which is perhaps the most important or common factor).

Freckelton and List (2009) emphasised that an obsessive preoccupation and interest with 'flames, cinders, colours, and heat' is common in individuals with autism convicted of arson, rather than it being a malicious intention to cause property damage or harm to others. It was also highlighted by McEwan and Freckelton (2011) that in most fire-setters, there is no intention to kill or cause any harm to other people. Instead, it is the fire itself which provides a psychological function for these individuals. Therefore, it has been strongly advocated that conventional punishment and retribution may not be appropriate with such individuals, as it would do little to stop them from thinking or fantasising about or setting fires – particularly for autistic individuals who have a preoccupation or fascination with a flickering flame (Freckelton, 2011; McEwan & Freckelton, 2011).

Property damage

Property damage is sometimes cited as being common in those with autism; however, this commonly happens as part of a meltdown, where they have uncontrolled behaviour and emotions, and any damage is due to a need to release severe anxiety and displace these feelings onto an object. Some autistic people believe 'better on an object than a person'; however, both are seen by bystanders as bizarre and potentially illegal, placing them in potential trouble with the police. Property damage is more common with autistic boys than girls, due to both their body strength and rage, as boys tend to externalise their anxiety more than girls.

Case study (the author)

A student of mine, an 11-year-old boy with severe autism and OCD (Obsessive Compulsive Disorder), when he has a meltdown, he would kick walls and doors, smash televisions, and smash anything in sight without any regard for their value. Many parents talk about their homes being smashed up, with door handles broken. They do not repair their homes as they know the likelihood of it happening again is extremely strong, even though their autistic child, mainly boys, would apologise and believe they can regulate themselves better next time.

The next time comes, and smashing occurs, with neighbours frequently calling the police due to the excess shouting and smashing, thinking 'domestic abuse' and a murder was taking place. In the case of my 11-year-old student, living in council accommodation, they were asked to move home, and so this has been a constant pattern over the last five years. By luck, his father was a builder, so he was able to repair walls and doors, but this inability to regulate their meltdowns is a constant story told by many parents of autistic boys.

Autism and cyber-dependent crimes

For those with autism, access to computers and the internet creates a world of intellectual stimulation with few emotional demands. It is perceived to be a safe, controlled, and reliable environment in which many with autism find comfort. It also affords a forum for working through obsessions and interests with few boundaries; however, caution should be noted regarding chat rooms, which are not age-locked, creating situations where a vulnerable young person may be chatting with an adult and could be easily influenced as a result. It is, therefore, very important to control their child's computer use and access to the internet, especially to potentially problematic and illegal websites.

Ledingham and Mills (2015) define cybercrime as "the illegal use of computers and the internet, or crime committed using computers and the internet". Within the legal context (e.g., in the United States, the UK, Australia, New Zealand, Germany, the Netherlands, and Denmark). They note two distinct types of cybercrime:

• Cyber-dependent crime, which can only be committed using computers, computer networks, or other forms of information communication technology, for example, including the creation and spread of malware for financial gain, hacking to steal important personal or industry data and distributed denial-of-service (DDoS) attacks to cause reputational damage; and

- Cyber-enabled crime, such as fraud, which can be conducted online or offline, but online may take place at unprecedented scale and speed (McGuire & Dowling, 2013; The National Crime Agency: NCA, 2016).

International law enforcement agencies have reported an apparently large number of autistic individuals, especially those with high ability/intelligence, among perpetrators of cyber-dependent crimes, such as hacking or spreading malware (Ledingham & Mills, 2015). This apparent relationship between cyber-dependent crime and autism is echoed in a survey of six international law enforcement agencies (UK, United States, Australia, New Zealand, Germany, the Netherlands, and Denmark) experiences and contact with autistic cybercriminals, which indicated that some autistic individuals commit cyber-dependent offences, such as: hacking; creating coding to enable a crime to be committed; creating, deploying, or managing a bot or bot-net; and malware (Ledingham & Mills, 2015).

Regarding cyber-dependent crime, some members of both autistic and especially high-ability autistic-like trait groups develop advanced digital skills required to commit cyber-dependent crime. The specific relationship between 'autism and the technical mind' has been previously speculated by Baron-Cohen (2012), being a fascination. Moreover, computer science students and those employed in technology are two of the groups who typically possess higher levels of autistic-like traits (Ruzich et al., 2015). These relationships are potentially significant, as cyber-dependent criminal activity requires an advanced level of cyber-related skills (such as proficiency in programming in Java, C/C++, disassemblers, and assembly language and programming knowledge of scripting languages, e.g., PHP, Python, Perl, or Shell). Therefore, there may be an association between autistic-like traits (e.g., hyper-focus/fixations/obsessions), and the potential to develop the advanced digital skills required for cyber-dependent crime.

Cyber-enabled crime is an online variant of traditional crimes (such as fraud) and shares common motivations such as financial gain, whereas the motivations for cyber-dependent crime can be based around a sense of challenge in hacking into a system or enhanced reputation and credibility within hacker communities (NCA, 2017). This may be pertinent for the relationship between cyber-dependent crime specifically and autism or autistic-like traits since cyber-dependent criminals typically have not engaged in traditional crime (NCA, 2017), and autism has been associated with generally being law-abiding and low rates of criminality.

Assessing the relationship between autistic-like traits and cyber deviancy in a sample of 296 college students, Seigfried-Spellar et al. (2014) found 179 (60%) engaged in some form of cyber-deviant behaviour (such as hacking, cyberbullying, identity theft, and virus writing), and the study distinguished between those who did and those who did not self-report cyber-deviant behaviour, with higher autistic-like trait scores among those reporting cyber-deviant behaviours, which included both cyber-enabled crimes such as cyberbullying and identity theft, as well as cyber-dependent crimes such as hacking and virus writing. In their conclusions, contrary to the researcher's expectations, hackers did not score higher on autism-like traits. However, virus writers, identity thieves, and cyberbullies scored more autism-like traits. In addition, individuals who engaged in hacking, identity theft, cyberbullying, and virus writing scored higher on autistic-like traits and reported poorer social skills, poorer communication, and poorer imagination compared to all other individuals engaging in computer-device behaviours.

Cyber-dependent crime may, therefore, distinguish high and lower autistic groups. The conclusion that autistic respondents were less likely to commit a cyber-dependent crime is also consistent with literature, suggesting that autistic people are generally law-abiding, if not more so, than the general population. However, research suggests that those with high ability/intelligence and autism are drawn to cyber-dependent crime.

Case study (Freckelton, 2020).

In 2002, Gary McKinnon, a Scottish system administrator, was charged with hacking into 97 United States computers over 13 months, removing critical files from the United States military system, deleting weapons logs, copying data and files, and leaving taunting messages. He was indicted by a federal grand jury in the Eastern District of Virginia on seven counts of computer-related crime and on an indictment in the District of New Jersey. He faced a potential sentence of imprisonment for ten years on multiple charges.

The United States applied to extradite Mr McKinnon in 2005 after the United Kingdom enacted the Extradition Act 2003 (UK), which implemented the 2003 extradition treaty with the United States. In 2006, a District Court Judge sent Mr McKinnon's case to the Secretary of State to determine whether he should be extradited. The decision was that he should be.

Mr McKinnon appealed against the decisions of the District Judge and the Secretary of State to the High Court. He failed, but his legal team raised two questions of general importance to be considered by the House of Lords, which in turn affirmed his extradition. A subsequent appeal to the European Court of Human Rights also failed, as did an application for judicial review to the High Court.

The principal ground for Mr McKinnon's opposition to extradition was his symptomatology of autism (Asperger's syndrome) and the stress that it was asserted that long-term imprisonment in a supermax prison in the United States would have on his mental state. In addition, his vulnerability in a prison environment was emphasised by his expert witnesses. The United States asserted that he would receive adequate treatment and care in its prisons.

Ultimately, after the legal processes had been exhausted, Theresa May, the Home Secretary, exercised her discretion not to extradite Mr McKinnon, stating:

Mr McKinnon is accused of serious crimes. But there is also no doubt that he is seriously ill. He has Asperger's syndrome and suffers from depressive illness. The legal question before me is now whether the extent of that illness is sufficient to preclude extradition... After careful consideration of all the relevant material, I have concluded that Mr McKinnon's extradition would give rise to such a hig h risk of him ending his life that a decision to extradite would be incompatible with Mr McKinnon's human rights.

She also determined to introduce an amendment to the extradition law. "This will mean that where prosecution is possible in both the UK and in another state, the British courts will be able to bar prosecution overseas if they believe it is in the interests of justice to do so."

Case study (Martin, 2018; Freckelton, 2020)

Lauri Love, diagnosed with autism, was charged on three indictments that between the period October 2012 and October 2013, he, working with others, made a series of cyber-attacks on the computer networks of private companies and United States Government agencies (including the U.S. Federal Reserve, U.S. Army, U.S. Department of Défense, Missile Defence Agency, NASA, Army Corps of Engineers, Department of Health and Human Services, U.S. Sentencing Commission and the FBI Regional Computer Forensics Laboratory) to steal and then publicly disseminate confidential information found on the networks. Love was arrested in 2014 after data stolen from U.S. government websites was found on one of his computers.

In most of the attacks, it was alleged that Mr Love gained unauthorised access by exploiting vulnerabilities in computer networks. Once inside the compromised computer systems, Mr Love and others, it was said, placed hidden 'shells' or 'backdoors' within the networks, allowing them to return and steal the confidential data, which included telephone numbers, social security numbers, credit card details, and salary information of employees, health care professionals, and service personnel. Thus, the charges that Mr Love faced bore many similarities to the case of Gary McKinnon. It was accepted at first instance that Mr Love, a man of 33 with both British and Finnish nationality, had Asperger's syndrome (high-functioning autism), although its severity was the subject of contest.

Mr Love appealed against District Judge Tempia's decision to send his case to the Secretary of State for the Home Department for her decision on whether to order his extradition to the United States of America under Part 2 of the Extradition Act 2003. On 14 November 2016, the Home Secretary ordered his extradition.

> The Court of Appeal heard that 33-year-old Lauri Love had severe mental health issues and was at a 'very high risk' of committing suicide if he was sent to the United States to face charges.
>
> In the judgment handed down by the Lord Chief Justice and Mr Justice Ouseley, it was found that Mr Love's extradition would have been against his human rights.
>
> There was no reason that Mr Love, who has autism (Asperger's syndrome), should not be prosecuted in the UK rather than the United States, the judgment added. Mr Love's lawyer, Mr Edward Fitzgerald QC, told the Court of Appeal the defence was not seeking immunity from justice, but said if Mr Love was sent to the United States, there was a significant risk he would not be fit to be tried.
>
> The evidence of Professor Baron-Cohen, Director of the Autism Research Centre, and an NHS (National Health Service) consultant specialising in the diagnosis of Asperger's syndrome, was that Mr Love was high functioning and could participate in a criminal trial and give instructions to his legal representative. His autism did not exist in conjunction with learning difficulties, attention deficit, or linguistic impairments. However, his autism was very severe because it caused him to become so absorbed in his interests that he neglected important areas in his life, such as his studies and his health. Professor Baron-Cohen did not accept that the protocols of the United States were sufficient to support a prisoner with autism, depression, and a high suicidal risk, such as Mr Love.
>
> Ultimately, the decision by the High Court to decline the extradition of Lauri Love constitutes a potent international precedent regarding the forensic relevance of autism spectrum disorder/Asperger's syndrome.

References

Al-Attar, Z. (2018). Interviewing terrorism suspects and offenders with an autism spectrum disorder. *International Journal of Forensic Mental Health, 17*(4), 321–337. https://doi.org/10.1080/14999013.2018.1519614

Al-Attar, Z. (2020). Autism spectrum disorders and terrorism: How different features of autism can contextualise vulnerability and resilience. *The Journal of Forensic Psychiatry & Psychology, 31*(6), 926–949. https://doi.org/10.1080/14789949.2020.1812695

Allely, C. S. (2022). *Autism spectrum disorder in the criminal justice system: A guide to understanding suspects, defendants and offenders with autism*. Routledge. https://doi.org/10.4324/9781003212195

Allely, C. S. (2019b). Firesetting and arson in individuals with autism spectrum disorder: A systematic PRISMA review. *Journal of Intellectual Disabilities and Offending Behaviour, 10*(4), 89–101. https://doi.org/10.1108/JIDOB-11-2018-0014

Allely, C.S. (2019c). *Sexual offending behaviour in young people with intellectual disabilities and autism spectrum disorder: autism and the criminal justice system. 38-72. Paper presented at Prevention, Intervention & Inclusion*, Glasgow, UK.

Allely, C.S. (2020). Case report: Autism spectrum disorder symptomology and child pornography. *Journal of Intellectual Disabilities and Offending Behaviour*, *11*(3), 171–189. https://doi.org/10.1108/JIDOB-11-2019-0026

Allely, C.S., & Creaby-Attwood, A. (2016). Sexual offending and autism spectrum disorders. *Journal of Intellectual Disabilities and Offending Behaviour*, *7*(1), 35–51. https://doi.org/10.1108/JIDOB-09-2015-0029

Allely, C.S., Kennedy, S., & Warren, I. (2019). A legal analysis of Australian criminal cases involving defendants with autism spectrum disorder charged with online sexual offending. *International Journal of Law and Psychiatry*, *66*, 101456.

Allen, D., Evans, C., Hider, A., Hawkins, S., Peckett, H., & Morgan, H. (2008). Offending behaviour in adults with Asperger syndrome. *Journal of Autism and Developmental Disorders*, *38*, 748–758.

Aspis, S. (2023). Supplementary written evidence submitted by Inclusion London (MHB115). Retrieved 21/01/2025. committees.parliament.uk/writtenevidence/114635/html/

Attwood, T. (2002). *Why does Chris do that?* (Revised ed.). London: The National Autistic Society.

Attwood, T., Henault, I., & Dubin, N. (2014). The autism spectrum, sexuality, and the law. London: Jessica Kingsley Publishers.

Ballan, M.S. (2012). Parental perspectives of communication about sexuality in families of children with autism spectrum disorders. *Journal of Autism and Developmental Disorders*, *42*(5), 676–684.

Ballan, M. S., & Freyer, M. B. (2017). Autism spectrum disorder, adolescence, and sexuality education: Suggested interventions for mental health professionals. *Sexuality and Disability*, *35*(2), 261–273. https://doi.org/10.1007/s11195-017-9477-9

Baron-Cohen, S. (1988). An assessment of violence in a young man with Asperger's syndrome. *Child Psychology & Psychiatry & Allied Disciplines*, *29*(3), 351–360. https://doi.org/10.1111/j.1469-7610.1988.tb00723.x

Baron-Cohen, S. (1995). Mindblindness*: An essay on autism and theory of mind*. Cambridge, MA: Bradford.

Baron-Cohen, S. (2012). Autism and the technical mind. *Scientific American*, *307*, 72–75.

Baron-Cohen, S., Leslie, A. M., & Frith, U. (1985). Does the autistic child have a "theory of mind"? *Cognition*, *21*(1), 37–46. https://doi.org/10.1016/0010-0277(85)90022-8

Barry-Walsh, J.B., & Mullen, P.E. (2004). Forensic aspects of Asperger's syndrome. *Journal of Forensic Psychiatry and Psychology*, *15*(1), 96–107. https://doi.org/10.1080/14789940310001638628

BBC News (2024). Teenager guilty of murdering Holly Newton. 15. 29 August 2024. Retrieved 04/09/2024. https://www.bbc.co.uk/news/articles/c8dpyz91vmgo

Bjørkly, S. (2009). Risk and dynamics of violence in Asperger's syndrome: A systematic review of the literature. *Aggression and Violent Behavior*, *14*(5), 306–312. https://doi.org/10.1016/j.avb.2009.04.003

Brendel, D.H., Bodkin, J.A., Hauptman, B., & Ornstein, A. (2002). 'I see dead people': Overcoming psychic numbness. *Harvard Review of Psychiatry*, *10*(3), 166–178.

Brown-Lavoie, S.M., Viecili, M.A., & Weiss, J.A. (2014). Sexual knowledge and victimization in adults with autism spectrum disorders. *Journal of Autism and Developmental Disorders*. 2014 September, *44*(9), 2185–2196. https://doi.org/10.1007/s10803-014-2093-y. PMID: 24664634; PMCID: PMC4131130.

Burdon, L., & Dickens, G.L. (2009). Asperger syndrome and offending behaviour. *Learning Disability Practice*, *12*(9), 14–20. https://ezproxy.uws.edu.au/login?url=https://search.proquest.com/docview/217734519?accountid=36155

Byers, E.S., Nichols, S., & Voyer, S.D. (2013). Challenging stereotypes: Sexual functioning of single adults with high functioning autism spectrum disorder. *Journal of Autism and Developmental Disorders*, *43*(11), 2617–2627. https://doi.org/10.1007/s10803-013-1813-z

CBS News (2017). Family of teen with autism mistakenly tackled by police calls for better training. 21 September 2017. Retrieved 19/06/2024. https://www.cbsnews.com/news/autistic-teen-who-was-roughed-up-by-police-speaks-out/

Cheely, C.A., Carpenter, L.A., Letourneau, E.J., Nicholas, J.S., Charles, J., & King, L.B. (2012). The prevalence of youth with autism spectrum disorders in the criminal justice system. *Journal of Autism and Developmental Disorders*. 2012 September, *42*(9), 1856–1862. https://doi.org/10.1007/s10803-011-1427-2. PMID: 22187108.

Chen, P.S., Chen, S.J., Yang, Y.K., Yeh, T.L., Chen, C.C., & Lo, H.Y. (2003). Asperger's disorder: A case report of repeated stealing and the collecting behaviours of an adolescent patient. *Acta Psychiatrica Scandinavica*, *107*, 73–76.

Chesterman, P., & Rutter, S.C. (1993). Case report: Asperger's syndrome and sexual offending.*The Journal of Forensic Psychiatry*, *4*(3), 555–562. https://doi.org/10.1080/09585189308408222

Collins, J., Horton, K., Gale-St Ives, E., Murphy, G., & Barnoux, M. (2022). A systematic review of autistic people and the criminal justice system: An update of king and murphy (2014). *Journal of Autism and Developmental Disorders*, *53*, 3151–3179. https://doi.org/10.1007/s10803-022-05590-3

Cooke, Y. (2019). Autistic man bit police officer on the arm after suffering a sensory meltdown outside McDonald's. *Somerset News*. 16:32, 22 October 2019. Retrieved 19/06/2024. https://www.somersetlive.co.uk/news/somerset-news/autistic-man-bit-police-officer-3455056

Corona, L.L., Fox, S.A., Christodulu, K.V., & Worlock, J. A. (2016). Providing education on sexuality and relationships to adolescents with autism spectrum disorder and their parents. *Sexuality and Disability*, *34*(2), 199–214. https://doi.org/10.1007/s11195-015-9424-6

Creaby-Attwood, A., & Allely, C. S. (2017). A psycho-legal perspective on sexual offending in individuals with autism spectrum disorder. *International Journal of Law and Psychiatry*, *55*, 72–80. https://doi.org/10.1016/j.ijlp.2017.10.009

Davis, B., & Schunick, W.G. (2002). *Dangerous encounters. Avoiding perilous situations with autism*. London: Jessica Kingsley Publishers.

Esan, F., Chester, V., Gunaratnam, I.J., Hoare, S., & Alexander, R.T. (2015). The clinical, forensic and treatment outcome factors of patients with autism spectrum disorder treated in a forensic intellectual disability service. *Journal of Applied Research in Intellectual Disabilities*. 2015 May, *28*(3), 193–200. https://doi.org/10.1111/jar.12121. Epub 2014 Nov 7. PMID: 25379816.

Fallon, C. (2021). Call for police to get mandatory neurodiversity training after officer assaulted young autistic boy in school. *Channel Four News*. 7 September 2021. Retrieved 18/06/2024. https://www.channel4.com/news/call-for-police-to-get-mandatory-neurodiv

ersity-training-after-officer-assaulted-young-autistic-boy-in-school?fbclid=IwAR1nhFgI
JsfujIJJcrIgNAXe2cpuJ_kiPDuRMOs2eL8uEllMnfl_N4lHyps

Farrington, D.P. (2007). Childhood risk factors and risk-focusedprevention. *The Oxford Handbook of Criminology*, *4*, 602–640.

Fitzgerald, M. (Ed.). (2013). *Recent advances in autism spectrum disorders – Volume I.* Intechopen. https://doi.org/10.5772/46001

Freckelton, I. (2020). Autism spectrum disorder and suitability for extradition: Love v the Government of the United States [2018] 1 WLR 2889; [2018] EWHC 172 (Admin) per Burnett LCJ and Ouseley J. *Psychiatry, Psychology and Law*. 2020 March 23, *27*(2), 181–191. https://doi.org/10.1080/13218719.2020.1727645. PMID: 32944120; PMCID: PMC7476620.

Freckelton, I. (2011a). Asperger's disorder and the criminal law. *Journal of Law and Medicine*, *18*, 677–691.

Freckelton, I. (2011b). Autism Spectrum Disorders and the Criminal Law. In *Book: A Comprehensive Book on Autism Spectrum Disorders*. Mohammadi, M.R. Intechopen. (pp. 249–272).

Freckelton, I., & List, D. (2009). Asperger's disorder, criminal responsibility and criminal culpability. *Psychiatry, Psychology and Law*, *16*(1), 16–40. https://doi.org/10.1080/13218710902887483

Godfrey, B. (2022). Dudley mum's legal fight over autistic son's conviction. *Correspondent*, BBC Midlands Today. 10 January 2022. Retrieved 28/07/2024. https://www.bbc.co.uk/news/uk-england-birmingham-59900767

Griffin-Shelley, E. (2010). An Asperger's adolescent sex addict, sex offender: A case study. *Sexual Addiction and Compulsivity*, *17*(1), 46–64.

Hammond, D.G., Adkin, T., & Elma, B. (2021). Autistic people and police brutality in the UK: Baron-Cohen the aggressor. *Boycott Spectrum 10k*. 24 October 2021. Retrieved 18/06/2024. https://emergentdivergence.com/2021/10/24/autistic-people-and-police-brutality-in-the-uk-baron-cohen-the-aggressor/

Happé, F., & Frith, U. (2006). The weak coherence account: Detail-focused cognitive style in autism spectrum disorders. *Journal of Autism and Developmental Disorders*, *36*(1), 5–25. https://doi.org/10.1007/s10803-005-0039-0

Hare, D. J., Gould, J., Mills, R., & Wing, L. (1999). *A preliminary study of individuals with autistic spectrum disorders in three special hospitals in England*. London: National Autistic Society.

Harris, M. (2017). Strategies for delivering sexual health education to adolescents with autism spectrum disorders: An integrative review of the literature. *Grace Peterson Nursing Research Colloquium*. 6. https://via.library.depaul.edu/nursing-colloquium/2017/Fall_2017/6

Hart-Kerkhoffs, L., Doreleijers, T.A.H., Jansen, L.M.C., van Wijk, A.P.H., & Bullens, R.A.R. (2009a). Offence-related characteristics and psychosexual development of juvenile sex offenders. *Child and Adolescent Psychiatry and Mental Health*, *70*(2), 266–272.

Hart-Kerkhoffs, L.A., Jansen, L.M., Doreleijers, T.A., Vermeiren, R., Minderaa, R.B., & Hartman, C.A. (2009b). Autism spectrum disorder symptoms in juvenile suspects of sex offenses. *The Journal of Clinical Psychiatry*. 2009 February, *70*(2), 266–272. https://doi.org/10.4088/jcp.08m04635. Epub 2009 Feb 10. PMID: 19210944.

Haskins, B. G., & Silva, J. A. (2006). Asperger's disorder and criminal behaviour: Forensic-psychiatric considerations. *Journal of the American Academy of Psychiatry & the Law Online*, *34*(3), 374–384.

Haw, C., Radley, J., & Cooke, L. (2013). Characteristics of male autistic spectrum patients in low security: Are they different from non-autistic low secure patients? *Journal of Intellectual Disabilities and Offending Behaviour*, 4(1/2), 24–32, 2050–8832.

Hellemans, H., Colson, K., Verbraeken, C., Vermeiren, R., & Deboutte, D. (2007). Sexual behaviour in high-functioning male adolescents and young adults with autism spectrum disorder. *Journal of Autism and Developmental Disorders*. 2007 February, *37*(2), 260–269. https://doi.org/10.1007/s10803-006-0159-1. PMID: 16868848.

Henry, C. (2018). *Fighting for my brother. Autism and the criminal justice system*. Research Project. University of Salford-Manchester. 10 December 2018. Retrieved 06/08/2024. https://hub.salford.ac.uk/acjs/2018/12/10/fighting-for-my-brother/

Hofvander, B. (2018). Offenders with autism spectrum disorder. In A.R. Beech, A.J. Carter, R.E. Mann, & P. Rotshtein (Eds.), *The Wiley Blackwell handbook of forensic neuroscience* (pp. 273–0). Hoboken, NJ: John Wiley and Sons Ltd. https://doi.org/10.1192/bjpo. bp.116.003889

Hofvander, B., Nilsson, T., Ståhlberg, O., Claesdotter, E., Moberg, P., Ahlbäck, K., & Hildebrand Karlén, M. (2023). Autism Spectrum Disorders in forensic psychiatric investigations–patterns of comorbidity and criminality. *Frontiers in Psychiatry*, *14*, 1168572. https://doi.org/10.3389/fpsyt.2023.1168572

Howlin, P. (2006). *Improving outcomes in adult life for people with autism*. Paper presented at the Wales 2nd International Conference on autism, Cardiff. www.awares.org

Howlin, P., Goode, S., Hutton, J., & Rutter, M. (2004). Adult outcome for children with autism. *Journal of Child Psychology and Psychiatry*. 2004 February, *45*(2), 212–229. https://doi.org/10.1111/j.1469-7610.2004.00215.x. PMID: 14982237.

Howlin, P., & Moore, A. (1997). Diagnosis in autism: A survey of over 1200 patients in the UK. *Autism*, *1*(2), 135–162. https://doi.org/10.1177/1362361397012003

Jackson, L. (2002). *Freeks, geeks and asperger syndrome*. London: Jessica Kingsley Publishers.

Kalyva, E. (2010). Teachers' perspectives of the sexuality of children with autism spectrum disorders. *Research in Autism Spectrum Disorders*, *4*(3), 433–437.

Kawakami, C., Ohnishi, M., Sugiyama, T., Someki, F., Nakamura, K., & Tsujii, M. (2012). The risk factors for criminal behaviour in high-functioning autism spectrum disorders (HFASDs): A comparison of childhood adversities between individuals with HFASDs who exhibit criminal behaviour and those with HFASD and no criminal histories. *Research in Autism Spectrum Disorders*, *6*(2), 949–957. https://doi.org/10.1016/j.rasd.2011.12.005

Kellaher, D.C. (2015). Sexual behavior and autism spectrum disorders: An update and discussion. *Current Psychiatry Reports*. 2015 April, *17*(4), 562. https://doi.org/10.1007/s11920-015-0562-4. PMID: 25749749.

King, C., & Murphy, G.H. (2014). A systematic review of people with autism spectrum disorder and the criminal justice system. *Journal of Autism and Developmental Disorders*. 2014 November, *44*(11), 2717–2733. https://doi.org/10.1007/s10803-014-2046-5. PMID: 24577785.

Kohn, Y., Fahum, T., Ratzoni, G., & Apter, A. (1998). Aggression and sexual offense in asperger's syndrome. *Israel Journal of Psychiatry and Related Sciences*, *35*(4), 293–299.

Kumagami, T., & Matsuura, N. (2009). Prevalence of pervasive developmental disorder in juvenile court cases in Japan. *Journal of Forensic Psychiatry & Psychology*, *20*(6), 974–987. https://doi.org/10.1080/14789940903174170

Ledingham, R., & Mills, R. (2015). A preliminary study of autism and cybercrime in the context of international law enforcement. *Advances in Autism*, *1*, 1–10. https://doi.org/10.1108/AIA-05-2015-0003.

Lehan Mackin, M., Loew, N., Gonzalez, A., Tykol, H., & Christensen, T. (2016). Parent perceptions of sexual education needs for their children with autism. *Journal of Pediatric Nursing*. 2016 November–December, *31*(6), 608–618. https://doi.org/10.1016/j.pedn.2016.07.003. Epub 2016 Aug 21. PMID: 27554640.

Lerner, M.D., Haque, O.S., Northrup, E.C., Lawer, L., Bursztajn, H.J. (2012). Emerging perspectives on adolescents and young adults with high-functioning autism spectrum disorders, violence, and criminal law. *Journal of the American Academy of Psychiatry and the Law, 40*, 177–190. *(PDF) Autism Spectrum Disorder and Criminal Responsibility: Historical Perspectives, Clinical Challenges and Broader Considerations within the Criminal Justice System.* Available from: https://www.researchgate.net/publication/317244722_Autism_spectrum_disorder_and_criminal_responsibility_historical_perspectives_clinical_challenges_and_broader_considerations_within_the_criminal_justice_system [accessed May 06 2025].

Lindsay, W.R., Craig, L., & Griffiths, D.M. (Eds.). (2019). *The Wiley handbook on what works for offenders with intellectual and developmental disabilities an evidence-based approach to theory, assessment and treatment.* London: Wiley.

McEwan, T.E., Harder, L., Brandt, C., & de Vogel, V. (2020). Risk factors for stalking recidivism in a dutch community forensic mental health sample. *International Journal of Forensic Mental Health, 19*(2), 127–141. https://doi.org/10.1080/14999013.2019.1661885

Mclelland, E. (2016). "Two policemen who chased a 33-year-old autistic man "because it was funny" are sacked". 7 April 2016.Daily Mail online. Retrieved 12/05/25. https://www.dailymail.co.uk/news/article-3528545/Two-policemen-chased-33-year-old-autistic-man-funny-sacked-gross-misconduct.html

Mahoney, M. (2009). Asperger's syndrome and the criminal Law: The special case of child pornography. https://www.harringtonmahoney.com/content/Publications/Aspergers-SyndromeandtheCriminalLawv26.pdf

Margari, A., De Agazio, G., Marzulli, L., Piarulli, F.M., Mandarelli, G., Catanesi, R., Carabellese, F.F., & Cortese, S. (2024). Autism spectrum disorder (ASD) and sexual offending: A systematic review. *Neuroscience & Biobehavioral Reviews*. 2024 July, *162*, 105687. https://doi.org/10.1016/j.neubiorev.2024.105687. Epub 2024 Apr 27. PMID: 38685290.

Martin, A.J. (2018). Lauri Love: Autistic hacking suspect wins US extradition appeal. *Sky News*. Mon 5 February 2018 13:59, UK. Retrieved 11/08/2024. https://news.sky.com/story/lauri-love-autistic-hacking-suspect-wins-us-extradition-appeal-11237738

Mawson, D., Grounds, A., & Tantam, D. (1985). Violence and Asperger's syndrome: A case study. *British Journal of Psychiatry, 147*, 566–569.

McCann, L. (2016). Supporting pupils with autism through sex and relationships education. Retrieved 08/08/2024. https://reachoutasc.com/wp-content/uploads/2016/04/17-21_Autism-sex.pdf

McEwan, T., & Freckelton, I. (2011). Assessment, treatment and sentencing of arson offenders: an overview. *Psychiatry, Psychology and Law, 18*(3), 319–328.

McGuire, M., & Dowling, S. (2013). Cyber crime: A review of the evidence. Retrieved 19/12/2017. https://www.gov.uk/government/uploads/system/uploads/attachment_data/file/246749/horr75-summary.pdf

Mehzabin, P., & Stokes, M.A. (2011). Self-assessed sexuality in young adults with High-Functioning Autism. *Research in Autism Spectrum Disorders, 5*(1), 614–621. https://doi.org/10.1016/j.rasd.2010.07.006

Mesibov, G., & Sreckovic, M. (2017). Child and juvenile pornography and autism spectrum disorder. In A. Lawrence, J. D. Dubin, & E. Horowitz (Eds.), *Caught in the web of the criminal justice system: Autism, developmental disabilities, and sex offenses* (pp. 64–93). London, UK: Jessica Kingsley Publishers.

Milton, J., Duggan, C., Latham, A., & Tantam, D. (2002). Case history of co-morbid Asperger's syndrome and paraphilic behavior. *Medicine Science and Law*, *42*(3), 237–244.

Mullen, P.E., Pathé, M., Purcell, R., & Stuart, G.W. (1999). Study of stalkers. *The American Journal of Psychiatry*. 1999 August, *156*(8), 1244–1249. https://doi.org/10.1176/ajp.156.8.1244. PMID: 10450267.

Murphy, D. (2010). Understanding offenders with autism-spectrum disorders: what can forensic services do? *Advances in Psychiatric Treatment*, *16*, 44–46.

Murrie, D.C., Warren, J.I., Kristiansson, M., & Diet, P.E. (2002). Asperger's syndrome in forensic settings. *International Journal of Forensic Mental Health*, *1*, 59–70. https://doi.org/10.1080/14999013.2002.10471161

National Autism Society (2022). Youth justice report. Retrieved 26/07/2024. https://nas.chorus.thirdlight.com/link/n4bhhjjwhbxk-as0nu1/@/preview/1?o

National Crime Agency (2016). NCA strategic cyber industry group. Retrieved 29/07/2024. https://www.nationalcrimeagency.gov.uk/publications/709-cyber-crime-assessment-2016/file.

National Crime Agency (2017). Pathways into cyber crime. Retrieved 29/07/2024. https://www.nationalcrimeagency.gov.uk/publications/791-pathways-into-cyber-crime/file.

Nichols, S., & Blakeley-Smith, A. (2010). I'm not sure we're ready for this …: working with families toward facilitating healthy sexuality for individuals with autism spectrum disorders. *Social Work in Mental Health*, *8*(1), 72–91.

O'Brien, C. (2014). 'My brother is not a murderer': How one woman gave up everything to fight for justice. *Mail Online*. 7 September 2014. Retrieved 06/08/2024. https://www.dailymail.co.uk/home/you/article-2743794/My-brother-not-murderer-How-one-woman-gave-fight-justice.html

Orsmond, G.I., Krauss, M.W., & Seltzer, M.M. (2004). Peer relationships and social and recreational activities among adolescents and adults with autism. *Journal of Autism and Developmental Disorders*. 2004 June, *34*(3), 245–256. https://doi.org/10.1023/b:jadd.0000029547.96610.df. PMID: 15264493.

Payne, K.L., Maras, K., Russell, A.J., & Brosnan, M.J. (2020a). Self-reported motivations for offending by autistic sexual offenders. *Autism*, *24*(2), 307–320. https://doi.org/10.1177/1362361319858860

Payne, K.L., Maras, K.L., Russell, A.J., & Brosnan, M.J. (2020b). Self-reported motivations for offending by autistic sexual offenders. *Autism*. 2020 February, *24*(2), 307–320. https://doi.org/10.1177/1362361319858860. Epub 2019 Jun 28. PMID: 31250659.

Payne, K.L., Maras, K.L., Russell, A.J., Brosnan, M.J., & Mills, R. (2020). Self-reported motivations for engaging or declining to engage in cyber-dependent offending and the role of autistic traits. *Research in Developmental Disabilities*, *104*, Article 103681. https://doi.org/10.1016/j.ridd.2020.103681

Peixoto, R.T., Chantranupong, L., Hakim, R., Levasseur, J., Wang, W., Merchant, T., Gorman, K., Budnik, B., & Sabatini, B.L. (2019). Abnormal striatal development underlies the early onset of behavioral deficits in Shank3B$^{-/-}$ mice. *Cell Reports*. 2019 November 12, *29*(7), 2016–2027.e4. https://doi.org/10.1016/j.celrep.2019.10.021. PMID: 31722214; PMCID: PMC6889826.

Peterson, C.C., Slaughter, V.P., & Paynter, J. (2007). Social maturity and theory of mind in typically developing children and those on the autism spectrum. *Journal of Child Psychology and Psychiatry, 48*, 1243–1250. https://doi.org/10.1111/j.1469-7610.2007.01810.x

Powell, J. (2021). Mum slams school as autistic son, 12, handcuffed by police on first day of term. *Mirror Newspaper website.* 19:41, 7 August 2021. Retrieved 18/06/2024. https://www.mirror.co.uk/news/uk-news/mum-slams-school-autistic-son-24711692

Pring, J. (2016). 'Cruel and inept' police locked up autistic man after he was attacked in hate crime. 9 May 2016. Retrieved 19/06/2024. https://www.disabilitywales.org/cruel-and-inept-police-locked-up-autistic-man-after-he-was-attacked-in-hate-crime/

Ravensberg, V., & Miller, C. (2003). Stalking among young adults: A review of the preliminary research. *Aggression and Violent Behavior, 8*(4), 455–469. https://doi.org/10.1016/S1359-1789(02)00075-7

Rawdon, N., Vinter, L.P., Allely, C., & Wheatley, R. (2024). Exploring the experiences of an autistic male convicted of stalking. *The Journal of Forensic Psychiatry & Psychology, 35*(3), 461–494. https://doi.org/10.1080/14789949.2024.2339537

Ray, F., Marks, C., & Bray-Garretson, H. (2004). Challenges to treating adolescents with Asperger's Syndrome who are sexually abusive. *Sexual Addiction & Compulsivity: The Journal of Treatment & Prevention, 11*(4), 1532, 265–285.

Robins, J. (2020). Petition for mercy on behalf of autistic man sentenced to life for joint enterprise murder. 29 April 2020 | 8:52 am. Retrieved 11/08/2024. https://www.thejusticegap.com/petition-for-mercy-on-behalf-of-autistic-man-sentenced-to-life-for-joint-enterprise-murder/

Robins, J. (2022). Neurodiversity & a shocking litany of wrongful convictions. www.newlawjournal.co.uk. 29 July 2022. Retrieved 07/08/2024. https://www.newlawjournal.co.uk/docs/default-source/article_files/comment_robins_29-july-2022b028e332-24d2-4486-a742-40b9edd2ace4.pdf?sfvrsn=28ceeb6_1

Ruble, L.A., & Dalrymple, N.J. (1993). Social/sexual awareness of persons with autism: A parental perspective. *Archives of Sexual Behavior, 22*(3), 229–240.

Rutten, A.X., Vermeiren, R.R.J.M., & Van Nieuwenhuizen, C. (2017). Autism in adult and juvenile delinquents: A literature review. *Child and Adolescent Psychiatry and Mental Health.* 2017 September 22, *11* 45. https://doi.org/10.1186/s13034-017-0181-4. PMID: 28947914; PMCID: PMC5609035.

Ruzich, E., Allison, C., Smith, P., Watson, P., Auyeung, B., Ring, H., Baron-Cohen, S. (2015). Measuring autistic traits in the general population: A systematic review of the Autism Spectrum Quoteitn (AQ) in a nonclinical population sample of 6,900 typical adult males and females. *Molecular Autism, 6*, 2. https://doi.org/10.1186/2040-2392-6-2.

Seigfried-Spellar, K.C., O'Quinn, C.L., & Treadway, K.N. (2014). Assessing the relationship between autistic traits and cyberdeviancy in a sample of college students. *Behaviour & Information Technology, 34*(5), 533–542. https://doi.org/10.1080/0144929X.2014.978377

Sevlever, M., Roth, M.E., & Gillis, J.M. (2013). Sexual abuse and offending in autism spectrum disorders. *Sexuality and Disability, 31*(2), 189–200.

Shine, J., & Cooper-Evans, S. (2016). Developing an autism specific framework for forensic case formulation. *Journal of Intellectual Disabilities and Offending Behaviour, 7*(3), 127–139. https://doi.org/10.1108/JIDOB-04-2015-0006

Sims, P. (2016). Autism, sensory differences and criminal justice. *National Autism Society.* 28 June 2016. Retrieved 26/07/2024. https://www.autism.org.uk/advice-and-guidance/

professional-practice/sensory-criminal-justice#:~:text=Attwood%20(2002)%20 makes%20the%20point,activity%2C%20not%20one%20for%20outside.

Siponmaa, L., Kristiansson, M., Jonson, C., Nyden, A., & Gillberg, C. (2001). Juvenile and young adult mentally disordered offenders: The role of child neuropsychiatric disorders. *The Journal of the American Academy of Psychiatry and the Law, 29*(4), 420–426.

Søndenaa, E., Helverschou, S.B., Steindal, K., Rasmussen, K., Nilson, B., & Nøttestad, J.A. (2014). Violence and sexual offending behavior in people with autism spectrum disorder who have undergone a psychiatric forensic examination. *Psychological Reports*. 2014 August, *115*(1), 32–43. https://doi.org/10.2466/16.15.PR0.115c16z5. Epub 2014 Jul 29. PMID: 25073065.

Stokes, M., & Newton, N. (2004). Autism spectrum disorders and stalking. *Autism*. 2004 September, *8*(3), 337–339. PMID: 15382361.

Stokes, M., Newton, N., & Kaur, A. (2007). Stalking, and social and romantic functioning among adolescents and adults with autism spectrum disorder. *Journal of Autism and Developmental Disorders*. 2007 November, *37*(10), 1969–1986. https://doi.org/10.1007/ s10803-006-0344-2. Epub 2007 Feb 2. PMID: 17273936.

Strunz, S., Schermuck, C., Ballerstein, S., Ahlers, C.J., Dziobek, I., & Roepke, S. (2017). Romantic relationships and relationship satisfaction among adults with Asperger syndrome and high-functioning autism. *Journal of Clinical Psychology, 73*(1), 113–125. https://doi.org/10.1002/jclp.22319

Sutton, L.R., Hughes, T.L., Huang, A., Lehman, C., Paserba, D., Talkington, V., Taormina, R., Walters, J.B., Fenclau, E., & Marshall, S. (2013). Identifying individuals with autism in a state facility for adolescents adjudicated as sexual offenders: A pilot study. *Focus on Autism and other Developmental Disabilities, 28*(3), 175–183.

Tantam, D. (1981). Lifelong eccentricity and social isolation. II: Asperger's syndrome or schizoid personality disorder? *British Journal of Psychiatry*. 1988 December, *153*, 783–791. https://doi.org/10.1192/bjp.153.6.783. PMID: 3256377.

Uljarevic, M., & Hamilton, A. (2013). Recognition of emotions in autism: a formal meta-analysis.*Journal of Autism and Developmental Disorders*.2013 July,*43*(7),1517–1526. https://doi.org/10.1007/s10803-012-1695-5. PMID: 23114566.

Van Bourgondien, M.E., Reichle, N.C., & Palmer, A. (1997). Sexual behavior in adults with autism. *Journal of Autism and Developmental Disorders, 27*(2), 113–125.

Ventura, F., Areias, G., Coroa, M., Araújo, A., Borges, J., Morais, S., & Madeira, N. (2022). Stalking behavior and high-functioning autism spectrum disorders – A case report. *The Journal of Forensic Psychiatry & Psychology, 33*(5), 639–645. https://doi.org/10.1080/ 14789949.2022.2098803

Weinman, C. (2023). Could my child with autism be arrested? What parents need to know. *Autism Parenting Magazine*. 29 September 2023. https://www.autismparentingmagazine. com/my-child-with-autism-arrested/

Welsh Assembly (2010). Autistic spectrum disorders a guide for criminal justice system practitioners in wales. December 2010.

Wing, L. (1981). Asperger's syndrome: A clinical account. *Psychological Medicine*. 1981 February, *11*(1), 115–129. https://doi.org/10.1017/s0033291700053332. PMID: 7208735.

Wing, L. & Gould, J. (1979). Severe impairments of social interaction and associated abnormalities in children: Epidemiology and classification. *Journal of Autism and Developmental Disorders, 9*, 11–29.

Woodbury-Smith, M.R., Clare, I.C.H., Holland, A.J., & Kearns, A. (2006). High functioning autistic spectrum disorders, offending and other law-breaking: Findings from a community sample. *The Journal of Forensic Psychiatry & Psychology*, *17*(1), 108–120. https://doi. org/10.1080/14789940600589464

Woodbury-Smith, M.R., Clare, I.C.H., Holland, A.J., Kearns, A., Staufenberg, E., & Watson, P. (2005a). A case-control study of offenders with high-functioning autistic spectrum disorders. *Journal of Forensic Psychiatry & Psychology*, *16*, 747–763 (23) (PDF) Autism spectrum disorder and criminal responsibility: historical perspectives, clinical challenges and broader considerations within the criminal justice system. Retrieved 26/07/2024. https://www.researchgate.net/publication/317244722_Autism_ spectrum_disorder_and_criminal_responsibility_historical_perspectives_clinical_ challenges_and_broader_considerations_within_the_criminal_justice_system

Woodbury-Smith, M.R., Robinson, J., Wheelwright, S.J., & Baron-Cohen, S. (2005b). Screening adults for Asperger syndrome using the AQ: A preliminary study of its diagnostic validity in clinical practice. *Journal of Autism and Developmental Disorders*, *35*, 331–335.

10 Failed by the Criminal Justice System

The Equality and Human Rights Commission (EHRC) report on inclusion (2020) and Slavny-Cross et al. (2022) warn that the UK criminal justice system (CJS) is failing those with learning disabilities and autistic people. The joint team surveyed 93 defence lawyers about autistic people they have represented in the last five years to find out about their defendants' experiences of navigating the CJS. Researchers found that the CJS is failing autistic people, and this should be a cause for concern. The study found that:

- Only 52% of autistic people were considered by the police to be vulnerable adults, even though the law recognises all autistic people as vulnerable.
- 35% of autistic defendants felt they were not given an 'appropriate adult' during police investigations, even though their diagnosis was known to police, and despite all autistic people being entitled under the law to have an appropriate adult present when being interviewed by the police.
- 18% of autistic defendants did not have an 'appropriate adult' present because their diagnosis was unknown to the police.

Appropriate adults act to safeguard the interests and rights of vulnerable defendants by ensuring that they are treated in a just manner, and can participate effectively during an investigation:

- Only 25% of autistic people in the study were given 'reasonable adjustments'.
- 38% were not given any, even though lawyers stated that this would have been beneficial. This is despite all autistic people being entitled to reasonable adjustments under the law.
- 33% did not receive any adjustments because their autism diagnosis was unknown at the time.
- Of the autistic people whose case went to trial, 22% were not given any reasonable adjustments, even though their lawyers stated that this would have been helpful.

Reasonable adjustments, such as using visual aids to assist with communication and allowing extra time to process information, can be made by the police to assist the detainee. Dr Rachel Slavny-Cross, who led the study, said, "Our research shows

DOI: 10.4324/9781003614432-10

quite clearly that autistic adults are not receiving fair treatment within the criminal justice system. Without reasonable adjustments or support, this could place them at a significant disadvantage" (EHRC, 2020). In 47% of the cases that included a trial by jury, the jury was not informed that the defendant was autistic. 59% of prosecution barristers and 46% of judges or magistrates said or did something during the trial that made them concerned that they did not have an adequate understanding of autism.

Dr Carrie Allison, another member of the research team, said

> *It's vital that jurors are provided with information about a defendant's autism and its implications, otherwise they are likely to misinterpret atypical behaviour exhibited by the defendant in court. Similarly, judges may fail to take into consideration mitigating factors that might otherwise influence sentencing.*
>
> (EHRC, 2020)

The study found that lawyers were more concerned that their autistic clients might engage in self-harm behaviours, compared with their non-autistic clients, and were more likely to report that their autistic clients experienced 'meltdowns' because of their involvement in the CJS. However, many were unaware of what might cause the meltdown and mitigate this as a precaution.

Dr Sarah Griffiths, a member of the research team, said

> *Autistic adults are particularly vulnerable to mental health problems, such as stress and heightened anxiety, with many autistic people experiencing meltdown and shutdown as a result (in interview and court settings). This is likely to have shaped their interactions with the criminal justice system and their ability to cope with the stress of being subject to criminal proceedings.*
>
> (EHRC, 2020)

However, a positive finding was that, in cases where their client was found to have committed a crime, 60% of judges saw the defendant's autism as a mitigating factor, and in these cases, the majority of autistic people were given a suspended or reduced sentence. Professor Sir Simon Baron-Cohen, Director of the Autism Research Centre at Cambridge and a member of the research team, added

> *There's an urgent need across the criminal justice system for increased awareness about autism. The police, lawyers, judges and jurors should be given mandatory training to be aware of how autism affects an individual's behaviour, so that autistic defendants are treated fairly within the criminal justice system.*
>
> (EHRC, 2020)

What most of the population view as 'normal life' is quite the opposite for a growing section of society. People with autism can find everyday interactions frightening, confusing, and extremely stressful as noted by a person with autism, "To me the outside world is a totally baffling incomprehensible mayhem which terrifies me. It is a meaningless mass of sights and sounds, noises and movement, coming from nowhere, going nowhere". Another stated, "I feel like an alien visiting a world I don't understand and that doesn't understand me, everything is unpredictable, random and frightening" (Slavny-Cross et al., 2022).

The prevalence of autism was finally recognised by the government through the introduction of the Autism Act (2009) and the recommendation that all staff in the CJS receive training in awareness of autism, also reinforced in the 'Independent Review of Mental Health in the Criminal Justice System' (Bradley, 2009). Both recognise the need for police officers to be able to identify the behavioural clues that may indicate someone with autism so that appropriate measures can be taken to ensure they are treated as vulnerable persons by the system. Officers first must be aware of the condition, and then, learn to apply certain techniques in the initial contact or interview which may increase the probability of appropriate responses and lead to a successful outcome of the encounter.

Why might someone with autism encounter the police?

- Offences relating to social naivety
- Offences of an aggressive nature, which are often related to an unexpected change in routine or to the environment, which may cause great anxiety and distress
- People with autism often adhere rigidly to rules and may become extremely agitated if other people break these rules
- Offences relating to a misunderstanding of social cues leading to reactions from others
- Repetition of words or actions annoying people
- Preoccupations with topics, objects, or people
- Problems making choices leaving them confused or scared in public
- Reaction to sensory experience causing a reaction which frightens others
- Wanting to be alone at any cost including becoming missing persons.

A person with autism may not understand the implications of their behaviour or the consequences of their actions, especially if their actions appear aggressive (Archer, 2024). They may run, failing to respond to an order to stop or drop to the floor, and begin rocking back and forth or avoiding eye contact with the officer. Police officers should not misinterpret these actions as a reason for increased use of force, as an autistic person may escalate into meltdown-like behaviour from fear, frustration, or confusion. The individual with autism cannot conceptualise meanness or acts of purposeful injury to others. They just want the circumstances to change and become less frightening but may not have the ability to formulate a way to implement such a change.

Indicators that an individual may have autism (Archer, 2024):

- They may avoid eye contact even if you move to be in their line of sight.
- They may be nonverbal (50% of autistic persons do not speak) or have limited vocabulary.
- They may speak in a monotone without expected inflexions.
- They may repeat exactly what you say.
- They may engage in repetitive physical actions, such as hand flapping, finger flicking, or twirling an object in their hands (stimming actions which may be their means to regulate themselves when anxious).
- They may rock back and forth, pace or engage in self-abuse (meltdowns are an expected response to fear, confusion, anxiety, or frustration as an effort to stop whatever has stimulated it).
- They may have an awkward gait or running style.
- They may not immediately respond to verbal commands or sounds.
- They may not understand your body language or recognise your commanding presence or uniform.
- They may be dressed inappropriately for the weather (they will have preferred items even if not suited to the season).
- They may not ask for help or show indications of pain even if an injury is apparent.
- They may carry an 'Attention' or 'Alert' card issued by an Autism Charity with details about their condition (see the below example).

Suggested responses by the police:

- Approach the person in a quiet non-threatening manner
- Understand that touching may cause a protective 'fight-or-flight' reaction
- Talk in a moderately calm voice
- Instructions should be simple and direct with no use of slang
- Seek all clues as to the cause of the situation and see whether the person is carrying an 'Attention' or 'Alert' card
- Maintain a safe distance until any inappropriate behaviour lessens

When questioned

If officers take a person into custody and even remotely suspect autism, then to reduce the risk they must be treated as vulnerable in line with the requirements of PACE 1984 (The Police and Criminal Evidence Act 1984) and will require constant watch during their stay.

Officers should prepare themselves for the fact that they will be unable to conduct 'normal' Tier 1 or 2 style interviews but may require a skilled vulnerable person trained interviewer to have any hope of achieving any progress. Proving 'Mens Rea' (the guilty mind) in most cases would be extremely difficult. People with autism may lack the skills to imagine the potential outcomes and consequences of their actions. That is not to say they cannot commit a crime; they just may not realise what they have done is wrong.

> *We know of two people whose first imprisonment was for non-paying a bill, both have a Learning Disability, and one person is also autistic. Neither had the capacity to budget or write and post a cheque as it was then. One person ended up feeling less stressed in prison and deliberately got himself imprisoned for the next twenty years. Both people received a small amount of support with everyday living and have been out of trouble for the last 10 years.*
> Local Government Association (2021)

Slavny-Cross et al. (2023) studied the experiences of 145 autistic and 116 non-autistic adults who had been arrested at some point in their lives. Autistic participants were nearly five times more likely to state that they were not given an appropriate adult, even though they believed they needed one, and felt less able to communicate with the police. Autistic participants felt less able to cope with stress, twice as likely to have experienced meltdowns in custody, and five times more likely to have experienced shutdowns because of their criminal justice involvement. We conclude that there are inequalities that autistic people face when navigating the CJS, and the degree to which they can participate effectively in the justice process. This has an impact on their mental health.

Researchers have raised concerns regarding autistic peoples' suggestibility and susceptibility to acceptance of something without protest during police interviews (Gudjonsson & Joyce, 2011; Stancliffe et al., 2015). In Slavny-Cross et al. (2023), autistic participants were more likely than non-autistic participants to agree with the statement "I felt unable to communicate with the police". When asked why they felt unable to communicate with the police, reasons such as finding it difficult to process what was being asked, not trusting the police, feeling 'too stressed', and finding the environment 'too noisy' were all endorsed. These findings highlight the communication difficulties that autistic people face when navigating the CJS. Wallace et al. (2021) found that autistic people are fearful of police contact because of the potential for police to misunderstand autistic behaviours and view these interactions as non-compliance and aggressive.

The lack of support during this time has been highlighted by many researchers, recognising their vulnerabilities. Slavny-Cross et al. (2023) indicated that both autistic and non-autistic participants reported similarly concerning levels of self-harm (35% vs. 24%) and thoughts about ending their life (54% vs. 42%) during the criminal justice process. However, the autistic group felt less able to cope with the stress of being involved with the CJS than the non-autistic participants did. Accessing support during involvement with the CJS is vital to prevent any impact on mental health for both autistic and non-autistic people. Both autistic and non-autistic people felt similarly unable to access the support they needed, which suggests that there is a general lack of support available.

Slavny-Cross et al. (2022) also found that lawyers of autistic defendants reported 29% of their autistic clients received their autism diagnosis during criminal proceedings, and 10% received their diagnosis after proceedings. Indeed, many autistic people are undiagnosed until adulthood, making it difficult for the police to identify them as autistic, and therefore as requiring adjustments and further support. Slavny-Cross et al. (2023) recommended that lawyers should suggest to defendants who they suspect might have autism to seek diagnosis, as it is easier to access support once a diagnosis is in place. That needs should be assessed irrespective of the presence of a diagnosis given the number of undiagnosed autistic adults who are likely to encounter the CJS, and long delays for assessment.

Regarding being stopped by the police, Rava et al. (2017) reported that 19.5% of autistic youth had been stopped and questioned by police by the time they were in their early 20s. Griffiths et al. (2019) reported that 18% of autistic adults had been stopped or arrested by the police. The National Autistic Society (2020b) in their study also found high levels of autistic young people being questioned by the police at home, along with being stopped and cautioned by the police (see Figures 16–18 for supporting data). The sample included 203 autistic people involved with the CJS with 167 family members, along with 40 criminal justice professionals inside and 115 professionals working with autistic people outside the CJS.

The study by National Autistic Society (2020) as noted earlier, highlighted the lack of reasonable adjustments by the police in custody, with providing an appropriate adult (24%) and the use of clear language (15%) being the most cited adjustments. Those that could be available but commonly are not separate waiting areas, more time to process information, easy read forms, and providing an advocate or intermediary. In essence, not enough is being offered for those with autism.

Looking at reasonable adjustments in court, the National Autistic Society (2020) found being told what to expect (29%) and assessment by a psychologist/psychiatrist (29%) to be the two most common adjustments, followed by offering an advocate (14%) and more time to process information (10%). Other allowances that would be helpful are: accommodation when giving verbal instructions, extra breaks during court hearings, opportunities to see the courtroom before the hearing, and a separate waiting time. In essence, again not enough is being offered for those with autism.

Looking at reasonable adjustments in prison, the National Autistic Society (2020) found a huge lack of reasonable adjustments. Choice of cell sharing (15%) and help contacting people (15%) were the most common adjustments, followed by help using services (9%, keyworker with knowledge of autism (9%), and easy-to-read forms (6%). Other allowances rarely offered are buddy schemes, extra support from staff, adjustments for education/employment, and a choice of activities.

In an innovative study by Bagnall et al. (2023), 32 autistic and 33 (age and IQ-matched) non-autistic adults took part in a novel virtual burglary scenario in either an 'innocent' or 'guilty' condition. In a subsequent mock police interview, innocent suspects were instructed to tell the truth about what they did, while guilty suspects were instructed to lie to convince the interviewer of their innocence. Results found investigative interviews are more socially and cognitively demanding for autistic than neurotypical mock suspects. In addition, verbal cues associated with deception can be displayed by autistic mock suspects even when truthful. The development of autism-focused suspect interview techniques is, therefore, crucial to resolving issues of interviewee welfare and the provision of best evidence. Therefore, discriminating between difficulty and deception in autistic suspects' interview accounts will be challenging.

Innocent autistic mock suspects displayed verbal cues associated with deception, as autistic mock suspects who told the truth reported fewer items of verifiable, extricating information to support their innocence, giving fewer verifiable details during an interview is not only consistent with liars' strategies to avoid disprovable claims, and may narrow the options for further investigation and elimination from enquiries. As such, our findings emphasise that investigative interviewers should be cautious when interpreting gaps or missing elements in autistic suspects' accounts. Bagnall et al. (2023) noted that increased anxiety may potentially contribute to autistic people displaying stress-adaptive (although atypical) behaviours during a suspect interview. For example, autistic people (automatically and voluntarily) use gaze aversion and repetitive movement to self-regulate hyperarousal, which may be misinterpreted by police interviewers as deception/lying. Although custody staff and interviewing officers are guided to consider signs of potential vulnerability, an autistic suspect may not be correctly identified due to a lack of specific questions about autism during the 'booking-in' phase in custody, or because a detainee chooses not to disclose being autistic out of concern of stigma. Therefore, a lack of awareness of a suspect's autism may lead to harsher interpretations of their behaviour during the interview.

Young and Brewer (2020) highlighted in their study of 32 diagnosed autistic adults, aged 20–64 years, on five different scenarios (order randomised) in which they assumed the role of a person under suspicion for committing a crime. Their difficulties in these tasks will not only likely lead to innocent suspects being unable to persuade police of their innocence but also impede their attempts to persuade judges and jurors of their innocence should the investigation produce charges against them. Developing an awareness of how autistic characteristics may contribute to biases in the justice system is critical from the perspective of training police and the judiciary and educating jurors in trials. In addition, police, judges, lawyers, and jurors must understand and acknowledge the implications that characteristics often associated with autism may have for the nature of testimony provided and behaviours observed in interview and courtroom settings.

Self-disclosure

Research by Crane et al. (2016) suggests that non-disclosure of existing diagnoses may be much higher, with 39% of their participants not disclosing their autism diagnosis. The decision not to disclose an autism diagnosis was linked to fears that they would experience discrimination and victimisation by police officers. An autistic person may only disclose their autism diagnosis if they are directly asked whether they are autistic. Asking an autistic person if they have a mental disability may not illicit a disclosure of an autism diagnosis, as many autistic people do not view their autism as a disability or mental illness, but rather, as an example of neurodiversity; also this relies on responding to an implied question. This is an example of how an autistic person may only answer questions posed, and unless specifically asked about autism will not self-disclose.

The London Metropolitan Police's records note 891 detainees listed as having autism (Metropolitan Police, 2022a). 2021 data from the same police force notes 391 arrests for people with autism (Metropolitan Police, 2023). This would suggest that autistic people do get involved with the police and do get arrested and, therefore, should be seen as a vulnerable group.

Capacity and culpability for criminal acts

There is no evidence that autism itself is a causal factor in offending behaviour, but features of the condition may predispose some autistic individuals to have contact with the CJS.

Alge (2019) discusses that 'Mens rea' and the 'reasonable man'. To ascribe culpability, criminal law relies on two fundamental elements: the 'actus reus' (guilty act) and the 'mens rea' (guilty mind). Although there are some exceptions, it is a basic tenet of English criminal law that both elements must be present for a defendant to be guilty of an offence, but it is the 'mens rea' (guilty mind) which is key, and provides the moral justification for punishment (Horder, 2016). The definition of 'mens rea' varies greatly depending on the offence in question, and may be dependent upon a defendant's intention, recklessness, or occasionally, negligence. These categories of 'mens rea' are in turn interpreted differently across different offences so that, for example, recklessness in criminal damage is defined differently from recklessness in manslaughter. The result is that a variety of objective, subjective, and twofold tests operate within the criminal law, so that juries and the judiciary may assess the culpability of a defendant's 'guilty mind' against the specific criteria for the offence with which they are charged.

How can we reliably assess an autistic defendant's culpability for an offence whose 'mens rea' is the absence of a reasonable belief in another party's state of mind, when it is precisely this lack of understanding of social communication and empathy which forms part of the diagnostic criteria for autism?

Section 1(2) of the Sexual Offences Act (2003) provides that "[w]hether a belief is reasonable is to be determined having regard to all the circumstances", and it is this caveat which renders the 'mens rea' not wholly objective, which is relevant to autistic defendants. Lord Justice Hughes ([2013] EWCA Crim 3) gives the example of a situation in which reasonableness of a belief could turn on a defendant's ability to read subtle social signals (Mental Health Online, 2013), and indeed in Sultan ([2008] EWCA Crim 6) the defendant was granted a retrial after evidence of his Asperger's syndrome/high-functioning autism had not been considered by the jury in the course of his rape trial (Casemine, 2008).

However, the characteristics of a defendant which may be considered while establishing a reasonable belief are far from settled. A 'wholly irrational' or 'delusional' belief in consent is unlikely to be deemed reasonable (Horder, 2016), but the line between an autistic defendant's obsessive compulsions and the jury's perception of an irrational or delusional belief may be a very fine one. Freckelton (2012) argues that the key to such cases is expert evidence about the "nexus between such conditions and accused persons' criminal responsibility". Given the wide spectrum of the condition, some autistic rape defendants will have an adequate understanding of consent; some may, depending on the context; and others may have extremely limited understanding despite functioning well in other respects. The only workable standard of 'all the circumstances' then becomes a subjective one, supported by medical evidence.

Experiences of court and fitness to plead

Following police contact, autistic suspects may move further through the CJS. They may face high levels of distress in the context of an interrogative interview or courtroom proceedings (North et al., 2008). Woodhouse et al. (2024) note that the sensory aspects of the courtroom (such as lighting and noise) can cause significant sensory overload and distress for autistic individuals, which may lead to negative experiences and/or difficulties with engagement, for example, an autistic 'shutdown' might leave an autistic person unable to communicate and a 'meltdown' might leave jurors thinking they are being obstructive and violent. These reactions to sensory overload may be misinterpreted by jurors, the judge, or prosecutor as indications of guilt or demonstrating deliberate acts of antisocial behaviour (Allely & Cooper, 2017; Berryessa, 2020).

Judges and juries often lack appropriate lived experience, knowledge, and awareness of how autistic characteristics impact offending behaviour, including criminal intent, behavioural control, and false perceptions about the potential for violence and aggression, and may lead to incorrect judgements (Berryessa, 2014, 2020; Caliman & Berryessa, 2023). Legal professionals tasked with supporting their clients may also lack appropriate knowledge. As a result, concerns have been raised as to whether the needs of autistic individuals are being met during criminal trials and whether juries may form inaccurate views of defendants (Berryessa, 2017; Cea, 2014).

Chaplin et al. (2017) highlight the need for police and court training to identify autistic behaviours in suspects and to take appropriate action to gain an assessment ideally before it reaches a court setting, the following case study highlights questionable behaviours and whether a suspect is 'fit to plead' in court. They question whether specialist court staff are available to make advice for such judgements, if not, then vulnerable suspects will not be treated fairly in a court setting. Chaplin et al. (2021) suggest such a service is possible, and in a trial, it reduced the number of cases going to court by dealing with them through diversion and liaison services. They note, "One of the main barriers to implementing such a model will be identifying sufficient professionals with the expertise to work in court settings with defendants with neurodiverse disorders".

Brewer et al. (2016) argue that there is recognition that for autistic individuals who are in contact with the courts, there is a lack of professionals trained to understand their special needs and vulnerabilities (Archer & Hurley, 2013; National Autistic Society, 2011). This is problematic when the difficulties individuals with autism experience are considered in relation to whether they will have a fair experience of the CJS. It is becoming increasingly common for mental health professionals (namely psychiatrists and psychologists) to be called to educate courts about autistic individuals accused of criminal conduct (Freckleton, 2013). However, it is also noted that while there are some signs of progress towards raising understanding of autism within the CJS, this is still locality-dependent (Archer & Hurley, 2013).

Autism can affect the individual's mental capacity and level of responsibility as well as the ability to be tried in a court of law (Berney, 2004). There is a lack of research specifically considering autistic individuals and 'fitness to plead'. It has been suggested that a detailed and reliable assessment of the individual's strengths and weaknesses is essential in concluding the person's capacity to make legal decisions (Murphy, 2010).

Records are hard to source, but the number of defendants found unfit to plead in England and Wales is so low (around 100 out of over 100,000 Crown Court defendants: 0.1% per year) that there is considerable professional concern that the procedure and test for identifying unfit defendants in England and Wales is not fit for purpose (Brewer et al., 2016; Rogers et al., 2008; Shah, 2012).

The Pritchard criteria fails to consider either decision-making capacity or individual autonomy, both of which have become increasingly relevant in clinical practice and civil proceedings (Brown et al., 2016). It is argued by Brewer et al. (2016) that mental health professionals are inconsistent in applying the legal criteria in their clinical assessments, making the clinical assessment of fitness-to-plead unreliable. Such concerns have led the Law Commission of England and Wales to publish two consultation papers in the area, which proposed significant legal and procedural reform. This includes the key recommendations that the Pritchard criteria should be replaced by a new legal test and that a defined psychiatric test to assist in the assessment of fitness to plead should be developed (Law Commission, 2010, 2014).

Case study (Chaplin et al., 2017)

Alf is a 30-year-old man with autism who stabbed his flatmate after believing he was colluding with the neighbourhood children by allowing them to play football at the front of the house, which was not the case. Following several heated exchanges and difficulty coping with the noise of the ball banging against the wall, he attacks his flatmate by punching him and saying, "make them stop". Whilst being assessed in court, he refuses to have someone represent him or to answer questions believing he had done nothing wrong. He believes his flatmate should be the one being sent to court as he lets children play outside the house when there is a sign stating clearly that ball

> *games on the green and in the close are strictly forbidden. Any attempts to interview or engage in reciprocal conversation are not possible as he is clear about what he has done and keeps repeating that he stabbed his flatmate who was breaking the rules. He is happy to tell people what happened but refuses to be cross-examined as he says it is unnecessary.*

Helm's (2021) study of legal professionals about enhanced vulnerable children and their pleas is indicated in Figure 10.1, which suggests this vulnerable group may struggle with the plea and court process and may plead guilty when they are not, to avoid a long trial. Pleading guilty via a 'plea bargain' can reduce any possible sentence by a third in length. Defence solicitors noted:

- "Clients with ADHD or Autism need very careful advice because the nature of the disorders means that clients can be both entrenched and very suggestible. In my experience, pleas have been mixed."
- "Often they enter early guilty pleas and have not been properly assessed and given adequate measures to ensure effective participation."
- "Some clients struggle with the thought of giving evidence, which may make them more likely to plead guilty. This is not solved by an intermediary at the point of the plea decision as it is another delay and meeting with an intermediary is seen as another hurdle for them to deal with. Many defendants give the impression that they just want to get the case over as quickly as possible, even if a guilty plea is the only way to do it. There is no way of knowing to what extent that is the real concern or if it is a euphemistic way to phrase a desire to plead

Have you noticed differences in plea decisions in childern with Autism, ADHD, or other disorders when compared to other children?
19 responses from legal professionals

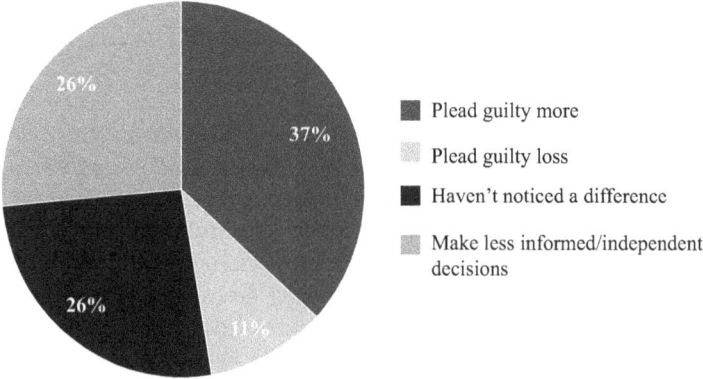

- Plead guilty more
- Plead guilty loss
- Haven't noticed a difference
- Make less informed/independent decisions

Figure 10.1 Differences in plea decisions according to SEND needs (Helm, 2021).

guilty, particularly with an appropriate adult there. Some defendants will insist on this, even where they have a runnable trial."

- "Respondents also noted how children with behavioural or developmental disorders may struggle to understand the guilty plea process, may feel set in their preferences regardless of advice, or evidence, or maybe overly reliant on parents or guardians. Yes. It is harder for young people with disorders to make informed decisions and they are less likely to plead guilty because they don't understand the implications/reduction in sentence for an early guilty plea".

Miscarriage of justice

There have been several cases where autism has not been taken seriously by the police and courts, which calls into account whether those with autism are treated fairly, and their prosecution legally sound.

RNZ (2022) and the Supreme Court of New Zealand (2022) highlight the case of Alan Hall who spent 19 years in prison for a murder he did not commit. He was sentenced to 36 years. However, in 2022 when New Zealand's highest court – the supreme court – quashed Hall's conviction because there had been a "substantial miscarriage of justice". Chief Justice Helen Winkelmann told the court that the crown's departure from accepted standards must "either be the result of extreme incompetence or of a deliberate and wrongful strategy to secure conviction". When Hall was arrested, police subjected him to lengthy interrogations, on one occasion for eight hours, and another for 15 hours, without a lawyer or support person present. He gave several different answers about no longer having the bayonet and his beanie in his possession, and these differing explanations were seen as evidence of guilt. Allely et al. (2024) commented that "it is imperative that ASD is identified and taken into consideration as early as possible during the criminal justice process. Failure to do so may contribute to a miscarriage of justice occurring, as it did for Alan Hall".

Innovative DAAY Court programme (Detention Alternatives for Autistic Youth Court)

Rava et al. (2017) note that by the time a child with autism reaches the age of 21, around 20% of them have been subjected to police questioning, and almost 5% have faced arrest. Those arrested, as indicated by Bowden et al. (2022), are at a higher risk of being charged with serious crimes, including offences against individuals and property, compared to non-autistic samples.

A judge in Las Vegas in 2008, inspired by research and direct encounters with autism children (Diaz, 2024), has taken action to address this issue by implementing a programme aimed at guiding vulnerable youth, part of the Las Vegas Eighth Judicial District's diversion programme. This initiative not only aims to prevent the perpetual cycle of incarceration among autism children but also to provide them with the necessary resources that will lead to their overall improvement. Its aim is as a diversionary court, to prevent young people with autism from entering the

CJS, combining the efforts of social workers, psychologists, attorneys, and parents to help the young people at risk.

The DAAY Court is a court-supervised programme for youth involved in the juvenile justice system with a primary diagnosis of autism. This programme addresses the client's access to appropriate services in a timely manner to reduce recidivism in the juvenile justice system (Clark County Court, 2024).

Many of the cases that come into Judge Bailey's courtroom are those of minors facing charges of battery, usually against their family members. Bailey's daughter has autism so was more aware of the issues at play. So instead of going into juvenile detention, autistic young people can choose to attend DAAY Court. Many of the young people who enter the programme get some form of therapy where they learn safe methods to deal with their emotions without losing control. They also can join after-school programmes with other at-risk kids to help with socialising.

In 2024, Nevada Governor Joe Lombardo officially recognised the programme, allowing it to get more funding. Lombardo's signature on Senate Bill 411 also allowed other jurisdictions across Nevada to create their own DAAY Court programme. So far, it seems to be working, as 86 children have graduated from the programme, with just six returning to court.

Case study (Diaz, 2024)

Angeleena has autism, frontal lobe epilepsy, mild cerebral palsy, ADHD, and anxiety. She has trouble with impulse control, leading to emotional and violent outbursts. It's been that way for a long time, Melody says. One especially bad time was when Angelina grabbed a steak knife and held it to her mother's face.

Her mother says "We went through this multiple times. The police have been called to my house 43 times". Her mother tried for years to get her daughter help, even calling treatment centres out of state, only to be told that they couldn't accommodate her daughter. "Nobody would take Angeleena. I felt like I was hitting a brick wall". After police came to her house in the winter of 2022 and Angeleena was arrested again, things changed. "I am so grateful that I called the police, and she got arrested. Isn't that a horrible thing to say? That changed everything for me". Her mother concludes "It was a life-changer, literally a life-changer. I can say that she probably would not be living with me today or alive today if I hadn't had DAAY Court".

References

Alge, D. (2019). *Autism, culpability and the criminal law.* 5(1). Retrieved 29/07/2024. https://repository.uwl.ac.uk/id/eprint/6189/1/Alge_New_Vistas_0501_2019_Autism,_culpability_and_the_criminal_law.pdf

Allely, C. S., McKinnel, T., & Chisnall, N. (2024). The contributory role of an autistic presentation to miscarriage of justice in a high-profile murder case in New Zealand. *Psychiatry, Psychology and Law, 31*(6), 1098–1113. https://doi.org/10.1080/13218719.2023.2260846

Allely, C.S. (2019c). *Sexual offending behaviour in young people with intellectual disabilities and autism spectrum disorder.* University of Salford. Retrieved 18/06/2024.

Allely, C.S., & Cooper, P. (2017). Jurors' and judges' evaluation of defendants with autism and the impact on sentencing: A systematic Preferred Reporting Items for Systematic Reviews and Meta-analyses (PRISMA) review of autism spectrum disorder in the courtroom. *Journal of Law and Medicine, 25*(1), 105–123.

Archer, N. (2024). When two different worlds collide (autism spectrum conditions and the criminal justice system). *Autism West Midlands.* Retrieved 05/07/2024. https://livingautism.com/two-different-worlds-collide-autism-spectrum-conditions-criminal-justice-system/

Archer, N., & Hurley, E.A. (2013). A justice system failing the autistic community. *Journal of Intellectual Disabilities and Offending Behaviour, 4*, 53–59. https://doi.org/10.1108/JIDOB-02-2013-0003

Bagnall, R., Cadman, A., Russell, A., Brosnan, M., Otte, M., & Maras, K.L. (2023). Police suspect interviews with autistic adults: The impact of truth telling versus deception on testimony. *Frontiers in Psychology, 14*, 1117415. https://doi.org/10.3389/fpsyg.2023.1117415

Berney, T.P. (2004). Asperger syndrome from childhood into adulthood. *Advances in Psychiatric Treatment, 10*, 341–351. https://doi.org/10.1192/apt.10.5.341

Berryessa, C.M. (2014). Judicial perceptions of media portrayals of offenders with high functioning autistic spectrum disorders. *International Journal of Criminology and Sociology, 3*, 46.

Berryessa, C.M. (2017). Educator of the court: The role of the expert witness in cases involving autism spectrum disorder. *Psychology, Crime & Law, 23*(6), 575–600.

Berryessa, C.M. (2020). Defendants with autism spectrum disorder in criminal court: A judges' toolkit. *Drexel Law Review, 13*, 841.

Bowden, N., Milne, B., Audas, R., Clasby, B., Dacombe, J., Forster, W., Kokaua, J., Gibb, S., Hughes, N., MacCormick, C., Smiler, K., Taylor, B., & Mirfin-Veitch, B. (2022). Criminal justice system interactions among young adults with and without autism: A national birth cohort study in New Zealand. *Autism.* 2022 October, *26*(7), 1783–1794. https://doi.org/10.1177/13623613211065541. Epub 2021 Dec 28. PMID: 34961358; PMCID: PMC9483704.

Brewer, R.J., Davies, G.M., & Blackwood, N.J. (2016). Fitness to plead: The impact of autism spectrum disorder. *Journal of Forensic Psychology Practice, 16*(3), 182–197. https://doi.org/10.1080/15228932.2016.1177285

Brown, P., Stahl, D., Appiah-Kusi, E., Brewer, R., Watts, M., Peay, J., & Blackwood, N. (2016). The fitness to plead assessment tool: Development and validation of a standardised instrument to assess the psycholegal capacities required to stand trial in England and Wales. Unpublished paper.

Caliman, Carolina R and Berryessa, Colleen, Legal Decision-Makers in Criminal Cases involving Autism Spectrum Disorder: A Review of the Research and a Call for Action (2023). *Forthcoming 2023, C.R. Caliman and C.M. Berryessa. Legal Decision-makers in Criminal Cases involving Autism Spectrum Disorder: A Review of the Research and a Call for Action. In B. Bornstein and M.K. Miller, Advances in Psychology and Law (Vol. 7). Springer.*

Casemine (2008). Sultan ([2008] EWCA Crim 6). Retrieved 29/07/2024. https://www.casemine.com/judgement/uk/5a8ff6f860d03e7f57ea4dd6

Cea, C.N. (2014). Autism and the criminal defendant. *Johns Law Review, 88*, 495.

Chaplin, E., McCarthy, J., & Forrester, A. (2017). Defendants with autism spectrum disorders: What is the role of court liaison and diversion? *Advances in Autism*, *3*(4), 220–228. https://doi.org/10.1108/aia-08-2017-0018

Chaplin, E., McCarthy, J., Marshall-Tate, K., Ali, S., Xenitidis, K., Childs, J., Harvey, D., McKinnon, I., Robinson L., Hardy, S., Srivastava, S., Allely, C.S., Tolchard, B., & Forrester, A. (2021). Evaluation of a liaison and diversion Court Mental Health Service for defendants with neurodevelopmental disorders. *Research in Developmental Disabilities*. 2021 December, *119*, 104103. https://doi.org/10.1016/j.ridd.2021.104103. Epub 2021 Oct 7. PMID: 34628339.

Clark County Court (2024). Eighth judicial district detention. *Alternative for Autistic Youth Court (DAAY)*. Retrieved 05/08/2024. https://www.clarkcountycourts.us/res/specialty-courts/DAAY_Flyer.pdf

Crane, L., Maras, K.L., Hawken, T., Mulcahy, S., & Memon, A. (2016). Experiences of autism spectrum disorder and policing in England and Wales: Surveying police and the autism community. *Journal of Autism and Developmental Disorders*, *46*(6), 2028–2041. https://doi.org/10.1007/s10803-016-2729-1

Diaz, J. (2024). This court program helps at-risk youth with autism avoid juvenile detention. 22 February 2024. 4:16 PM ET. Retrieved 29/07/2024. https://www.npr.org/2024/02/22/1233217782/court-program-for-autistic-youth

Equality and Human Rights Commission (2020). Inclusive justice: A system designed for all. June. Retrieved 05/07/2024. https://www.equalityhumanrights.com/sites/default/files/ehrc_inclusive_justice_a_system_designed_for_all_june_2020.pdf

Freckelton, I. (2012). Expert evidence by mental health professionals: The communication challenge posed by evidence about autism spectrum disorder, brain injuries, and huntington's disease. *International Journal of Law and Psychiatry*, *35*, 372–379.

Freckleton, I. (2013). Autism spectrum disorder: forensic issues and challenges for mental health professionals and courts. *Journal of Applied Research in Intellectual Disabilities: JARID*, *26*, 420–434. 10.1111/jar.12036.

Griffiths, S., Allison, C., Kenny, R., Holt, R., Smith, P., & Baron-Cohen, S. (2019). The Vulnerability Experiences Quotient (VEQ): A study of vulnerability, mental health and life satisfaction in autistic adults. *Autism Research*, *12*(10), 1516–1528. https://doi.org/10.1002/aur.2162

Gudjonsson, G., & Joyce, T. (2011). Interviewing adults with intellectual disabilities. *Advances in Mental Health and Intellectual Disabilities*, *5*(2), 16–21. https://doi.org/10.5042/amhid.2011.0108

Helm, R. (2021). Incentivized legal admissions in children part 2: Guilty pleas. Retrieved 22/10/2022. https://evidencebasedjustice.exeter.ac.uk/wp-content/uploads/2021/09/Child GuiltyPleas_FullReport.pdf

Horder, J. (2016). *Ashworth's Principles of the Criminal Law*. Oxford: OUP.

Law Commission. (2010). *Unfitness to plead (Consultation Paper no.197)*. London, England: The Stationery Office.

Law Commission. (2014). *Unfitness to plead: An issues paper*. London, England: The Stationary Office.

Local Government Association (2021). People with a learning disability and autism in the criminal justice system. Local Government Association. Retrieved 07/05/25. www.local.gov.uk/publications/people-learning-disability-and-autism-criminal-justice-system

Mental Health Online (2013). B v R [2013] EWCA Crim 3, [2013] MHLO 7. Retrieved 29/07/24. https://www.mentalhealthlaw.co.uk/B_v_R_(2013)_EWCA_Crim_3,_(2013)_MHLO_7#:~:text=HUGHES%20LJ%20said%2C%20in%20the,if%20there%20might%2C%20independently%20of

Metropolitan Police (2022a). People with autism arrested for violent crime in 2021. Retrieved 19/06/2024. https://www.met.police.uk/foi-ai/metropolitan-police/d/march-2022/people-with-autism-arrested-for-violent-crime-in-2021/

Metropolitan Police (2022b). Autistic-individuals-under-arrest-strip-searched-2020. Retrieved 29/07/2024. https://www.met.police.uk/SysSiteAssets/foi-media/metropolitan-police/disclosure_2022/september_2022/autistic-individuals-under-arrest-strip-searched-2020.xlsx

Metropolitan Police (2023). People-autism-arrested-violent-crime-2021. Retrieved 29/07/2024. https://www.met.police.uk/SysSiteAssets/foi-media/metropolitan-police/disclosure_2022/march_2022/people-autism-arrested-violent-crime-2021.xlsx

Murphy, D. (2010). Understanding offenders with autism-spectrum disorders: What can forensic services do? *Advances in Psychiatric Treatment, 16*, 44–46.

National Autistic Society. (2011). Criminal justice system and ASDs. Retrieved 26/03/2013. https://www.autism.org.uk/working-with/criminal-justice/criminal-justice-system-and-asds.aspx

National Autistic Society (2020a). Obsessions and repetitive behaviour – A guide for all audiences. 14 August 2020. Retrieved 26/07/2024. https://www.autism.org.uk/advice-and-guidance/topics/behaviour/obsessions/all-audiences

National Autistic Society (2020b). Youth justice report. 6 October 2022. Retrieved 14/07/2024. https://www.autism.org.uk/what-we-do/news/youth-justice-report

North, A.S., Russell, A.J., & Gudjonsson, G.H. (2008). High functioning autism spectrum disorders: An investigation of psychological vulnerabilities during interrogative interview. *The Journal of Forensic Psychiatry & Psychology, 19*(3), 323–334.

Payne, K.L., Maras, K.,L. Russell, A.J., & Brosnan, M.J. (2020). Self-reported motivations for offending by autistic sexual offenders. *Autism.* 2020 February, *24*(2), 307–320. https://doi.org/10.1177/1362361319858860. Epub 2019 Jun 28. PMID: 31250659.

Payne, K.L., Russell, A., Mills, R., Maras, K., Rai, D., & Brosnan M. (2019). Is there a relationship between cyber-dependent crime, autistic-like traits and autism? *Journal of Autism and Developmental Disorders.* 2019 October, *49*(10), 4159–4169. https://doi.org/10.1007/s10803-019-04119-5. PMID: 31267290; PMCID: PMC6751221.

Rava, J., Shattuck, P., Rast, J., & Roux, A. (2017). The prevalence and correlates of involvement in the criminal justice system among youth on the autism spectrum. *Journal of Autism and Developmental Disorders, 47*(2), 340–346. https://doi.org/10.1007/s10803-016-2958-3

RNZ (2022). Alan Hall's murder conviction quashed after 37 years. 8 June 2022. Retrieved 11/08/2024. https://www.rnz.co.nz/news/national/468736/alan-hall-s-murder-conviction-quashed-after-37-years

Rogers, T.P., Blackwood, N.J., Farnham, F., Pickup, G.J., & Watts, M.J. (2008). Fitness to plead and competence to stand trial: A systematic review of the constructs and their application. *Journal of Forensic Psychiatry & Psychology, 19*, 576–596. https://doi.org/10.1080/14789940801947909

Shah, A. (2012). Making fitness to plead fit for purpose. *International Journal of Criminology and Sociology, 1*, 176–197.

Slavny-Cross, R., Allison, C., Griffiths, S., & Baron-Cohen, S. (2022). Autism and the criminal justice system: An analysis of 93 cases. *Autism Research*, 1–11. https://doi.org/10.1002/aur.2690

Slavny-Cross, R., Allison, C., Griffiths, S., & Baron-Cohen, S. (2023). Are *autistic people disadvantaged by the criminal justice system? a case comparis*on. Autism: *The International Journal of Research and Practice.* Jul 2023, 27(5), 1438–1448.

Stancliffe, R.J., Tichá, R., Larson, S.A., Hewitt, A.S., & Nord, D. (2015). Responsiveness to self-report interview questions by adults with intellectual and developmental disability. *Intellectual and Developmental Disabilities*, *53*(3), 163–181. https://doi.org/10.1352/1934-9556-53.3.163

Supreme Court of New Zealand (2022). Oral Judgement of the court. Retrieved 11/08/2024. https://www.courtsofnz.govt.nz/assets/cases/2022/2022-NZSC-71.pdf

The Bradley Report (2009). Independent review of people with mental health problems or learning disabilities in the criminal justice system. April 2009. Retrieved 05/07/2024. https://lx.iriss.org.uk/sites/default/files/resources/The%20Bradley%20report.pdf

Wallace, D., Herbert, J., Tyler, D., & McGee-Hassrick, E. (2021). Interactions between individuals on the autism spectrum and the police: The fears of parents, caregivers, and professionals. *Policing: A Journal of Policy and Practice*, *15*, 950–964. https://doi.org/10.1093/police/paaa059

Woodhouse, E., Hollingdale, J., Davies, L.,Zainab Al-Attar, Susan Young, Luke P. Vinter, Kwaku Agyemang, Carla Bartlett, Colleen Berryessa, Eddie Chaplin, Quinton Deeley, Ian Freckelton, Felicity Gerry, Gisli Gudjonsson, Katie Maras, Michelle Mattison, Jane McCarthy, Richard Mills, Peter Misch, David Murphy & Clare Allely. (2024). Identification and support of autistic individuals within the UK Criminal Justice System: A practical approach based upon professional consensus with input from lived experience. *BMC Medicine*, *22*, 157. https://doi.org/10.1186/s12916-024-03320-3

Young, R.L., & Brewer, N. (2020). Brief report: Perspective taking deficits, autism spectrum disorder, and allaying police officers' suspicions about criminal involvement. *Journal of Autism and Developmental Disorders*. 2020 June, *50*(6), 2234–2239. https://doi.org/10.1007/s10803-019-03968-4. PMID: 30830490.

11 The Study and Results

Methodology

This book uses two online questionnaires (see Appendices 2 and 3): one for adults with autism, and another for parents with autistic children. Each survey offered participants the option to be interviewed, giving consent and anonymity for their responses (consent was recorded on their questionnaire forms).

Only adults older than 18 years were interviewed. At the start of each interview, consent was again requested, and the interviews were to be recorded. The interviewer again repeated that anonymity would be provided for their interviews, with the option of participants not answering any question posed. Data was stored on a password-secure computer. As this was a private research project and not conducted through a university, no ethics committee application was sought. The author has a PhD and has experience with successful ethics committee applications and is a member of an ethics committee himself. No quotes were used, but each interview helped to formulate the chapters being written and as confirmation of the topics being investigated. The interview script was semi-structured and drawn from the online questionnaire items., each interview took approximately one hour in length.

Participants were approached via Facebook and in-person autism-related groups. Whilst the samples were not large ($N = 15$ adult survey, $N = 10$ parent survey), this reflects the sensitive nature of the survey, asking about meltdowns, abuse experienced, and criminal activity. Whilst the lack of responses is noted, there are many case studies featured in this book.

In addition, the author has used social media contacts (Facebook and Linkedin) to gain expert interview participants. These interviews allow expert views of the subject matter being investigated, namely crime, meltdowns, restraint, sexual crimes, and autism in general. Each expert interview has helped to formulate the chapters of this book, and whilst no quotes have been used from them, they have been very useful in confirming the book was heading in the right direction.

Results

Results will be discussed as being from the autistic 'adult sample', and the 'parent sample' regarding their autistic child.

DOI: 10.4324/9781003614432-11

Sample

The adult sample contained roughly 50% males and 50% females; however, in the parent sample it was mainly females (mothers) that responded. I noted an error in that I did not record the gender of their autistic child.

73% of the adult sample participants were in the 31–50-year age group, with 20% being in the 12–18-year age group. In the parent survey, parents were mainly talking about children in the 12–18-year age group (50%) and then the 5–11-year age group.

60% of the adult group was in England compared to 90% of the parent group. 20% of the parent group were outside the UK and Europe, and 13% in Scotland and Wales.

Autism

60% of the adult sample had a formal diagnosis compared to 90% of the parent-led sample.

33% of the parent sample had been diagnosed by the NHS and 27% diagnosed privately. In the parent sample, 60% of their autistic children had been diagnosed by the NHS (CAMHS) and 30% privately.

47% of the adult sample had been diagnosed when they were 31–50 years old, and another 20% when they were 12–18 years old. In the parent's sample children, 60% were diagnosed between the ages of 5 and 11 years old, and another 30% between the ages of 12–18 years old.

60% of both adult and parent samples saw autism as a condition (social model of disability) and 40% as a disorder (medical model of disability). This suggests both groups see the unique qualities that autism brings, being part of their personality.

Of the strengths that come with autism, adults saw the following as major strengths:

- A strong sense of justice (I have a strong sense of justice and will fight and be vocal for what I think is right.)
- Loyalty (I'm fiercely loyal. Once I let you into my heart, you can trust me implicitly.)

Parents saw the following as major strengths in their autistic children:

- Expertise in their favourite topics (My special interest has been a way for me to succeed in education and my career, even when the social and psychological odds were stacked against me from the start.)
- Honesty (I feel like due to my autism I am probably the most trustworthy, honest, and loyal person anyone could ever meet, I genuinely feel.)

Asking 'How does Autism affect you?' Adults saw the following as major effects:

- Not seeming to understand what others are thinking or feeling

- Having a very keen interest in certain subjects or activities
- Finding it hard to make friends or preferring to be on their own
- Finding it hard to say how you feel

Parents saw the following as major effects in their autistic children:

- Not seeming to understand what others are thinking or feeling
- Having a very keen interest in certain subjects or activities
- Finding it hard to say how you feel

Regarding 'who' triggered the autism diagnosis. The adult sample said that it was very mixed, with 27% by adults themselves, and 20% by both their doctor/mental health worker and family members. With parents it was evenly split: their child (30%), parents (30%), and the school (30%).

Regarding coping with their autism, the main strategies by both adult and parent samples were:

- Hiding some signs of autism by copying how others behave and play
- Withdrawing in situations they find difficult

Parents noted the events that triggered the diagnosis in their child were:

- Showing signs of severe anxiety
- Several prolonged stress sick leaves
- Poor mental health in the workplace linked to meltdowns, etc.
- A repeated cycle of burnout that I have been trying to figure out the root cause of
- Mental health crisis and exhaustion from masking all my life
- One of my much younger cousins was diagnosed early. I realised that many of the things he did that triggered the diagnosis were things I had done as a child as well
- Family fall out and thinking things differently to my siblings
- My study and work recognise traits
- I was struggling in life
- When I was in prison the special needs department referred me for assessment on release
- Was unwell
- Struggling with moving to secondary school

Parents noted triggers for their child's diagnosis were:

- Isolating him/herself
- Eating disorder
- Unable to socialise
- Yes, when we went to see a paediatrician regarding attention-deficit/hyperactivity disorder (ADHD), she referred us

- Adoption, post-adoption behaviours
- Being on holiday and a stranger (who worked with autistic children) commenting on how well I was coping with my son
- Mother (me) got her diagnosis at age 56, referred child aged 9 for diagnosis, finally diagnosed at age 12
- The way she reacted to her rabbit dying
- Not wanting to do schoolwork, far behind in schoolwork it is too hard
- Emotional dysregulation in all situations of challenge, speech impairment, low gait and muscle tone, anger outbursts, and hurting peers.

33% of the adult sample also had ADHD and 47% had mental health issues. In the parent sample, 50% of their children also had ADHD and 20% had mental health issues. Interestingly, 80% of the adult sample were on medication for related autism issues, compared to 90% of the parent/child sample, a surprisingly high number. 73% of the adult group had/or currently self-medicated to cope with their autism.

Interestingly, 70% of the adult sample felt that they struggled with addictions; alcohol and illegal drugs were frequently mentioned, for example,

- I have had difficulties with addiction to alcohol, illegal drugs (cannabis), caffeine, and sex/masturbation. All these things are great for stimming/ emotional regulation but can be unhealthy in excess. The trick is regulating my use of them.
- Alcohol helps with my sensory process if the environment is too loud and chaotic
- Lots of drinking and cannabis use to cope with social situations when I was young
- Alcohol really helps with my sensory process if the environment is too loud and chaotic.

Parents noted fewer addictions in their children, with 80% saying no; however, one parent noted:

- Gaming, social media, and vaping

School

Adults noted only 20% of their teachers recognised their autism in primary school, and 27% in secondary school. Parents noted that 60% of their child's teachers recognised their autism in primary school, but only 40% of their secondary school teachers.

Unfortunately, 94% of adults said that they gained no help in school for their autism, compared to parents talking about their children, with 30% gaining no help. Of the 70% of parents who said their child gained support this was mainly:

- Extra time
- Movement breaks

- Fidget toys
- A standing desk
- Wobble cushion
- Use of devices (laptop, iPad, tablet)

Both the adult and parent samples felt they were unfairly blamed for their (child's) 'impulsiveness' at school 50% of the time, and 87% of adults and 80% of parents felt they were blamed for things out of their control (autistic traits).

Adults felt that very few of their teachers understood autism, compared to 'some' in parents talking about their child's teachers, indicating more awareness in today's teachers.

Interestingly, 33% of adults said that they were suspended/expelled from school, compared to 40% of parents talking about their autistic children. Reasons noted by the adults with autism were:

- Too difficult to deal with, they didn't know how to deal with a 16-year-old girl having multiple panic attacks and meltdowns causing severe issues such as going mute.
- I got suspended (I think a few times). If I got a detention, I would not go and it would escalate to a suspension. I also think I got suspended for repeatedly not going to school (which makes no sense as a punishment, but it worked for me).
- I did not go into lessons with a boy who was rude to me, and I walked out when I got overwhelmed.
- In retrospect, I'd call it autistic burnout. It's only recently that this has a name.
- I only focused on lessons I found interesting that's why.

Parents noted the following reasons in their children:

- Impulsiveness led to my child hitting and hurting some children when he was unable to express emotions correctly
- Not being understood
- Resulting from throwing chairs

Whilst none of the autistic adults noted being suspended/expelled, parents commented on it in more cases in their children.

91% of adults with autism thought autistic young people are drawn to drugs by mixing with negative social groups, parents thought this was in 67% of cases regarding their autistic children.

A large percentage of both adults with autism and parents felt that half or more of young people in pupil referral units/alternative education were autistic.

Meltdowns/shutdowns

Looking at meltdowns/shutdowns at school, adults with autism recall the following were their main triggers:

- Sensory overload: noise/smell

- Stress and anxiety about their day
- Communication difficulties: not being understood
- Being overwhelmed by multiple tasks
- Things not going to plan
- Unexpected requests of them by teachers

Parents thought their child's main triggers at school were:

- Bullying
- Sensory overload: noise/smell
- Unexpected events, for example, a fire alarm
- Unexpected changes to routine, for example, supply teachers/change of seating/ friends not at school
- Stress and anxiety about their day
- Communication difficulties: not being understood
- Being overwhelmed by multiple tasks
- Things not going to plan
- Unexpected requests of them by teachers

These meltdowns manifested mainly as 'assaults on other children/students' with both the adult autistic and parent groups. Parents also noted 'damage to property and assaults on other children', in 25% of cases. Adults with autism also noted that they ran away because of meltdowns.

Interestingly, because of meltdowns, adults noted it caused their peers to avoid them, and extra help to be offered in class and during unstructured times. Parents, regarding their children, also noted peers avoiding them and extra help in class (but not during unstructured times), but increased suspensions and exclusions.

Adults with autism noted their triggers were now mainly unexpected changes to their routine, stress and anxiety about their day, and being overwhelmed by multiple requests; this resulted in meltdowns with property damage, assaults on others, stealing, withdrawal from situations, and getting very angry. They pointed out that in most cases this resulted in friends/others avoiding them.

Looking at the responses of parents regarding meltdowns/shutdowns in public, these were caused by sensory overload (noise, smell) and things not going to plan. This resulted in property damage, and other children and adults getting hurt. Parents noted in all cases they were perceived they be indirectly/directly blamed as bad parents.

Victimisation

As children, the adult sample noted all had received emotional abuse by other children and parents, followed by physical abuse. Parents of autistic children noted very high cases of physical abuse and then emotional abuse in their child, from both other children and adults, some may have been teachers or support staff. Case studies in this book have noted that less qualified support staff have been the perpetrators of such abuse. Interesting schools tend to place the least qualified staff with the neediest young people, and in cases of students with autism, many teachers perceive the learning support staff to be the main educators for the child in their classrooms, allowing them to focus on other learners. Legally the teacher has the ultimate duty towards all learners in their classroom and they are responsible for managing the interventions by learning support staff; however, this does not tend to happen due to large class sizes and overworked teaching staff.

Risk factors of crime

The autistic adults felt that late diagnosis of autism and bullying as a child, and in some cases child abuse, had led them towards criminal acts. The parents noted that the factors that they felt led their child into crime would be a diagnosis of autism that came too late.

Police involvement

By some margin, 5–11 years old was the time when most autistic adults were first spoken to/arrested by the police, followed by 12–18 years old. Forty percent of the autistic adults said that they were involved with criminal activities, of whom 50% responded to the question about criminal activities. Violence towards others and stealing are the main crimes committed, followed by violence towards property and drug use/drug dealing as lesser crimes committed. This disparity may come from adults not classifying certain acts as criminal, such as drug use.

When asking why autistic adults may become involved with crime, the following reasons were suggested:

- "Not feeling fully integrated into society, making it easier to accept behaviour not accepted by society."
- "I think it's complex and depends on a lot more factors than neurotype: class race and gender are all much larger factors. I do think there is a strong link between undiagnosed autism and substance abuse, but I also believe this should be treated as a public health concern rather than a criminal one."
- "I think our brains are different."
- "I see many autistic women in jail so there must be a link... People think we don't want to engage but we communicate differently which can lead to being misunderstood... therefore a meltdown occurs for one example."
- "While I definitely accept responsibility for my actions, I do feel the need to copy what others are doing to fit in resonates (maybe) more strongly in Autistic people. If the Autistic person has found themselves with a group of anti-social people, then the desire to copy the behaviours and 'fit in/be accepted' may quite easily outweigh the punishment for the crime, particularly at a younger age, when the full ramifications are not understood."

Only 7% of the autistic adults had been in prison, and this was when they were 19–30 years old, being there 1–5 times. Interestingly, 25% of the autistic adult sample had experienced being in care.

Conclusion

Both survey responses reflect the empirical chapters in this book: the lack of support and awareness in school, and the lack of understanding of meltdowns, victimisation, and abuse due to their difference.

Interestingly, both the adults and parents of autistic children said that because of their meltdowns, they were excluded by their peers and friends. It was also felt unfair that parents were seen as 'bad parents' due to their child's meltdowns in public.

The indications of the many triggers regarding meltdowns reflect the empirical data found in other studies. This suggests that many triggers at school could be avoided (fire alarms, unexpected changes to the school day, not being understood, noise and smells, and unexpected requests by teachers).

Also surprising was the young age (5–11 years old) when autistic children were first spoken to by the police. This is a highly vulnerable age which makes them susceptible to negative influences.

It is pleasing to read that those parents of children with autism felt there was more support available at school; however, there was a rise in suspensions and exclusions which might reflect less understanding in secondary schools. This also reflects the latest UK government school statistics indicating a significant rise in school suspensions and exclusions.

12 Discussion

The empirical review for this book has been widespread and covered many topics which have not been combined before into one book; hopefully, this will allow connections and new thinking to occur. Topics evolved organically as investigations commonly do.

Several main themes have occurred whilst writing this book:

- Meltdowns are the result of unsuitable learning situations taking place at schools, by educators who misunderstand or are unaware of, an autistic child's needs.
- The young autistic person who has a meltdown is commonly blamed unfairly by educators for their meltdowns, and educators do not take responsibility for, or understand fully the consequences of, their actions which may have triggered the meltdown; or may not appreciate how to create an inclusive learning environment.
- Due to the misunderstanding of meltdowns, parents of young autistic people are often sent to alternative education settings, have managed moves, or are pressured to homeschool, as the result of the school's inability to support their child's learning needs.
- The intense anger that comes from meltdowns/dysregulation leads to self-harming and hurting others, property damage, and goes beyond school into the community. The lack of knowledge about the cause of these meltdowns seems to lead to police involvement and potential arrest.
- Bullying and victimisation at school is where many young people first encounter hostility, being blamed and bullied for being different, not just by their peers but also teachers. Reporting bullying rarely resulted in a reduction and it was easier to exclude the victim than deal with the wider cause. Some choose to bully back and have revenge on those who bully them, but their lack of social skills and restraint can mean they are criminally responsible for their actions, no matter how significant their justification.
- Restraint and seclusion are commonly used to cope with a child's meltdowns, suggesting that the young person is blamed for the school's inability to support their needs. Restraint and seclusion whilst commonly used, are unrecorded in schools, more so in special schools. Police involvement commonly takes place where the school lacks inclusive practices, again blaming the young autistic child.

DOI: 10.4324/9781003614432-12

- The lack of suitable education for autistic young people, academic and social, means many do not understand social and sexual relationships, leading to choosing the internet for information, and this places them at risk of unfiltered and dangerous information and chatrooms.
- The lack of appropriate sex and relationship education in schools means that many young autistic people are unskilled and leave school with misunderstandings about relationships, leading to incidents of stalking and sexual crimes, for example, inappropriate touching.
- Many autistic people struggle to judge the age of others around them, and therefore when making friends online and collecting images of the opposite/ same sex, they may collect images which are of an inappropriate age, classed as 'child pornography'.
- Many autistic young people are perceived as naïve and too trusting, and therefore vulnerable to being taken advantage of, causing some to be unwittingly involved with criminal activities, called 'mate crime'. This can also similarly lead to being involved in knife crime.

Each of the above themes will now be discussed.

Meltdowns are the result of unsuitable learning situations taking place at schools, by educators who misunderstand or are unaware of, an autistic child's needs.

Schools are under pressure to educate more and more young people, and without additional funding, resulting in a pressure pot: increased student numbers, lack of SEND training, very low staffing in classrooms, and lastly undiagnosed SEND needs. The result is students with SEND needs are placed in environments which are unsuitable to their needs. Meltdowns may look like an overreaction to a single event, but they are the culmination of lots of smaller events, of which the last may be the 'straw that broke the camel's back' or the 'tip of the iceberg'. Minor or routine actions may have preceded large and sudden reactions due to the cumulative effect of previous smaller actions. These might build up due to bullying at breaktime, or being pushed in the corridor, but the last straw was their book not being given to them or being asked to move seats. This is misunderstood by teachers and leads to the downplaying of the role of the school and teacher in a young person having a meltdown or shutdown. Sadly, this leads to the blame being unfairly placed on the young person, a negative label put on the result of the meltdown, e.g., assault or property damage, which may result in police involvement or a 'managed move' out of mainstream education 'for their good', and into alternative education with other perceived 'disruptive students'. This also means peers may avoid an autistic child due to their meltdowns which look unpredictable and dangerous.

The young autistic person who has a meltdown is commonly blamed, unfairly by educators, for their meltdowns, and educators do not take responsibility for their actions which may have triggered the meltdown, or the lack of actions to create an inclusive learning environment.

School leaders talk about offering inclusive learning and environments to students, however, the words become meaningless unless supported by action, in that teachers feel supported to offer an adapted curriculum to all the learners in their classrooms, and schools provide enough additionally trained SEND staff to support the needs of their students with diagnosed and undiagnosed learning differences. Do teachers have the knowledge and time to create adaptive and inclusive resources? – not that I have seen in the many schools I have taught in. All I have seen are teaching assistants having to adapt as they enter classrooms, trying to make sense of the lesson being taught as they have no prior knowledge of the lesson, nor have targeted resources to use.

Legally a mainstream classroom teacher is required to adapt their learning to the needs of many types of learners in their classroom. The UK teaching standards (Department for Education, 2021a) include having a clear understanding of the needs of all pupils, using and evaluating distinctive teaching approaches to engage:

- Those with special educational needs
- Those of high ability
- Those with English as an additional language
- Those with disabilities

In addition, there is a need to adapt learning for:

- Those from low-income families, commonly called 'Pupil Premium (PP)'
- Those who are looked after by local authorities, commonly called 'looked after children (LAC)'

Also, to manage behaviour effectively to ensure a good and safe learning environment (Department for Education, 2021b):

- Have clear rules and routines for behaviour in classrooms, and take responsibility for promoting good and courteous behaviour both in classrooms and around the school, following the school's behaviour policy
- Have high expectations of behaviour, and establish a framework for discipline with a range of strategies, using praise, sanctions, and rewards consistently and fairly
- Manage classes effectively, using approaches which are appropriate to pupils' needs to involve and motivate them
- Maintain good relationships with pupils, exercise appropriate authority, and act decisively when necessary.

Secondary school teachers tend to have at least 20 classes to teach a week with up to 20 different sets of students to know and cater for.

The question posed is, is it possible or realistic for teachers to manage the above for multiple classes of 25–30 young people? If not, then how are inclusive classrooms possible?

With reductions in SEND funding, SEND funding is often not being ring-fenced in schools and is commonly used to prop up main school budget deficits (e.g., staffing, electricity costs, etc). Increasing student numbers with undiagnosed learning difficulties increases the pressures each year. It is no wonder that young people, even with diagnosed needs, are poorly supported in classrooms. In the case of autistic young people who find mainstream classrooms a sensory overload, it is no wonder many have meltdowns. Schools use restraint and seclusion on an increasing basis to cope with increased pressures to secure pupil numbers, which reduces pressure on their school budgets, without regard to being able to provide for the needs of such pupils.

The reduction of special schools in the UK, which offer students specialist educational support, and the pressure on mainstream schools to accept most students with high educational needs, even with Educational Health Care Plans (EHCPs), means many high-needs students are placed in schools which are unable and unsuitable to meet their needs.

I was introduced to the 'spoons' theory recently, which is a great way to understand why meltdowns may happen. McCann (2020) explains the theory as:

- A child with autism starts the school day with a full drawer of spoons equalling the amount of stress/anxiety they can cope with during a day (which may be only half as many as a typical child), many spoons could have already used up in dealing with the demands of getting to school. Depending on various factors such as whether they slept, if they ate breakfast without dramas, if mum remembered to say goodbye the right way if their clothes were itching their skin, if their routine was changed, or any number of other seemingly incidental events…they may be starting the day with, say, only five spoons instead of ten.
- Then they need to start using their spoons at school. Each set of instructions, each set of work demands, each time they must organise themselves, follow a complex set of instructions or cope with change, and each social interaction may cost the autistic person a spoon or two if complex and stressful. If there are sensory sensations that are overwhelming, then another spoon is used to regulate and keep calm. If they must work in a group, more than one spoon may be needed. Break times are not relaxing, another spoon or two is used up in coping with all the social interaction, noise and lack of structure. Some manage to save a spoon by shutting off and taking the time to be alone so that they can cope with the next set of lessons.
- So, you may have a child or young person who seems okay in the morning but always seems to lose it in the afternoon, they won't join in anything at break times and pace around the perimeter of the yard or social space; or a child who has meltdowns some days but is fine on other days; or parents ask you what you are doing to their child as they always have a meltdown as soon as they come out of school…and getting them to do homework is impossible; or you may have a colleague at work who seems not to be able to speak to you on some days, unable to socialise and seems distracted and distressed.

- You might assume you need more structure in the afternoons. You might assume you need to teach the child some social skills so they can make friends at break times. You might assume the parent isn't disciplined enough. You might put all kinds of practical support in place, but it doesn't work.
- It may just be that the autistic person has used up all their spoons. They have no communication, organisation, sensory, social or intellectual energy left. They might just be able to keep it together in the morning but then are far too exhausted to carry on in the afternoon. Some days there may be no spoons to deal with the things they usually seem okay with. They might even be able to keep it together through the day but cannot contain themselves in the safety and familiarity of their home. Some even manage to borrow spoons from the next day but there will be a day when there are no spoons left to borrow, and the person has a major meltdown.

However, when all spoons are used up, a meltdown is likely, therefore the spoons theory is a good way to understand the cumulative effect of an autistic person's day at school. The use of self-stimming or self-stimming is seen as self-soothing and can help to replenish spoons, the ability to manage the stress that each day brings. See Appendix 4 for a list of Stimming strategies used by autistic individuals.

Due to the misunderstanding of meltdowns, parents of young autistic people are leveraged into alternative education, have managed moves, or their parents are pressured to homeschool, as the result of the school's inability to support their child's learning needs.

UK statistics point to high numbers of students who are diagnosed with autism, but more importantly, also many with undiagnosed SEND needs are at risk of being suspended or permanently excluded from school. Even with a diagnosed need and an EHCP (statutory funded SEND provision), schools find it very hard sometimes to support their level of need. The numbers have increased substantially over the last year (2023–24) without an official or obvious reason being provided. Can covid explain this, or more likely changes in school behaviour policies and the very long waiting times for autism and ADHD assessments?

Personally speaking, as a secondary school SENDCo the author is consulted as to whether his school can accommodate children with EHCPs transitioning to secondary education. The local authority last year sent this author 14 such children to consider, whilst some schools receive 30 or more consultations each year, requiring responses within a 14-day timeframe.

In real terms, there are very few of these children who the school can realistically support adequately. Most require a specialist provision but there are so few special school places available, so local authorities push such children into mainstream schools. Whilst LAs may talk about putting the child first, it's often more about money, or the lack of it, which means there are only a small number of local state-owned special schools with available places. This is where the problem starts. There is a reluctance to send the child to an independent special school which will cost considerably more (state special schools may cost UK£30,000–40,000 a year compared to independent special schools costing UK£60,000 a year per young person, some can be UK£100,000 plus depending on need).

Many children with high needs are pushed into mainstream secondary schools, where they have already failed at the primary school stage. Therefore, even before the child starts in year 7, the school knows they are unable to meet their needs (e.g., providing an autism-friendly workstation in each classroom, which may be fine in a primary school where the child is situated in one room mainly). In secondary schools, this would unrealistically mean an autism-friendly workstation would be required in 10+ classrooms, for example, tutor room, Science, Maths, English, Geography, History, French, Art, ICT, and so on.

In many cases, the child is going to significantly struggle and become dysregulated in every classroom along with the lunch hall and at break times. So, it is no surprise that within a year or so, their meltdowns have gained in frequency and severity, and teachers are concerned and struggling to educate them. They may choose not to attend school as they and their parents see that it is not good for their mental well-being, or they develop 'emotionally based school avoidance (EBSA)'. This sounds like it's the child's fault, but in real terms, it is a reaction to the school's lack of inclusive practices.

The National Autistic Society (2024c) points to the various means a school uses to manage autistic young people, including the use of suspensions, internal and external, part-time timetables, exclusion from school trips and after-school activities, and managed moves and off-rolling. This book also investigated the high numbers of mainstream and special schools using restraint and seclusion to cope with autistic young people.

Timpson (2019) found that

there are schools inappropriately routinely using part-time timetables, where schools allow children to attend for only part of the school day, to legitimise an informal exclusion. Though this can be necessary in exceptional cases, many parents and carers spoke of long-term arrangements spanning several years to which they had not consented, which simply amounted to their child not being offered a full-time education.

In some cases, parents can argue that their autistic child is being denied the right to attend school on a full-time basis because the school does not have the resources to provide the pupil with the support they require on a full-time basis, which would be discrimination arising from disability unless it can be justified.

Growing concerns around the use of 'off-rolling' were highlighted by Timpson (2019)

There are times when a child is taken off the school roll for legitimate reasons, such as if they have moved out of the area or because their parents have independently chosen to home educate them. However, some children are made to leave their school and are removed from the school roll without a formal permanent exclusion or by the school encouraging the parents to remove their child from the school, which is done in the school's interests, and at the school's request.

Exclusion can generate feelings of isolation, inferiority, injustice, and anger, along with making the young person with autism and their parents feel rejected. The question needs to be asked how change can be made, so that autistic young people get the support they need in schools?

Lord Timpson has in 2024 become the new Labour Minister of State in charge of prisons, with an understanding of the 'school-to-prison pipeline' due to his work on rehabilitating prisoners, many with histories of school failure, permanent exclusions, and literacy/cognitive difficulties.

The intense anger that comes from meltdowns/dysregulation leads to self-harming and hurting others, property damage, and goes beyond school into the community. The lack of knowledge about the cause of these meltdowns seems to lead to police involvement and potential arrest.

Research points to meltdowns as misunderstood by teachers and schools, and behaviour policies as discriminatory in how they place the blame on the child. In some cases where the police are called, the blame is again put on the young person, and they are the ones who ultimately lose out due to poor practices in schools. Moving a young person with diagnosed or undiagnosed autism to alternative education is not the solution, it's just moving the problem and only for a short time. The real solution is to fix the practices in schools. Bad parenting is also commonly blamed which ignores the child's autism and/or ADHD diagnosis.

In Scotland, Maureen Mckenna (Simpson, 2023) formerly the director of education at Glasgow City Council, oversaw a 90% drop in school exclusions, both permanent and temporary, over 14 years. Over the same period, violence in Glasgow's education settings was also reduced by half. This drop was achieved by a 'zero-tolerance policy' by making schools manage their behaviour concerns rather than allowing them to exclude students and transport such students to another provider. Also, she shut many of the pupil referral units in Glasgow, and funnelled the money and expertise into the schools, helping them to become more inclusive. The Mayor of London has just commissioned McKenna to work on London's high exclusion problem.

Making schools more inclusive is part of the solution, but also the realisation that some SEND students need specialist support in smaller classroom settings with a high staff ratio in a special school. The current strategy of throwing money into schools to offer some support ignores the many meltdown triggers for autistic students in mainstream noisy and chaotic classrooms of 30 students. No matter how much money is thrown at schools, unless schools set up their own internal special school provision, a child with severe autism will not learn in a noisy class of 25–30 students.

Bullying and victimisation at school is where many young people first encounter hostility, being blamed and bullied for being different, not just by their peers but also teachers. Reporting bullying rarely resulted in a reduction and it was easier to exclude the victim than deal with the wider cause. Some choose to bully back and have revenge on those who bully them, but their lack of social skills and restraint can mean they are criminally responsible for their actions, no matter how significant their justification.

Many with autism report bullying, and many research studies support the view that those with autism are bullied more than others with learning and physical disabilities. Doing the perceived 'right thing' by ignoring or reporting incidents to teachers does not tend to result in reductions and can in some cases make it worse. Those who choose to bully back or others, tend to not do it to gain power over others, as per traditional concepts of bullying, but to inflict revenge, and this can be linked to a typical trait of a 'sense of justice' that many with autism manifest. The danger is those with autism will get into trouble and inflict revenge which is criminal, not appreciating their own anger/strength, nor what is criminal and what is not.

Restraint and seclusion are commonly used to cope with a child's meltdowns, suggesting that the young person is blamed for the school's inability to support their needs. Restraint and seclusion whilst commonly used, are unrecorded in schools, more so in special schools. Police involvement commonly takes place where schools lack inclusive practices, seemingly blaming the young autistic child.

Research notes that schools are not required by law to register each time restraint and seclusion is used, therefore the practice goes on unchecked (campaigners for Callum's Law, discussed previously, are trying to introduce this into UK schools). Again, this reflects the lack of understanding of the triggers to autistic meltdowns, lacking indeed an awareness that many mainstream teaching strategies and school environments are the cause of meltdowns and resulting dysregulation.

Research and case studies into the numbers of autistic young people and adults being held under the UK's Mental Health Act in autism assessment units under false pretences as a suitable residential unit for those with autism supports the view that autism is effectively marginalised and criminalised in the UK (National Autistic Society, 2024a; Sky News, 2019; Joshi, 2019; Care Quality Commission, 2022). In Victorian days many families would send their children with disabilities away, to the coast for their health, saving families the embarrassment which might affect their standing in society and affect the marriage prospects of their other children. However, in the UK, young people with autism who have severe meltdowns are sent to such units and other residential care homes for 'their safety', despite evidence suggesting they are far from safe in them (Nicholls, 2021; Public Health England, 2015; The Care Quality Commission, 2022). Therefore, are they sent away for the safety of society, in a similar way as prison safeguards society?

If one took an alternative perspective of this situation, if the causes of meltdowns were better understood by schools, parents, and medical professionals, then such units would not be needed, and autistic individuals would be helped and supported in more suitable environments. This sounds utopian, and of the author's 11-year-old student with autism and OCD who is school phobic. He wants to come to school but is afraid; he has explosive meltdowns and uses OCD strategies to try to control his home environment. His high anxiety means he is stuck and unable to move forward and is not accessing psychiatric and medication because of his phobia of leaving the home setting. There is a huge amount of control being placed on him, but it's unhelpful in accessing professional support, for example, he will not go to CAMHS clinics to see psychiatrists and refuses to take any form of medication.

If one sees autism as the primary need, and his OCD and anxiety as secondary, then his OCD reflects his means to create order in a world he sees as lacking and causes him anxiety. If one goes back further, he struggled to create order in his primary school and this led to occasional meltdowns, and by the time he left there, they had created a safe and dependable environment. His move to secondary school, with only one boy moving with him from his primary school, fractured his safe and dependable environment. The support he needed was removed and this led to helplessness. In essence, he was not ready to move schools, especially not to a mainstream secondary on two sites and not autistic-friendly due to sensory overload.

The environment is crucial, and many autistic young people are not suited to mainstream education; however, authorities still send them there due, I contest, to budgetary constraints. This is not putting the young person first!

The lack of suitable education for autistic young people, academic and social, means many do not understand social and sexual relationships, leading to choosing the internet for information, which places them at risk of unfiltered and dangerous information and chatrooms.

Evidence indicates autistic young people have delayed maturity, and this leads them to struggle with social relationships. This also leads many parents and teachers to believe they are too vulnerable and unprepared for sex and relationship education.

Autistic teenagers need to have information given to them in a way that they can understand and tailored to their abilities. Whilst schools may help, many families find that they need to ensure that their teen understands what they need to do. Autism Awareness Australia (2024) suggests many autistic people identify as being gay or lesbian, a greater percentage than neurotypicals.

> *Parents can't put their heads in the sand and pretend things won't change.*
> *Teenagers will be teenagers regardless of autism!*
> Autism Awareness Australia (2024)

A recent conversation by the author with the headteacher of a local autism school regarding sex education illuminated the challenges involved in pre-empting possible sexual offences amongst their students. The proposal was a graphic educational programme, to make the education explicit but which they feared would be shocking to parents. The understanding was to avoid vague terms and to challenge terms used which might be confusing, as autistic teenagers are likely to take terms very literally. For example, talking about a boy's voice breaking could cause anxiety as the term commonly used is incorrect, it doesn't 'break', it changes.

Singer (2024) suggests that talking about sex can be difficult for any parent, but for families with adolescents with autism, the topic can be particularly challenging. These teens often lag developmentally behind their typically developing peers.

They may need help understanding the basics of consent and figuring out how to set appropriate boundaries. Those who are beginning to explore romantic relationships may need more explicit instruction on the social norms that go along with dating. The Sparks programme has several elements to it, as their guidance explains:

- We talk about the difference between a friend and a romantic partner, and someone you have a crush on who doesn't reciprocate.
- A lot of times being more explicit and concrete can be helpful. Saying "Don't let anyone do what you don't want them to do" is vague. We are more specific. We say, "Here are some things that might come up if you have a romantic partner. You can decide if you want them to happen or not. For example, do you want to kiss someone with your mouth closed? Do you want someone to touch your neck?" Part of this is learning about boundaries and part is exploring possible sensory issues or trigger zones.
- We use the same overall curriculum but make it more visual. When teaching about puberty and lifespan development, we have pictures of babies, kids, teens, and adults, and ask them a mix of questions, like which people here would have a period drive a car or date another teenager. We do some labelling of anatomy to help teach those terms. Young people mostly seem to find ways to understand their anatomy and biology. It's more the social and emotional piece that they struggle with.
- Sexting and online pornography have changed so fast. For kids who spend a lot of time on the internet, it's already in their lives. It's important to address it from a developmental perspective, but it's also potentially a legal issue. Parents often don't like to talk about it. But if teens are already accessing online pornography, we want to give them enough information to navigate it safely. We spend a lot of time on the difference between over and under-18 appropriateness and legality.

'Intimate Relationships and Sexual Health: A Curriculum for Teaching Adolescents/ adults with High-functioning Autism Spectrum Disorders and Other Social Challenges' by Catherine Davies and Melissa Dubie is seen as a good resource for autistic young people.

The National Autistic Society (2024b) have an in-depth website for sex education. It offers advice to make the teaching of many important topics more visual, for example:

Sex and Relationship Education

This could be supported visually by drawing stick figures or using photographs, of each significant person in this individual's life, including themselves, their family members, support workers, teachers, and doctors, if appropriate. You may want to use a different piece of paper for each person. The pictures should be placed in the middle of the paper and connections should be made to a variety of drawings, words or photographs that surround this person. These other pictures or words should symbolise this person's role for the individual concerned and perhaps other members of the family. You could change the person in the centre from the autistic person to mum, dad or a sibling, as this may help your child to understand how other people view the relationships in the family. You may want to discuss another family that is different from your own – perhaps one headed by a single parent or vice versa, a family with two same-sex partners or vice versa.

The aim should be to educate both appropriately but in simpler terms explicitly with visuals and models.

The lack of sex and relationship education in schools means that many young autistic people are unskilled and leave school misunderstanding relationships, leading to incidents of stalking and sexual crimes taking place, for example, inappropriate touching.

With more suitable and explicit sex and relationship education the young autistic person will have a better understanding of consent and appropriate relationships. The use of social stories will help to explain the fine line between a consenting relationship and stalking, from appropriate touching to non-consensual touching which might lead to possible arrest.

The aim must NOT be to avoid such education, as their bodies are growing as per their peers, but to tackle his head on. Mainstream school educators may not be the most suitable people in this regard, and the explicit material needed for those with autism might be too strong for neurotypical students, and teachers may be uncomfortable with teaching such material.

This places a burden on parents, specialist teachers, and health authorities to make sure this curriculum is covered over several years, offering opportunities for questions and discussions. A single session will not be enough, as per their neurotypical peers.

The number of autistic young people finding themselves in trouble regarding sex and relationship education should be enough of a wake-up call.

Many autistic people struggle to judge the age of others around them, and therefore when making friends online and collecting images of the opposite/same sex, they may collect images which are of an inappropriate age, classed as 'child pornography'.

The use of social stories and visuals of family members and others will help to educate regarding puberty, ageing, and consent. The more explicit the better is suggested by experts in this area.

Bloor et al.'s (2022) study of the challenges faced by mainstream school educators regarding sex and relationship education for autistic students notes:

- Participants suggest that the appropriate age to introduce sex education should be based on their intrigue or their bodily reactions accompanying puberty.
- As autism is an individualised condition it is difficult to identify what is more appropriate, especially if learning is within a group context.
- To promote engagement and concentration, participants identified that resources need to be relatable to autistic learners to support their understanding. The national curriculum prevents real-life photos from being used which is problematic as

cartoon images do not look the same as real life, thus limiting understanding and potentially causing confusion. This is particularly problematic in autistic learners who find abstract concepts challenging to understand since autistic people are less inclined to attend to and process abstract information, instead preferring more concrete representations.

- Participants suggested that using the correct terminology for body parts is vital as it could identify safeguarding concerns such as sexual abuse. There is a particular dependency on teachers in this regard as autistic learners may not be able to effectively communicate concerning this topic. Learners may not even be aware of what a safeguarding scenario is if they have not been educated on it; highlighted by Kathleen that it is 'easy' for autistic individuals to be sexually abused. Emmaline suggests that learners may avoid using correct anatomical terms because they view them as 'dirty words' but both participants here highlight the dangers of using alternative words due to their ambiguous nature: if learners are prevented from communicating proficiently what they mean, then this may lead to (potentially problematic) miscommunication.

- It is important to acknowledge, celebrate, and act safely on sexual impulses. An ableist perspective and thus assumptions of autistic learners' comprehension of social skills could influence how teaching is delivered to explore and manage sexual impulses healthily. In the example above, Larry details how an individual may advance upon another without consent, but if they have not been taught the social skills around sex and relationships then this may have problematic implications.

- An individualised condition and resources may not be 'fit for all' – and therefore should be tailored to individual learners' needs. This highlights the importance of inclusive and accessible settings for autistic learners, to improve the quality and understanding of sex education.

- The tailoring of resources through the likes of using realistic photographs and conducting one-on-one teaching may be a way to address the needs of autistic learners by making the information more concrete through increasing focus and engagement, as it is applicable to them (as opposed to, for instance, cartoon genitalia). This is an example of how sex education can be made more accessible for autistic learners by providing concrete examples that utilise processing and comprehension strengths.

The lad I was working with ended up being put on the sex offender register because the stuff he was getting taught in this class, he thought in his head that 'oh now I know what to do; I can go and do that'

(George, in Bloor et al., 2022)

I've seen search histories of teenage boys with autism that I've worked with... and you can see on the search history they're just clicking the link, and they've ended up somewhere really dark, sometimes illegal... nobody had that discussion with them about what's online. And the fact that some of it is illegal and is out there in the dark web realistically, really easily accessible. Horrendous stuff online... like that's what they think sex is like and they don't understand it's not.

(Genny, in Bloor et al., 2022)

Bloor et al. discuss that autistic individuals are protected more in school if they act inappropriately because staff, families, and learners are aware of how conditions may influence sexual behaviours. Because of this, it could be challenging for learners to understand the transition to acting appropriately outside of school, if they do not yet understand sexually appropriate behaviours. Outside of school, individuals face repercussions within the judicial system such as being arrested and consequentially can cause a lack of independence as being placed on the sex offender register may prevent individuals from living areas and applying for particular jobs.

This book has discussed some of the inappropriately aged online material accessed by autistic young people and adults, particularly that classed as child pornography. Commentators argue that a change in the law requires making the collection and distribution separate offences, with allowances made for those with autism regarding the collection for private use.

Research doesn't always point to them being used for masturbation, but often more to learn about relationships from perceived like-minded, and (perceived) same-aged individuals. The collection is compulsive and excessive in the same way a fixation might be for trainspotting.

Allely (2018) discusses that in cases of child pornography investigations for those with autism, many of the images were not opened, and it was the compulsive nature of collecting that was the overriding intention. Many autistic individuals explore the internet for sexual education or to satisfy their sexual needs, because of little or no sexual outlets with their peers/friends. The challenge is when an autistic adult has the social maturity of a 14-year-old, but they are 27 years old. It seems logical they would seek out someone of the same social and emotional maturity; however, this places them in a position at odds with the law.

They feel more comfortable with them, etc. Thus, it may be that if and when they consume child pornography, this is likely better understood as a way for them to try to understand relationships and sexuality, rather than as a precursor to any sexual offending behaviour towards a minor.

Issues also occur when autistic individuals are completely unaware that what they have done is illegal. One of the contributory factors that explains this is their impaired ability to recognise the facial expressions of the children in the images they are viewing. Interestingly, autistic individuals who come across child pornography material online may not even think to question the legality of viewing such material. Asking themselves, how could something which is illegal be so freely available on the internet?

Allely also notes

> *It may possibly be the case that some autistic individuals inadvertently download and view child pornography because they are unable to accurately guess the age of the individuals in the images. Such issues are only further exacerbated by the fact that the boundaries or distinction between an adult and a minor can be 'blurry'. In fact, it is frequently intentionally blurred by the media, pop culture and legal 'adult' porn. The legality and severity of the offence is determined by the age of the victims in the images being viewed by the defendant, which only further highlights the need to consider the contributory role of autism symptomology in such cases.*

Allely argues

> *there is clearly an urgent need for more appropriate disposition of diversion from the criminal justice system for individuals with autism who are charged with possession of child pornography. Indeed, there is an increasing amount of discussion in the literature regarding the 'unduly harsh' or 'draconian sentences' faced by individuals with autism after being found guilty of violating child pornography statutes.*

Many autistic young people are perceived as naïve and too trusting, and therefore vulnerable to being taken advantage of, causing some to be unwittingly involved with criminal activities, called 'mate crime'. This can also lead to being drawn by malign influences into knife crime.

Autistic young people and adults, due to their delayed social skills are vulnerable and susceptible to being taken advantage of. Being naïve and too trusting comes from their literal understanding of the world. In a similar way they struggle to judge emotions regarding fear, they also struggle to read body language. 'Mate Crime' can easily happen where social skills have not been taught, maybe through social stories. The question needs to be posed, can these skills be taught where an autistic adult has the mental capacity of a child?

References

Allely, C. (2018). The role of autism symptomatology in certain specific child pornography offences. *Clare Allely's latest blog entry*. Retrieved 30/07/2024. https://www.gu.se/en/gnc/the-role-of-autism-symptomatology-in-certain-specific-child-pornography-offences#:~:text=Another%20important%20issue%20to%20consider,compulsive%20and%20obsessive%20features%20of

Autism Awareness Australia (2024). Teens and young adults: Sexuality. Retrieved 29/07/2024. https://www.autismawareness.com.au/teens/sexuality

Bloor, D., Ballantyne, C., Gillespie-Smith, K., Wilson, C., & Hendry, G. (2022). Investigating the challenges of teaching sex education to autistic learners: A qualitative exploration of teachers' experiences. *Research in Developmental Disabilities, 131*, 104344. https://doi.org/10.1016/j.ridd.2022.104344

Care Quality Commission (2022). Out of sight – Who cares? Restraint, segregation and seclusion review. 25 March 2022. Retrieved 22/07/2024. https://www.cqc.org.uk/publications/themed-work/rssreview

Department for Education (2021a). Teachers' standards. Updated 2021. Retrieved 11/07/2024. https://assets.publishing.service.gov.uk/media/5a750668ed915d3c7d529cad/Teachers_standard_information.pdf

Department for Education (2021b) Teachers' standards guidance for school leaders, school staff and governing bodies. Retrieved 11/07/2024. https://assets.publishing.service.gov.uk/media/61b73d6c8fa8f50384489c9a/Teachers__Standards_Dec_2021.pdf

Joshi, A. (2019). 'She's not an animal': Autistic teen girl locked up 24 hours a day. Thu 31 October 2019 21:37, UK. Retrieved 18/07/2024.

McCann, L. (2020). Spoon theory & autism. Retrieved 11/07/2024. https://reachoutasc.com/spoon-theory-and-autism/

National Autistic Society (2024a). Number of autistic people in mental health hospitals: Latest data. 21 June 2024. Retrieved 24/07/2024. https://www.autism.org.uk/what-we-do/news/number-of-autistic-people-in-mental-health-ho-20

National Autistic Society (2024b). Sex education – A guide for parents. https://www.autism.org.uk/advice-and-guidance/topics/family-life-and-relationships/sex-education/parents-and-carers

National Autistic Society (2024c). Unlawful and unofficial exclusion. Retrieved 12/07/2024. https://www.autism.org.uk/advice-and-guidance/topics/education/exclusions/exclusion-england/unlawful-and-unofficial-exclusion#:~:text=disability%20discrimination%20helpful.-,Managed%20moves%20and%20off%2Drolling,as%20a%20'managed%20move'

Nicholls, T. (2021). Transforming care: Our stories. National Autism Society. Retrieved 22/07/2024. https://www.challengingbehaviour.org.uk/wp-content/uploads/2021/03/transformingcareourstories.pdf

Public Health England (2015). Prescribing of psychotropic drugs to people with learning disabilities and/or autism by general practitioners in England. Retrieved 10/04/25. www.gov.uk/government/publications/psychotropic-drugs-and-people-with-learning-disabilities-or-autism/psychotropic-drugs-and-people-with-learning-disabilities-or-autism-introduction

Simpson, F. (2023). Interview: Maureen McKenna, education expert advising London's VRU. Tue 26 September 2023. Retrieved 29/07/2024. https://www.cypnow.co.uk/features/article/interview-maureen-mckenna-education-expert-advising-londons-vru#:~:text=Mckenna%20was%20formerly%20the%20director,and%20temporary%20%E2%80%93%20over%2014%20years.

Singer, E. (2024). Sex education and autism. SPARK. Retrieved 29/07/2024. https://sparkforautism.org/discover_article/sex-education-and-autism/

Sky News (2019). Line 18: 'My autistic son deserves a life but he's locked up'. Fri 12 April 2019 14:31, UK. Retrieved 19/07/2024. https://news.sky.com/story/line-18-my-autistic-son-deserves-a-life-but-hes-locked-up-11539937

Timpson, E (2019). Timpson review of school exclusion. May 2019. Retrieved 12/07/2024. https://assets.publishing.service.gov.uk/media/5cfe7d8de5274a0906be72c8/Timpson_review.pdf

13 Conclusion

Beginning this book, this author perceived himself as an 'insider' with relevant knowledge from working as a SENDCo (special needs and disabilities coordinator) in primary and secondary schools, along with line management experience with a team of specialist teachers and also acting as a specialist teacher myself in an autism school. However, as soon as he began to investigate further, he could see he was an 'outsider' trying to make sense of the lived experience of having autism as a young person and how schools try, and mostly fail, to support their needs.

At the time of researching this book, the author was offered a new role as the joint SENDCo and Safeguarding manager at a specialist autism school. From the research conducted for this book, he knew that each needed its own staff member, and that the safeguarding element was substantial. He turned down the role and whilst writing this conclusion believes it was the correct choice. In his opinion, no single person could do both roles well, keeping students safe.

The book has been an eye-opener for him. He knew about unfair school behaviour policies, and schools using exclusions as an alternative to putting in the support needed. He knew that Educational, Health, and Care Plan (EHCP) funding was inadequate and that schools were not given enough funding to provide the provisions listed in legally binding EHCP documents. What he didn't know, however, grew and grew, and was shocking to read.

The idea and realisation that UK schools in the 20th century, in 2024, were using restraint for young people with autism was shocking, as were the numerous accounts of young people being held under false premise in 'autism assessment units', sent for their benefit/safety, and stuck there as they are held under the sectioning properties of the UK's 'Mental Health Act'. This is not how modern society is meant to treat vulnerable citizens, and it is more reminiscent of Victorian values and the introduction of mental sanitoriums to treat those who are perceived as different. However, for autism, there is no electric shock treatment to use to make them 'normal' and fit to return to society.

It seems very clear that there is a lack of understanding of autism in both the medical and educational professions, with a lack of understanding of the triggers of meltdowns. To then blame the autistic person for their meltdowns seems morally wrong, and then to lock them up seems abhorrent. The use of restraint as a replacement for trained specialist staff, which seems to be merely a cheaper control

DOI: 10.4324/9781003614432-13

method, is also wrong. The long campaign for Calum's Law demonstrates not only the lack of awareness of the problems faced in school but also indicates that policymakers are putting saving money before the needs of the child. Frustratingly, the campaign for Calum's law has been going for 14-plus years with no sign it will be introduced! Schools and their staff need to be accountable for their actions, and whilst this book is entitled *Autism and Crime*, the use of restraint and seclusion is straight out of prison playbooks. Locking up young people, and using the Mental Health Act as reasoning to protect the individual and society at large is again about control and not about understanding.

This book identifies meltdowns as a reaction to the autistic person's environment, and using the 'social model of disability', autistic people are disabled by society's treatment of their challenges. Autistic children learn early on that the world around them is illogical and chaotic and needs to be managed. Many develop obsessive-compulsive disorder strategies to manage the environment around them and to reduce their meltdowns.

The lack of awareness of autism, especially in girls, means that many go through childhood and school without diagnosis and struggle and many having 'shutdowns' from dysregulation. Anxiety and depression, along with self-harming and anorexia, are sadly too common, but CAMHS (the UK's mental health service) are so under-resourced that they readily treat these secondary symptoms without questioning the cause. Today he interviewed a 30-year-old lady who this week gained her autism diagnosis, she said that she masked too well, and so it was no surprise she was never diagnosed. She is also awaiting an attention-deficit/ hyperactivity disorder (ADHD) assessment. When he asked about anxiety, she quickly opened up that this was present from late primary school to this day, and she said that her father, a doctor, had tried to find a reason for it. She did not blame her parents as they tried their best. What struck me was that because she was doing well at school she was not screened by the school for autism or ADHD, as there is an incorrect perception that autism and ADHD are related to school academic failure and low intelligence. Only those that kick off and make trouble gain attention and possible assessment. An autistic girl who masks well but still comes over as shy and reserved, who would not make eye contact, is left alone to suffer in silence. We look to teachers and medical professionals as experts, but they are not.

Sadly, today's society uses a deficit model, and to gain help via an assessment one needs to fail. To gain an EHCP in the UK, a young person needs to be substantially behind their peers academically and therefore has been allowed to fail. This places the high-ability autistic young person at a disadvantage, they are doing too well to be diagnosed, but at what cost to their mental and emotional well-being?

Symptoms of autism make them highly vulnerable, and the term 'mate crime' suggests that it is common for autistic young people to be taken advantage of, and their immaturity, delayed social skills, and trusting nature places them in great danger. They are told by parents and others that they need to have friends; however, they are very happy to be left alone. In their efforts to please their parents, they place themselves in significant harm's danger by befriending others and pleasing others who will take advantage of their kindness.

Looking at criminal acts, again we see autistic symptoms make them an easy target for criminal elements, their social naivety along with pressures to have friendships is a recipe for potential disaster. Many autistic young people lack peer examples of how one should find relationships with others, and in schools, their social naivety is accepted when they touch the hair or bottoms of staff members. Outside of school, these same actions are seen as assault and the police act accordingly. It is accepted that autistic people find it hard to judge the ages of others, and they see themselves as children. Therefore, wishing to be around others their age may lead them to seek out younger people for relationships, but also to watch them to better understand them. Cases where the police have been called to playgrounds due to teenagers with autism are too common. This is the same for the collection of child pornography. The fixations on objects or people are a major symptom of autism which can be for anything that takes their fancy, from train sets to the collection of scientific facts, the search for UFOs, to obsessions with people, which can be classed as stalking (sometimes of celebrities) and collections of weapons. This author believes that it's about the collection of information to understand, rather than a conscious act to harm or stalk. This leads many into cybercrime in the search for knowledge, by breaking into restricted government websites to gain the 'latest' information.

Meltdowns are a cause for many criminal arrests due to their sometimes-violent nature: property damage and violence towards other people can be commonplace; however, these unconscious acts are misunderstood. If one sees them as the culmination of stressors, maybe using the spoons theory, then society and educators/parents can do a lot to reduce the stress load on autistic people. However, the world is random, random things happen each day and most non-autistic (neurotypical) people can cope with this. An autistic person struggles, badly.

A train breaking down, a car crash, or buses not running on time – most take it in their stride. However, for an autistic person their planned route to avoid crowds of people is changed, they find themselves with an unplanned route, using a bus they don't know, a driver who may not be friendly to them, crowds of people who may touch them, too much noise and who knows what smells! The list goes on, and these small things will quickly add up to overload causing dysregulation and potentially a meltdown. They can't cope so they fling their arms out to try and move out of the way, they hit a few people by this action, and they are shouted at, and the police are called. No one cares about 'why', it's 'what'. 'What' they did to others in their attempt to get out of an environment of sensory overload.

Overall, coming to this subject and completing the research for this book, I can conclude that on the surface one should be concerned with the level of crime that autistic individuals are drawn into or commit. However, when looking deeper one can see there is no real desire to commit criminal offences, they are unfairly blamed for their physical property and violence towards others, as their meltdowns are a culmination of many events which they have struggled to cope with. Does this mean they should be blamed, by societal rules this author would say yes, but morally he would say no.

Many meltdowns in school environments are caused by them being educated in unsuitable schools, placed in mainstream schools with huge sensory issues, rather than specialist schools for autism, where class sizes are much smaller and are staffed by suitably trained educators. The use of restraint even in residential care homes is unwise from trained staff, even more worrying is the use of restraint and seclusion by untrained staff in mainstream schools. There are enough media reports to suggest this is unregulated and undocumented and should stop immediately. Its use is of course the result of meltdowns, which are the result of autistic young people, cases from three years old, being placed in unsuitable educational environments and taught/cared for by unsuitability and untrained staff.

Schools and parents need to start early to educate autistic young people regarding relationships, consent, and boundaries, but this seems to be put off due to their cognitive age, rather than recognising and respecting their chronological age. Saying "they are too immature to get it" is putting off a problem which needs much longer to teach than neurotypical young people, who can rely on their peers to fill in any gaps. Parents wrapping them up in cotton wool is an unwise strategy, but one commonly used by parents who would struggle and be embarrassed to teach in the explicit way they need. Autistic young people enjoy the predictability of using computers and searching the internet. Leaving autistic young people to gain sex and relationship advice from the internet has been seen to have poor outcomes, but where else do they turn? Conflicting peer and adult advice is unhelpful for vulnerable autistic teenagers, where they need to be taught using social stories and more explicit sex and relationship advice.

This book focussed on sexual crimes as this is where most autistic young people struggle, and there is a huge amount of research in this area. Autism symptoms include a strong sense of justice, and this can be a protective factor, which makes when they are seen to commit a crime much harder for them to make sense of. If they do not recognise, that they have committed a crime, then it's going to be much harder for them to make sense of any punishment. To gain early parole (an early release from prison) following a crime one needs to admit to the crime and show understanding of their motive. Autistic prisoners may find this factor a barrier to their release, meaning they may be held in prison beyond their early release date.

Crimes committed by individuals with autism vary; a review of court decisions in Freckelton (2011a, 2011b) found that offenders with autism tended to commit the crimes found in Table 13.1. Reading through it one can see how they can easily be charged with criminal offences due to their autism traits.

Society, social services, the police, and courts by using prisons, residential units, and autism assessment units, and using the Mental Health Act as reasoning to protect 'the public' and support the 'autistic individual' is questionable. Many such units use restraint and seclusion as a form of control by staff with little expertise in autism.

Whilst one should not condone any criminal offence, when taking a legal perspective, both 'actus reus' (guilty act) and 'mens rea' (guilty mind) are required for a court to prosecute successfully. We are talking about an intention to offend. In the case of child pornography, both the collection and distribution-sharing of images are treated the same. However, in the case of a person with autism who will only collect for private use, this unfairly treats them as criminals. Many cases of

Table 13.1 Table of offences by autistic people

Crime committed	Related to autistic symptoms
• Arson • Stalking	• Fascination with flames • Fixations • Lack of sex and relationship education • Unable to read facial expressions and emotions, so struggles to see fear in others
• Knife use and collection	• Fixations
• Computer crimes, stalking, and getting into hard systems	• Fixations to find out information • Hyperfocus
• Child pornography	• Information gathering regarding relationships with others their age (or their perceived age) • Collection does not always mean use or sharing
• Intensive anger hurting people	• Meltdowns caused by dysregulation and impacted by sensory overload
• Intensive anger to kill people	• Fixations and blame • Meltdowns caused by dysregulation and impacted by sensory overload
• Carrying drugs after being befriended	• 'Mate crime' due to being too trusting • Will go to the nth degree to retain relationships, even if they are unsuitable and damaging to them
• Sexual offences	• Lack of sex and relationship education • Unable to read facial expressions and emotions, so struggles to see fear in others • Unable to understand consent • Unable to understand masturbation being a private stimming activity

autistic individuals have been overturned due to a better understanding of intention concerning autism (theory of mind).

Sadly, many autistic individuals are questioned and arrested based on an unfair assumption that they intend to commit an offence. This is the case with child pornography and cybercrime. In the case of physical damage and violence against others which resulted from a meltdown, these need to be treated compassionately by any arresting officer with autism training; otherwise, they will quickly jump to the wrong conclusion and traumatise the autistic person even more, with further meltdowns when put into a police van to be driven to a police station for questioning and held in a holding cell. The sensory overload of such reactions by police will likely mean they are physically restrained. Media reports of five-plus officers pinning down a young person with autism can be found in this book.

In a similar vein, media reports of a non-verbal autistic teenager being arrested by the police for waiting at the back of his grandparent's home in the playground with other but younger children. Even when he tried to explain he was autistic it was ignored, and his grandparents only knew what had happened after they contacted the police to report a missing person. Autism training in the police force is vital.

This book has been an epic journey for me, and this author now has a much more informed understanding of autism, the challenges autistic young people face, and how they can easily be misunderstood to be committing criminal offences when they are not. He hopes you have also gained from this experience.

References

Freckelton, I. (2011a). Asperger's disorder and the criminal law. *Journal of Law and Medicine, 18*, 677–691.

Freckelton, I. (2011b). Autism spectrum disorders and the criminal law. In M.R. Mohammadi (Ed.), *A comprehensive book on autism spectrum disorders* (pp. 249–272). IntechOpen.

Appendix 1

Stimming

Stimming is seen by many as a soothing action that helps to maintain an autistic person's emotional and mental well-being, and to cope with the daily hassles of life (Neyleen Rivero Cárdenas, 2023).

Visual stimming

- Watching the sun filter through a window (I spend hours on that)
- Aligning objects
- Finding patterns on tiles (or anywhere else) (sometimes I make stories with those patterns, it's fun, especially when it's a party and you're already banned from using your phone because "you should socialise more")
- Sorting objects by colours/shapes (all the time! My candy must be eaten in a certain order or else I won't enjoy it properly, obviously)
- Focusing and blurring the gaze (my mom says it's disturbing)
- Stare at one spot and blur the rest (preferably a specific colour (yellow), but anything will do)
- Using glow sticks/other toys (I love my glow bracelets! It's the best (and bearable) part of carnivals)
- Visual sensory toys
- Looking at a painting (not so much)
- Watching dust motes in the light (I could do that for hours, it's like a dance)
- Blinking rapidly (or not blinking at all, there's no middle ground)
- Looking at shiny things (my eyes are left with spots, but it's worth it)
- Watching satisfying videos (ASMR, kittens, people cooking, etc.) (KITTENS)
- Staring at lights or fans (and following them until you get dizzy)
- Moving objects in front of the eyes (usually very close)
- Looking at things from the "corner of the eye" (out of the corner of the eye)
- Turning lights on and off (drove my mom crazy with that when I was younger)
- Watching the rain fall/watching a thunderstorm (I LOVE rainy days)

Tactile stimming

- Hugging something or someone (I love hugging my friends/family)
- Petting an animal (my dog loves petting as much as I love petting him)

- Touching an object to feel its texture (but when it's a bad texture tm, yikes)
- Touching objects in passing (the bark of a tree, a railing, the wall, etc.) (all the time)
- Touching hair (stretching it, rolling it, tucking it behind the ear, etc.) (it's relaxing)
- Touching fingertips (with a pattern or without) (tickles a little, doesn't it?)
- Touching the corners of the lips
- Stroking lips with fingertips or tapping (yes)
- Touching lips, biting lips or running tongue over lips (I did that before I read that and then laughed at the coincidence)
- Touching a sensory toy (pop it, slime, etc.) (I have so many slimes and pop, it's almost ridiculous)
- Scratching your head or any other part of your body (scalp)
- Clenching and unclenching fists
- Squeezing the button on pens (drives everyone crazy for some reason, which I don't understand, why something so relaxing is so irritating to others?)
- Playing with jewellery (rings, bracelets) (I wear a lot, especially rings, so I spend all day twirling them on my finger)
- Wrapping/twisting fingers around fabric, t-shirt straps, or other (long sleeves)
- Bumping wrists (as in clapping)
- Pinching the tip of the nose, eyebrows, etc. (sometimes)
- Bumping teeth together repeatedly (oh yes)
- Rubbing hands against clothing or others (the fabric of my jeans has the perfect texture to do that, then my hands have like electricity and it's so much fun)
- Squeezing your hands/fists (great with nails that are a little long)
- Rubbing the palms of your hands/fingers (it itches and tingles, but relaxes?)
- Playing with twisting a rubber band (not so much)
- Playing with your fingers/hands (and doing complicated dances with them at the same time)
- Splashing hands in cold water
- Running your hand over your forehead (once or twice maybe)
- Wiping your hand over your eye (squeezing it)
- Rolling objects between hands
- Braiding hair (me, my friends, any hair that stands still in front of me will be braided, in exams, I used to do it on my friends' hair to relax and they would calm down too, which was a plus)
- Pretending to play an instrument (air guitar, triangles, maracas, etc.)
- Spelling with sign language (I only know a few words, mental note, I'd like to learn more)
- Breaking leaves or pieces of tree bark while walking ("It's like leaving a trail of breadcrumbs")
- Breaking into many pieces and/or folding sugar envelopes (yep)
- Pulling out body hair (one at a time) (painful but satisfying)

Olfactory stimming

- Smell something repeatedly (yeah)
- Smelling new (it's such a good smell!)
- Smelling your pets (especially if it's freshly bathed)
- Smelling your loved ones (everyone smells differently, and their smell calms you down, my mom's/little brother's makes me fall asleep every time, my dad's makes me hungry, he always smells like some food I don't recognise)
- Smelling essential oils/ candles (not so much)
- Using diffusers/incense (a lot! My dad and I do it all the time and it makes my mom climb walls because she doesn't like the smell of incense, so now we do it when she's not home xd)
- Smelling clothes you've just washed (I love the lavender smell of my freshly washed clothes)
- Using bath bombs (I don't use them, but I think I might)
- Smelling food (if it smells bad, I won't eat it)

Taste stimming

- Eating something for the feel of its texture (texture is everything, if it doesn't have good texture, forget it, I'm not going to eat that)
- Sucking on the sleeves of t-shirts (and nibbling on them, all my favourite sweaters have little holes in them from all the nibbling)
- Repeatedly eating/sucking/slurping on something (definitely, pens, my fingers, fabrics)
- Eating something to taste it (yes)
- Eating spicy/sour/etc. food for the sensation it gives you (sour yes, sometimes, but spicy is a big no-no)
- Eating raw pasta (then I regret it because it gives me a stomach-ache)
- Eating play dough/wax/ paper or other inedible things (it stings) (like so much paper my mom says I will grow leaves someday, play dough tastes weird)
- Thumb sucking/ hair (all the time, really, all, the time)
- Throat clearing/coughing repeatedly (it's more the motion than doing it...not sure if I'm making myself clear)
- Running tongue over teeth (yep)
- Grinding teeth (I used to do it when I was a kid, not so much anymore)
- Eating very slowly (this one, my younger brother and I are very slow eaters)
- Eating candy, lollipops, chewing gum (keeping my mouth busy helps me think)
- Nail biting (if I had a dollar every time I was told "stop biting your nails," I'd be a multimillionaire)
- Eating the skin of fingers, lips, etc. (my lips peeling, my dad tries to stop me from doing it by giving me lip balms, but the taste just makes me eat them more lol) (my favourite flavour is blue raspberry)

- Biting the inside of my cheeks and sucking the blood (more the little skin than the blood, but sometimes I get out of hand and end up with sores, I've been scolded for that a few times) (my mom is a dentist, so)

Auditory/verbal stimming

- Hearing/singing the same song/songs on loop (I will become obsessed with a song and listen to it on loop for days, the last one was Dark Paradise and its playback was constant for a whole week)
- Listening to a specific part of a song on loop (Athena's part in My Goodbye from Epic the Musical)
- Listening to the sound of rain (I play videos with that sound to sleep)
- Repeating phrases from movies /series/ mantras/catchphrases (yeah, repeating dialogues is my thing)
- Repeating words (I'll start repeating a word and then a sentence and it'll be an endless loop)
- Listen to any repetitive sound (YES)
- Grunting (especially if I'm feeling uncommunicative that day)
- Yelling (not so much, talking very loudly yes, but not to the point of shouting, I think)
- Whispering/mumbling
- Whistling/humming (yes, I hum all day long)
- Putting my ear close to the speakers (NO) (I tried it once) (Never again)
- Turning on a household appliance to listen to it (The sound of my laptop is comforting)
- Listening to music (at a very high volume) with headphones (definitely yes, everyone asks me if it doesn't bother me and I'm like "No? If it bothered me, I wouldn't do it")
- Snapping my fingers (I can't snap my fingers, feel my pout from the screen, I never learned how it's so hard)
- Count out loud (and one, two, three, and one, two, three) (the waltz beat sticks with me for hours, I keep hearing my old dance teacher)
- Clicking your tongue (with a rhythm, obviously)
- Recite something from memory (a poem, numbers, etc.) (there's a poem I learned when I was very young, like, 3–4 years old, and I still recite it, it's "The Pink Slippers" by José Martí)
- Drumming (another thing that bothers others for some reason that I don't understand for the life of me) (I've been told that the sound is annoying, but I swear I don't understand why)
- Listening to the sound of a seashell (I have a lot of seashells, like, a lot, and hearing the waves is super relaxing)
- Listening to nature sounds (minus crickets, I hate the sound of crickets/crickets)
- Beatboxing/rapping (I can't do that TwT)
- Making beats with my fingernails on a surface (yeah, another annoying sound for others, relaxing for me)
- Snorting (not much)

- Pretending to tickle the other person but with 'tiki tiki tiki tiki' sounds (I love doing that, tickling or just poking someone's cheek by making that sound is fun) (kids love it as much as I do)

Proprioceptive/vestibular stimming

- Jumping (in the same place, small jumps when I get excited)
- Jumping rope (I would do it, but my balance sucks)
- Use a balance board (I repeat, my balance sucks)
- Shake my head sideways (YES)
- Twisting and turning (especially if it's a swivel chair, my mom uses one in her office and when she's not working, I'm on top of it, twisting and turning)
- Dancing (I have three left feet and can't carry a beat even if it kills me in public, but I like to dance in private with impromptu moves, sometimes without music) (The times my mom has caught me cooking and moving to the beat of music in my head are countless) (I die of embarrassment every time because she just looks at me with an amused smile and it's embarrassing, people)
- Walking up and down the aisle (especially if I'm studying)
- Flapping/flapping (I get really excited, and my hands can't help it, ok?)
- Moving feet, hands, etc. (sometimes in sync) (or rather, almost all the time in sync and rhythm with something)
- Walking on tiptoe, standing on the side of one foot or heel (I love that, a lot, I do that for no apparent reason)
- Swinging (not everyone?)
- Contract and relax some muscle (ouch, no, it's painful, they always ride on top of each other and it's a pain to put them back in place)
- Rocking back and forth (again, not everyone?)
- Shrugging shoulders (if they get too tight)
- Using a weighted blanket (I've never done that, as far as I can remember)
- Opening and closing doors (nope)
- Hanging from places (MONKEY BARS, MONKEY BARS)
- Lying face down on something (in my bed, sometimes I wake up in that position, my mom just sighs, because my little brother and I do it and she's just resigned to finding us in the weirdest sleeping positions)
- Hitting your head (or another part of your body) against something or with your hands (it hurts, don't recommend it)
- Running (exercise, ugh)
- Spinning around in a chair with wheels (I think I mentioned this already, but I LOVE doing that)
- Swinging on a pendulum (yes)
- Shake your head to a rhythm

Other stimming/combined

- Doodling (if my notes don't have doodles/drawings, they are not my notes)
- Looking for patterns on tiles or any other object (it's funny)

- Reading license plates and the like (and forgetting them five seconds later but then you remember and start finding patterns)
- Memorising things (you never remember what you need, but you remember that obscure fact you read at 4 a.m. about jellyfish)
- Playing an instrument (I don't know how to play one, but I'd like to learn violin)
- Keyboarding (YES)
- Painting (mandalas, patterns, etc.) (I LOVE it) (Seriously, mandalas are my life)
- Assemble something with Lego (My little brother and I have a huge bag of Lego) (Technically, they are his, but I like them better, so he gave them to me and now they are ours).
- Using a stimming toy (e.g., anti-stress) (Er, I've broken more than I should by squeezing or biting them too hard)
- Lying on the floor/cold surface (especially if your brain is going too fast)
- Mentally counting/ mentally repeating things (definitely yes)
- Crafts that require repetition/patterns (crochet, knitting, bracelet making, macramé, etc.) (I love knitting)
- Collecting objects and sorting them, classifying them, observing them, etc. (organise my seashell collection in order of size/colours)
- Hatha yoga or any sport that requires repetition (I like yoga, but I don't like to exercise, so it's something I do once in a while)
- Folding my ears in on themselves (I used to do that all the time as a kid)
- Do stretching (and rattle your bones, all my friends cringe every time I do that)
- Doing puzzles/jigsaw puzzles/Rubik's cube (YES, YES, YES)
- Read the same book/books over and over (Guilty, I have my favourites)
- Shuffle cards, coins, etc. (Cards)
- Popping bubble wrap (PLOP, PLOP, PLOP)
- Doing sudoku, looking for patterns! (ONE OF MY FAVORITE THINGS IN THE WORLD)

Reference

Neyleen Rivero Cárdenas (2023). NOT complete but EXHAUSTIVE list of STIMMING. Retrieved 16/08/2025. https://www.reddit.com/r/AutismTranslated/comments/11lyiye/not_complete_but_exhaustive_list_of_stimming/?rdt=44196

Appendix 2

Adult Autism Survey

This project builds on the recent books by Dr Neil Alexander-Passe, the author of *Dyslexia, Neurodiversity, and Crime: investigating the school-to-prison pipeline* (2023). His new book on 'ADHD and Crime' (2024) is due out very soon!

This is a very important project to highlight the injustices in society (school and criminal justice system).

The author aims to write a new book *Autism and Crime* in 2024–25, so is seeking volunteers to:

- Complete this survey
- Offer to be interviewed over zoom (I will keep your name anonymous)

Please answer honestly, it's an important survey (you cannot be identified by taking the survey).

IMPORTANT: If you are under the age of 18, please complete this with a parent/adult.

Thank you

Dr Neil Alexander-Passe

About you...

1 Are you Male, Female or other?

- Female
- Other gender
- Prefer not to say

2 Your age?

- 5–11 yrs old (primary school age)
- 12–18 yrs old (secondary school age)
- 19–30 yrs (young adult)
- 31–50 yrs
- 51 yrs plus

3   Where do you live?

- Scotland, Wales, or Northern Ireland
- Outside the UK, in Europe
- Outside the UK, outside Europe

Autism diagnosis...

4   Do you have a formal autism diagnosis?

- Yes
- No

5   Who diagnosed your Autism?

- CAMHS or the National Health Service (NHS) if an adult
- Privately
- Never diagnosed

6   What age were you when you were first diagnosed with autism?

- 5–11 yrs old (primary school)
- 12–18 yrs old (secondary school)
- 19–30 yrs old (young adult)
- 31–50 yrs old
- 51 yrs plus
- Not applicable, never diagnosed

7   How do you define autism?

- ASD (as a disorder)?
- ASC (as a condition)?

8   What positive things does Autism give you? (please click as many that are relevant)

- Expertise in their favourite topics (My special interest has been a way for me to succeed in education and my career, even when the social and psychological odds were stacked against me from the start.)
- Hyperfocus (My autistic strength is hyperfocus. I get through way more work than my colleagues and it's always accurate and of excellent quality.)
- A strong sense of justice (I have a strong sense of justice and will fight and be vocal for what I think is right.)
- Creativity (I enjoy being creative: it not only brings me joy, it's a useful tool in all parts of life.)
- Attention to detail (I tend to have such high attention to detail, which as an artist, helps me to create many wonderful artworks.)
- Honesty (I feel like due to my autism I am probably the most trustworthy, honest and loyal person anyone could ever meet, I genuinely feel.)

- Loyalty (I'm fiercely loyal. Once I let you into my heart, you can trust me implicitly.)
- Creative problem solving (One of my autistic child's strengths is his uncanny ability to figure out solutions to problems that are amazingly creative, inventive, and often downright ingenious.)
- Less influenced by socially derived biases (A great strength of autism can be seeing the world in a different way, questioning and breaking norms which others blindly follow.)
- Excellent memory (My memory. I retain ridiculous and usually pointless details and facts. It's usually a strength and I love it when people are amazed by the cool memory game and challenges I show them.)
- Other:

9 How does Autism affect you? (please tick as many as relevant)

- Not seeming to understand what others are thinking or feeling
- Unusual speech, such as repeating phrases and talking 'at' others
- Liking a strict daily routine and getting very upset if it changes
- Having a very keen interest in certain subjects or activities
- Getting very upset if you are asked to do something
- Finding it hard to make friends or prefer to be on their own
- Taking things very literally – for example, may not understand phrases like "break a leg or its raining cats and dogs"
- Finding it hard to say how you feel
- Other:

10a Who triggered the referral for your first autism diagnosis?

- Me
- My parents
- My teachers/school
- Other family
- I wanted to be diagnosed
- Being arrested, so the police
- My doctor/mental health worker
- Not applicable, never diagnosed

10b How do you cope with your autism? (please click as many that are relevant)

- Hiding some signs of autism by copying how others behave and play
- Withdrawing in situations they find difficult
- Appearing to cope better with social situations
- Showing fewer signs of repetitive behaviours

11. What event triggered the initial referral for diagnosis?

_____

12. Please can you describe your initial diagnostic process?

_____

13. Do you have any secondary diagnosis?

- ADHD
- Mental Health issues
- Conduct disorders
- Dyslexia
- No other conditions
- Other:

14 Have you ever been medicated for your autism?

- Yes
- No

15 What does it feel like to be medicated for autism?

  _____

16 Do you still take medication for your autism?

- Yes
- No
- Sometimes
- Not applicable

17 Did taking autism medication have any negative effects on you? (tick as many as relevant)

- Could not sleep
- Did not want to eat (may have caused weight loss)
- Frustration
- Anxiety
- Risk-taking
- Self-harming yourself
- Attempted suicide
- Depression
- Drug taking (illegal drugs)
- Felt numb
- Not applicable, never taken medication
- Other:

18 If you are not now taking the medication, why? _____

19 Have you ever self-medicated to cope with the negative effects of autism? (caffeine drinks, alcohol, vaping, or illegal drugs)

- Yes
- No

20 Do you think you have/have had difficulties with addictions, e.g., computer gaming, illegal drugs, alcohol, caffeine, vaping, sex? Please can you explain more about it. _____

All about school...

21 Did your school recognise your autistic traits?

- PRIMARY SCHOOL (5–11 yrs) – Yes
- PRIMARY SCHOOL (5–11 yrs) – No
- SECONDARY SCHOOL (12–18 yrs) – Yes
- SECONDARY SCHOOL (12–18 yrs) – No

22 What help did your school give you for your autism? (tick as many as relevant)

- No help at all
- Fidget toy
- Movement breaks
- Standing desk
- Extra time
- Other:

23 Do you think your teachers understood your autism? Please describe the good and bad ones _____

24 Were you 'unfairly' blamed for your impulsiveness at school?

- Yes
- No

25 Do you think they were unfairly blamed for things out of your control?

- Yes
- No

26 Do you think schools and teachers understand autism?

- All of them (100%)
- Some of them (50%)
- Very few of them (25%)
- None of them (0%)

27 Have you 'ever' been suspended/expelled?

- Yes
- No

28 If suspended/expelled, why do you think you were?

_____

29 How many times have you been suspended/expelled from school (primary and secondary schools)?
Never been expelled

- 1–3
- 4–6
- 7+

30 Have you ever been sent to a PRU (pupil referral unit) or a similar alternative education provision for suspended/excluded children?

- Yes
- No

31 Was attending a PRU (pupil referral unit) or a similar alternative education provision suitable for you?

- Yes
- No
- Not applicable, never went to a PRU/alternative provision

32 What was it like attending a PRU (pupil referral unit) or a similar alternative education provision? _____

33 Why do you think kids with autism maybe vulnerable at a PRU (pupil referral unit) or a similar alternative education provision? _____
_____

34 Do you think that kids with autism are drawn to drugs and crime from attending a PRU (pupil referral unit) or a similar alternative education provision? Mixing with the other kids there.

- Yes
- No

35 What percentage of kids at PRUs (pupil referral units) or a similar alternative education provision do you think have autism?

- 0–25%
- 26%–50%
- 51%–75%
- 76%–100%

MELTDOWNS/SHUTDOWNS, what causes them/triggers and outcomes?

36 At SCHOOL what caused/triggered your meltdowns/shutdowns?

- Bullying
- Sensory overload: noise/smell
- Unexpected events, e.g., a fire alarm

- Unexpected changes to routine, e.g., supply teachers/change of seating/ friends not at school
- Stress and anxiety about your day
- Communication difficulties: not being understood
- Being overwhelmed by multiple tasks
- Things not going to plan
- Unexpected requests of them by teachers
- Other:

37 At SCHOOL how did your meltdowns/shutdowns present?

- Damage to property
- Assaults on adults/teachers Assaults on other children/students
- Other:

38 At SCHOOL what resulted from your meltdowns/shutdowns?

- Extra help in class
- Extra help in unstructured times, e.g., break and lunchtimes
- Suspension
- Exclusion
- Being spoken to by the police/arrested
- Sent to an alternative provision/PRU
- Asked to change school/or to be home-educated
- Other children/students avoiding you
- Staff avoiding you/change of classes to more understanding teachers
- An EHCP being applied for (government extra funding for your education)
- CAMHS/mental health practitioner/psychiatrist referral
- Medication being prescribed
- Other:

39 As an ADULT, what caused/triggered your meltdowns/shutdowns?

- Bullying
- Sensory overload: noise/smell
- Unexpected events, e.g., a fire alarm
- Unexpected changes to routine, e.g., train breaking down, missing a bus, losing something
- Stress and anxiety about your day
- Communication difficulties: not being understood
- Being overwhelmed by multiple tasks
- Unexpected requests on them by others
- Other:

40 As an ADULT, how did your meltdowns/shutdowns present?

- Damage to property
- Assaults on others Other:

- As an ADULT, what resulted from your meltdowns?
- Tick all that apply.
- CAMHS/mental health practitioner/psychiatrist referral
- Being spoken to by the police/arrested
- Having to move home
- Friends, people you know avoiding you
- Other:

41   How you ever been prescribed medication to help your meltdowns/shutdowns, if so what and did it help? _____

Victimisation (I am very sorry to ask, but its relevant/important)
Research suggests many young people with autism are abused when young.

42   Were you bullied as a child, how?

- Sexual abuse (by other children/adults)
- Physical abuse (by other children/adults)
- Emotional abuse (by other children or parents) Other:

43   Were you bullied as an adult, how?

- Sexual abuse
- Physical abuse
- Emotional abuse
- Other:

Risk factors

44   Are there any factors you think are relevant to you committing criminal acts?

- Being male
- Being single (unmarried or not in a long-term relationships)
- Having no children
- Having learning difficulties as a child
- Being bullied as a child
- Late diagnosis of autism
- Late diagnosis of other difficulties, e.g., ADHD, mental health issues
- Struggling to find long-term employment
- Difficulties in the workplace
- Substance misuse
- Being in care
- Having a single parent
- Parents not working
- Childhood abuse
- Other:

Autism and crime...

45 What age were you when you were FIRST spoken to or arrested by the police?

- 5–11 yrs old (primary school)
- 12–18 yrs old (secondary school)
- 19–30 yrs old (young adult)
- 31–50 yrs old
- 51 yrs plus
- Not applicable, I have never been spoken to by the police/or arrested

46 Have you been involved in criminal activities?

- Yes
- No

47 Please can you describe what criminal activities you have been involved with (please tick any that are relevant)?

- Violence towards others (verbal and physical aggression)
- Violence towards property (criminal damage)
- Antisocial behaviour
- Stealing
- Burglary
- Drugs
- Gangs
- Fraud and forgery
- Driving under the influence of drugs or alcohol
- Sexual crimes
- Other:

48 Do you think there is a link between autism and crime?

- Yes
- No
- Unsure

49 If so, please explain why? _____

Autism and prison...

50 Have you ever been in prison?

- Yes
- No

51 What age were you when you first went to prison or a secure child/youth unit?

- 5–11 yrs old (primary school)
- 12–18 yrs old (secondary school)
- 19–30 yrs old (young adult)
- 31–50 yrs old

- 51 yrs plus
- Not applicable, I have never been to prison or a secure/youth unit

52 How many times have you been in prison or a secure child/youth unit?

- Never been
- 1–5 times
- 6 times plus

53 Have you ever been in care?

- Yes
- No

Would you be open to being interviewed about your autism experience?

You will receive a copy of the interview to check and will remain anonymous (any names will be changed).

- If yes, please complete this box with your name and email address as consent

Thank you for your honest answers, your time is appreciated.

Appendix 3

Parent Autism Survey

This project builds on the recent books by Dr Neil Alexander-Passe, the author of *Dyslexia, Neurodiversity, and Crime: investigating the school-to-prison pipeline* (2023). His new book on 'ADHD and Crime' (2024) is due out very soon!

This is a very important project to highlight the injustices in society (school and criminal justice system). I am very interested in meltdowns, the triggers, and what happened after them.

The author aims to write a new book "Autism and Crime" in 2024–25, so is seeking volunteer parents to

- Complete this survey
- Offer to be interviewed over zoom (I will keep your name anonymous)

Please answer honestly, its an important survey (you can not be identified by taking the survey).

Thank you

Dr Neil Alexander-Passe

About you...

1 Are you Male, Female or other?

- Male
- Female
- Other gender
- Prefer not to say

2 Your age? (parent's age)

- 19–30 yrs (young adult)
- 31–50 yrs
- 51 yrs plus

3 Where do you live?

- England
- Scotland, Wales, or Northern Ireland
- Outside the UK, in Europe Outside the UK, outside Europe

4   How many children do you have?

- 1–2
- 3–4
- 5–6
- 6+

5   How many of your children have autism?

- 1
- 2
- 3
- 4

Your child with autism, the one you feel best fits this study
The child who has been in trouble at school, maybe how has had really bad meltdowns

6   Your child's age?

- 5–11 yrs old (primary school age)
- 12–18 yrs old (secondary school age)
- 19–30 yrs (young adult)

Autism diagnosis…

7   Do they have a formal autism diagnosis?

- Yes
- No

8   Who diagnosed their Autism?

- CAMHS or the National Health Service (NHS) if an adult
- Privately
- Never diagnosed

9   What age were they when first diagnosed with autism?

- 5–11 yrs old (primary school)
- 12–18 yrs old (secondary school)
- 19–30 yrs old (young adult)
- Not applicable, never diagnosed

10   How would you define autism?

- ASD (as a disorder)?
- ASC (as a condition)?

11   What positive things does Autism give them? (please click as many that are relevant)

- Expertise in their favourite topics (My special interest has been a way for me to succeed in education and my career, even when the social and psychological odds were stacked against me from the start.)

- Hyperfocus (My autistic strength is hyperfocus. I get through way more work than my colleagues and it's always accurate and of excellent quality.)
- A strong sense of justice (I have a strong sense of justice and will fight and be vocal for what I think is right.)
- Creativity (I enjoy being creative: it not only brings me joy, it's a useful tool in all parts of life.)
- Attention to detail (I tend to have such high attention to detail, which as an artist, helps me to create many wonderful artworks.)
- Honesty (I feel like due to my autism I am probably the most trustworthy, honest and loyal person anyone could ever meet, I genuinely feel.)
- Loyalty (I'm fiercely loyal. Once I let you into my heart, you can trust me implicitly.)
- Creative problem solving (One of my autistic child's strengths is his uncanny ability to figure out solutions to problems that are amazingly creative, inventive, and often downright ingenious.)
- Less influenced by socially derived biases (A great strength of autism can be seeing the world in a different way, questioning and breaking norms which others blindly follow.)
- Excellent memory (My memory. I retain ridiculous and usually pointless details and facts. It's usually a strength and I love it when people are amazed by the cool memory game and challenges I show them.)
- Other:

12 How does Autism affect them? (please tick as many as relevant)

- Not seeming to understand what others are thinking or feeling
- Unusual speech, such as repeating phrases and talking 'at' others
- Liking a strict daily routine and getting very upset if it changes
- Having a very keen interest in certain subjects or activities
- Getting very upset if you are asked to do something
- Finding it hard to make friends or preferring to be on their own
- Taking things very literally – for example, may not understand phrases like "break a leg or its raining cats and dogs"
- Finding it hard to say how you feel
- Other:

13 Who triggered the referral for their first autism diagnosis?

- They asked for a diagnosis
- You as a parent
- Their teachers/school
- Other family
- Being arrested, so the police
- Their doctor/mental health worker
- Not applicable, never diagnosed

14 How do they cope with their autism? (please click as many that are relevant)

- Hiding some signs of autism by copying how others behave and play
- Withdrawing in situations they find difficult

- Appearing to cope better with social situations
- Showing fewer signs of repetitive behaviours

15   Was there an event that triggered their initial referral for diagnosis?

_____

16   Please can you describe their initial diagnostic process? _____

_____

17   Do they have any secondary diagnosis?

- ADHD
- Mental health issues
- Conduct disorders
- Dyslexia
- No other conditions

18   Have they ever been medicated for autism?

- Yes
- No

19   What do they say the medication makes them feel like? _____

_____

20   Do they still take medication for autism?

- Yes
- No
- Sometimes
- Not applicable

21   Did taking autism medication have any negative effects on them? (tick as many as relevant)

- Anger and violence towards others or property
- Could not sleep
- Did not want to eat (may have caused weight loss)
- Frustration
- Anxiety
- Risk-taking
- Self-harming yourself
- Attempted suicide
- Depression
- Drug taking (illegal drugs)
- Felt numb
- Not applicable, never taken ADHD medication

22   If they are not now taking the medication, why?_____

_____

23 Have they ever self-medicated to cope with the negative effects of autism? (caffeine drinks, alcohol, vaping, or illegal drugs)

- Yes
- No

24 Do you think you have/have had difficulties with addictions, e.g., illegal drugs, alcohol, caffeine, vaping, sex, computer gaming? Please can you explain more about it. _____

All about school...

25 Did their school recognise their autistic traits?

- PRIMARY SCHOOL (5–11 yrs) - Yes
- PRIMARY SCHOOL (5–11 yrs) - No
- SECONDARY SCHOOL (12–18 yrs) - Yes
- SECONDARY SCHOOL (12–18 yrs) - No

26 What help did their school give them for their autism? (tick as many as relevant)

- No help at all
- Fidget toy
- Movement breaks
- Standing desk
- Extra time

27 Do you think their teachers understood their autism? Please describe the good and bad ones _____

28 Were they 'unfairly' blamed for their impulsiveness at school?

- Yes
- No

29 Do you think they were unfairly blamed for things out of their control?

- Yes
- No

30 Do you think schools and teachers understand autism?

- All of them (100%)
- Some of them (50%)
- Very few of them (25%)
- None of them (0%)

31 Have they 'ever' been suspended/expelled?

- Yes
- No

32   If suspended/expelled, why do you think they were? _____

_____

33   How many times have they been suspended/expelled from school (primary and secondary schools)?

- Never been expelled
- 1–3
- 4–6
- 7+

34   Have they ever been sent to a PRU (pupil referral unit) or a similar alternative education provision for suspended/excluded children?

- Yes
- No

35   Was attending a PRU (pupil referral unit) or a similar alternative education provision suitable for them?

- Yes
- No
- Not applicable, never went to a PRU/alternative provision

36   What was it like for them to attend a PRU (pupil referral unit) or a similar alternative education provision? _____

37   Why do you think kids with autism maybe vulnerable at a PRU (pupil referral unit) or a similar alternative education provision?

_____

38   Do you think that kids with autism are drawn to drugs and crime from attending a PRU (pupil referral unit) or a similar alternative education provision? Mixing with the other kids there.

- Yes
- No

39   What percentage of kids at PRUs (pupil referral units) or a similar alternative education provision do you think have autism?

- 0–25%
- 26%–50%
- 51%–75%
- 76%–100%

MELTDOWNS/SHUTDOWNS, what causes them/triggers and outcomes?

40   At SCHOOL what caused/triggered their meltdowns/shutdowns?

- Bullying
- Sensory overload: noise/smell

- Unexpected events, e.g., a fire alarm
- Unexpected changes to routine, e.g., supply teachers/change of seating/ friends not at school
- Stress and anxiety about their day
- Communication difficulties: not being understood
- Being overwhelmed by multiple tasks
- Things not going to plan
- Unexpected requests of them by teachers
- Other:

41 At SCHOOL what happened during their meltdowns/shutdowns?

- Damage to property
- Assaults on adults/teachers' assaults on other children/students
- Other:

42 At SCHOOL what resulted from their meltdowns/shutdowns?

- Extra help in class
- Extra help in unstructured times, e.g., break and lunchtimes
- Suspension
- Exclusion
- Being spoken to by the police/arrested
- Sent to an alternative provision/PRU
- Asked to change school/or to be home educated
- Other children/students avoiding you
- Staff avoiding you/change of classes to mire understanding teachers
- An EHCP being applied for (government extra funding for your education)
- CAMHS/mental health practitioner/psychiatrist referral
- Medication being prescribed

43 What caused their meltdowns/shutdowns in PUBLIC or in the HOME?

- Sensory overload, noise, smell
- Things not going to plan
- Too many people
- Not getting their own way
- Other:

44 What happened during their meltdowns/shutdowns in PUBLIC or in the Home?

- Property damage
- Children got hurt
- Adults got hurt

45 What resulted in their meltdowns/shutdowns in PUBLIC or in the HOME, the reaction of others?

- Called a bad parent
- The police were called

- Had to move home/area
- Have they ever been prescribed medication to help their meltdowns/ shutdowns, if so what and did it help?

Victimisation (I am very sorry to ask, but its relevant/important)
Research suggests many young people with autism are abused when young.

46   Were they bullied as a child, how?

- Sexual abuse (by other children/adults)
- Physical abuse (by other children/adults) Emotional abuse (by other children/ adults)
- Other:

Risk factors

47   Are there any factors you think are relevant to them committing criminal acts?

- Being male
- Having learning difficulties as a child
- Being bullied as a child
- Late diagnosis of autism
- Late diagnosis of other difficulties, e.g., ADHD, mental health issues
- Struggling to find long-term employment
- Difficulties in the workplace
- Substance misuse
- Childhood abuse
- Other:

Would you be open to interviewed about your child's autism experience?

You will receive a copy of the interview to check and will remain anonymous (any names will be changed).

- If yes, please complete this box with your name and email address as consent.

Thank you for your honest answers, your time is appreciated.

Index

For Product Safety Concerns and Information please contact our EU
representative GPSR@taylorandfrancis.com
Taylor & Francis Verlag GmbH, Kaufingerstraße 24, 80331 München, Germany

www.ingramcontent.com/pod-product-compliance
Lightning Source LLC
Chambersburg PA
CBHW050349270326
41926CB00016B/3658

9 7 8 1 0 4 1 0 1 3 7 8 5